APPROACHES
TO
SEMIOTICS

edited by

THOMAS A. SEBEOK

assisted by

DONNA JEAN UMIKER

22

SPEAKING
AND
SEMIOLOGY

MAURICE MERLEAU-PONTY'S
PHENOMENOLOGICAL THEORY OF
EXISTENTIAL COMMUNICATION

by

RICHARD L. LANIGAN

1972

MOUTON

THE HAGUE · PARIS

LIBRARY OF CONGRESS CATALOG CARD NUMBER: 72-189696

Printed in Belgium, by NICI, Printers, Ghent.

With Gratitude To
DR. THOMAS J. PACE
Friend, Professor, and Colleague

ACKNOWLEDGMENTS

The author wishes to thank Dr. Thomas J. Pace, to whom this book is dedicated, for his constructive criticisms which lent form and substance to the present study when it was presented as doctoral dissertation in the School of Communication at Southern Illinois University in 1969. In addition, Dr. Pace must be credited with stimulating the author's interest in the intimate relationship between communication and philosophy, especially existential phenomenology. Also, I would like to thank Dr. Earl E. Bradley, Dr. Lewis E. Hahn, Dr. Ralph Micken, Dr. C. Horton Talley and Dr. Dorothy Higginbotham for their part in the examination and critique of the original dissertation manuscript. The instruction afforded me in the seminars of Dr. George Kimball Plochmann and Dr. William D. Smith must also be mentioned.

Special gratitude is due Mr. Alan M. Cohn, Humanities Librarian of Morris Library at Southern Illinois University, for his consistent vigilance and effort in obtaining publications necessary to this study, particularly those in French, and for his advantageous direction in the use of specialized indices.

Personal thanks go to Mr. Ronald Levaco whose mutual interest in film and phenomenology provided a great deal of insight through our frequent dialogues and debates on semiology. While on a personal note, I must mention my deep regard for the understanding and love that my wife, Antoinette Mercier, has shown throughout the writing of the book.

Finally, I should note that even with the good advice and criticism of friends and colleagues, no one but myself is accountable for the analysis I offer in the present study.

Grateful acknowledgment is extended to the publishers of the various books quoted in the present study. Specific credit to each publisher and author is duly noted in full footnote citations and a second time in the bibliography.

RICHARD L. LANIGAN
May 1971

TABLE OF CONTENTS

Introduction   15

I. Existential Communication as Phenomenology   21
  1. Existential Communication   21
     1.1. The Philosophical School of Paris   24
     1.2. The Return to Phenomena   26
  2. The Apparent Antinomy of Existential Communication   27
     2.1. Phenomenalism   27
     2.2. Phenomenology   29
        2.2.1. Investigating Particular Phenomena   30
        2.2.2. Investigating General Essences (Eidetic Intuiting)   31
        2.2.3. Apprehending Essential Relationships Among Essences   31
        2.2.4. Watching Modes of Appearing   32
        2.2.5. Exploring the Constitution of Phenomena in Consciousness   33
        2.2.6. Suspending Belief in the Existence of the Phenomena   33
        2.2.7. Interpreting Concealed Meaning   34
  3. Communication as Existentialism   35
     3.1. Existence as Indirect Communication   35
     3.2. Existence as Direct Communication   37
     3.3. Existence as Authentic and In-authentic Communication   38
     3.4. Existence as Primordial Communication   39
  4. Merleau-Ponty's Philosophy as Existential Phenomenology   41
     4.1. Philosophy qua Philosophy   41
     4.2. Merleau-Ponty's Method   43

4.3. Gesture : Communicating the Existential Phenomena   46

II. Existential Phenomenology as Semiology   51
  1. The Cartesian Dualism : Semiotic Phenomenalism . . .   51
    1.1. The Semiology of Charles Sanders Peirce   52
    1.2. The Semiology of Charles W. Morris   54
    1.3. The Semiology of C. K. Ogden and I. A. Richards   58
    1.4. The Semiology of Bertrand Russell   60
      1.4.1. Applying the Theory of Types to ordinary
             Language   63
      1.4.2. Applying the Theory of Descriptions   64
  2. Dualistic Synthesis : Semiotic Existentialism   65
    2.1. The Semiology of Karl Jaspers   65
    2.2. The Semiology of Martin Heidegger   71
    2.3. The Semiology of Jean-Paul Sartre   74
  3. Semiotic as Existential Phenomenology   75
    3.1. Semiology as Problematic   76
    3.2. The Semiology of Roland Barthes   78
    3.3. The Semiology of Maurice Merleau-Ponty   81
      3.3.1. Semiology as Semiotic in Merleau-Ponty . .   82
      3.3.2. Signs and Signification   85
      3.3.3. Immanence and Transcendence in Semi-
             ology   90
      3.3.4. Meaning in Semiology   93

III. Perception : The Lived-Body Experience   97
  1. The Primacy of Perception (Description)   98
    1.1. Sensation   98
    1.2. Intellection   99
    1.3. Seeing   102
    1.4. Other   106
      1.4.1. Myself, My "Psyche"   108
      1.4.2. Introceptive Image   109
      1.4.3. Visual Body   110
      1.4.4. "Psyche" of the Other   111
    1.5. Perception   115
      1.5.1. Spatiality   115
      1.5.2. Temporality   117
      1.5.3. Perception as Synopsis   119

1.6. Body 125
   1.6.1. Freedom 129
   1.6.2. The Lived-Body 130
2. Radical Reflection as *Gestalt* 133
  2.1. Epoché 134
  2.2. Primordial Situation 135
  2.3. Radical *Gestalt* 136
   2.3.1. Film : A Temporal Paradigm 140
   2.3.2. Radical Reflection as Method 144
    2.3.2.1. Pre-Objective Phenomena 144
    2.3.2.2. Reffective Reduction 145
3. Radical *Cogito* 147
  3.1. Pre-Conscious 148
  3.2. *Cogito* 149
  3.3. Intentionality 151

IV. Expression : Existential Phenomenology as Speaking . . . 155
1. Expression as Phenomena 156
2. Language 160
  2.1. Silence 164
  2.2. Chiasm 167
  2.3. Film : A Semiotic Paradigm 169
3. Tongue 175
  3.1. Literature 179
  3.2. Myth 181
4. Speaking 184
  4.1. The Speaking Subject 187
  4.2. Speech : A Definition 190
  4.3. Dialogue As Maieutic 194
  4.4. Film : Maieutic Icon 196
  4.5. Speaking As Maieutic 199

V. Introduction to the Prose of the World 202

Bibliography 210

I. Primary Sources 210
  A. Merleau-Ponty's Books, Articles, Lectures, and Essays
    in the Chronological Order of Publication; Annotated . 210
  B. Translations of Merleau-Ponty's Original French Trea-
    tises in the Chronological Order of Publication; Anno-
    tated 218

II. Secondary Sources   221
   A. Reviews of Merleau-Ponty's Treatises   221
   B. Analyses of Merleau-Ponty's Treatises   222
      1. Books   222
      2. Articles and Essays   224
      3. Unpublished Materials   235

III. Additional References   235
   A. Books   235
   B. Articles and Essays   240
   C. Unpublished Materials   243

Index   244

KEY TO FOOTNOTE ABBREVIATIONS

M. M.-P.   =   Maurice Merleau-Ponty

Structure   =   *The Structure of Behavior*
(La structure du comportement)

Phenomenology   =   *Phenomenology of Perception*
(Phénoménologie de la perception)

Sense   =   *Sense and Non-Sense*
(Sens et non-sens)

Praise   =   *In Praise of Philosophy*
(Éloge de la philosophie)

Signs   =   *Signs*
(Signes)

Visible   =   *The Visible and the Invisible*
(Le visible et l'invisible)

Themes   =   *Themes from the Lectures at the Collège de France : 1952-1960*
(Résumés de cours. Collège de France. 1952-1960)

Humanism   =   *Humanism and Terror : An Essay on the Communist Problem*
(Humanisme et terreur. Essai sur le problème communiste)

Primacy   =   *The Primacy of Perception and Other Essays*

INTRODUCTION

I am speaking. This principium of knowledge, indeed of existence, is the foundation of Maurice Merleau-Ponty's phenomenological theory of existential communication. What is to be learned from an inquiry into the phenomenon of speaking is not an inclusive answer to the innumerable questions posed by man's being, his history, or his fellow men. Rather, the act of speaking is an on-going process of questioning in which a person develops a style of living with himself, his environment, and his neighbor.

Questions can indeed be total; but answers, in their positive significance, cannot. Like a passion that one day just ceases, destroyed by its own duration, a question burns out and is replaced by an unquestioned state of affairs.[1]

The reality of *man speaking* is an expanding problem that is a partial concern of sociology, psychology, philosophy, anthropology, and communication theory. Yet, it is a reality that is fundamentally bound by the act of "speaking" in all of its dimensions, whether personal or interpersonal. This is to say, "disclosing fundamental meaning-structures through all its many fissures, our age calls for a philosophical interpretation".[2] This judgment reflects Merleau-Ponty's basic contention that our age has become an "unquestioned state of affairs" or an age of science in which technology has reified man in an attempt to solve his problems in a world of other objects. The apparent security that science offers is not a final answer, although it is treated as such in many instances of human interaction. Life in a world so defined by science is at best an illusion of the moment for which questioning is a necessary step to progress beyond the illusion. The questioning necessarily begins outside science in philosophy.

---

[1] M. M-P., *Signs* (Evanston, Ill.: Northwestern University Press, 1964), pp. 3-4.
[2] M. M-P., *Signs*, p. 13.

Philosophy is not science, because science believes it can soar over its objects and holds the correlation of knowledge with being as established, whereas philosophy is the set of questions wherein he who questions is himself implicated by the question.[3]

Such a point of view is not anti-science in a fanatical sense, but merely the assertion of philosophy's superiority in allowing man to question in terms of his life-world for those answers that will allow him to exist in the world of fact. In short, the basic questions of value that are vital to man's existence must be precedent to the questions of fact. Science must be considered as another means of questioning reality, not as its sole answer.[4]

The writings of Merleau-Ponty suggest that his use of phenomenology as a method allowed him to incorporate the facts of science in the realm of man's life-world or *Lebenswelt*. By his careful scrutiny of perception and the conditions for perception, he conceived a theory of signs or semiology that is applicable to man's existential presence, most notably in man's speaking. In point of fact the relation between Merleau-Ponty's concepts of semiology and speaking suggest an original definition of man's being-in-the-world. A phenomenological analysis of man speaking is thus an inquiry into man's existence in the world and the conditions of the world's presence for man. Merleau-Ponty's systematic interest in the objective and subjective nature of man speaking constitutes a unique theory of communication that is methodologically a *phenomenology* and ontologically an *existentialism*.[5]

The concern of this study is to extricate Merleau-Ponty's original conclusions from his writings with respect to semiology and speaking. The method of extrication appears most practical given the nature of Merleau-Ponty's style which is to formulate conclusions and results as "ready-made" with the question of verification left to the auditor.[6] A systematic exploration of Merleau-Ponty's work will require a general

---

[3] M. M-P., *Visible* (Evanston, Ill.: Northwestern University Press, 1968), p. 27.
[4] See Walter Fales, "Phenomenology of Questions", *Philosophy and Phenomenological Research* IV (September, 1943), pp. 60-75.
[5] An accurate explication of M. M-P's phenomenology and his existentialism occurs respectively in James Daly, "Merleau-Ponty's Concept of Phenomenology", *Philosophical Studies* XVI (1967), pp. 137-164, and Raymond Bayer, "Merleau-Ponty's Existentialism", *University of Buffalo Studies* (Monographs) XIX, no. 3 (1951), pp. 95-104. Cf., M. M-P., "La Philosophie de l'existence", *Dialogue* V, no. 3 (December, 1966), pp. 307-322.
[6] The efficacy of this procedure has been demonstrated by Herbert Spiegelberg, *The Phenomenological Movement,* 2nd ed. (The Hague: Martinus Nijhoff, 1965), II, 559.

consideration of the scope and meaning of existential communication followed by a detailed examination of semiology and speaking. The union between the semiology and speaking will become apparent in the explication of the "lived-body experience" which in turn suggests the direction of Merleau-Ponty's ontological speculations when he died.

The primary source material for the present inquiry is drawn from the various copyrighted translations of Merleau-Ponty's treatises and articles. Because these translations are readily available, often from more than one translator, for comparison with the original French and represent a faithful rendering of Merleau-Ponty's thought, they have been used in deference to the French editions. Where doubt and the possibility of ambiguity occur, the English is parenthetically followed by the French usage. The one exception to these guidelines will be discussed momentarily.

As an author, teacher, and sometime editor-in-chief and political director of *Les Temps Modernes,* Merleau-Ponty was prolific in his composition of books and articles. Hence, it may be helpful to briefly sketch the development of his writing from the first published book to the volume he was working on when he died. A detailed listing of his work appears in the bibliography of this study.

His first published book, *La Structure de comportement* in 1942,[7] is a detailed analysis of the traditional approaches to psychology with a methodical examination and critique of Behaviorism, Gestalt Psychology, Realism, Naturalism, and Idealism. Three years later, in 1945, his second work, *Phénoménologie de la perception,*[8] was published. This is a landmark volume in the history of phenomenology as it was the first French work to appear with "phenomenology" in the title, indicating a specific philosophic use of the method. The volume is respectively devoted to sections on "traditional prejudices and the return to phenomena; the body; the world as perceived; Being-for-itself, and Being-in-the-world". This book is considered to be Merleau-Ponty's major treatise and contribution to philosophy. It is necessary to note at this point that the Colin Smith translation is used in the present study, but where necessary, obvious errors have been corrected.

---

[7] *The Structure of Behavior,* trans. Alden L. Fisher, (Boston: Beacon Press, 1963); New French Ed. preceded by "A Philosophy of Ambiguity" by Alphonse de Waehlens, (Paris: 1949).
[8] *Phenomenology of Perception,* trans. Colin Smith (New York: Humanities Press, 1962).

In most cases only a word or short phrase is in question, hence the bulk of the Smith translation is still utilized *as corrected*.[9]

No major treatise was to follow for some time, although Merleau-Ponty collected a number of his essays and journal articles which progressively resulted in the publication of *Humanisme et terreur*,[10] *Les Adventures de la dialectique*,[11] and *L'Œil et l'esprit*.[12] Selections from all three works have appeared in translation under the title *The Primacy of Perception*.[13] Next came *Éloge de la philosophie*[14] which is a short volume containing Merleau-Ponty's inaugural address given on January 15, 1953, when he entered the Collège de France. Minor themes were expressed in short essays of introduction in *Les Philosophes célèbres*, which he edited in 1956.[15] Continuing his thematic writing style, he published two more collections of essays drawn from various journal pieces which appeared under the respective titles, *Signes* (in 1960)[16] and *Sens et non-sens* (in 1961).[17]

Finally, the volume *Le Visible et l'invisible* was published posthumously in 1964.[18] It was to be Merleau-Ponty's second, major work and final statement of his philosophy as it had progressed from the statement in *Phenomenology of Perception*. When he died he had completed approximately one hundred sixty-two pages of text devoted to Part I — "the visible". He also left about one hundred twenty pages of working notes that were to be used in writing the remaining two parts of the book — "nature" and "logos". In point of fact, this last section on *logos* was to have been the statement of Merleau-Ponty's theory of communication in its ontological status. The posthumous publication of a fragment[19] and working notes entitled

[9] "For purposes of neither teaching nor research can this translation [Smith's] alone be relied upon". Aron Gurwitsch, "Review: *Phenomenology of Perception*", *Philosophical Review* LXXIII (July, 1964), pp. 417-422, quotation, p. 422.
[10] Trans. John O'Neill, Boston: Beacon Press, 1969.
[11] Paris: Éditions Gallimard, 1955.
[12] Paris: Éditions Gallimard, 1964.
[13] James M. Edie (ed.) (Evanston, Ill.: Northwestern University Press, 1964).
[14] *In Praise of Philosophy*, trans. John Wild and James Edie (Evanston, Ill.: Northwestern University Press, 1963).
[15] Paris: L. Mazenod, 1956.
[16] Trans. Richard C. McCleary (Evanston, Ill.: Northwestern University Press, 1964).
[17] Trans. H.L. and P.A. Dreyfus (Evanston, Ill.: Northwestern University Press, 1964).
[18] Claude Lefort (ed.), trans. Alphonso Lingis (Evanston, Ill.: Northwestern University Press, 1964).
[19] "Pages d'Introduction à la Prose du Monde", Introductory Note by Claude Lefort, *Revue de Métaphysique et de Morale* LXXII, no. 2 (April-June, 1967), pp. 139-153.

La Prose du Monde[20] indicate that Merleau-Ponty had begun work on the problem of communication in the 1950's but apparently abandoned the theme of these notes until his projected writing in *The Visible and the Invisible* supplied the new ontological theme for his philosophy of communication.

Another posthumous work, *Résumés de cours. Collège de France. 1952-1960,*[21] contains Merleau-Ponty's synopsis of lectures which he delivered at the college. This collection of "themes" as they originally appeared in the annual resumes is a concise summary of his philosophic development during his tenure at the college.

Although his topical writings range over psychology, socio-anthropology, politics, film, and philosophy, Merleau-Ponty hypostatized communication (speaking) as the foundation of each area of knowledge insofar as speaking is the vehicle of creation and preservation of knowledge in each. This central thesis can be seen in a careful reading of almost any of his essays and is unquestionably present in his books.

While the primary task of this study is to extricate Maurice Merleau-Ponty's phenomenological theory of existential communication, reference to other theorists is made where they explain Merleau-Ponty by means of agreement or disagreement.

By extricating Merleau-Ponty's theory of communication one finds in his writings a specific theory of semiology which forms the base of a theory of perception and a theory of expression. The dialectical operation of perception and expression form an explanation for thought and action at the personal, interpersonal, and social levels of human involvement. Merleau-Ponty's communication theory is a pioneering effort to combine the best methodology of psychology and philosophy, in his view, to explain man's unique character as *homo loquens.* In Merleau-Ponty's work one can see the genesis of methodology that is compromising of both *phenomenology* and *structuralism* which are the major approaches to the study of *homo loquens.*[22] Thus, it is not of minor importance to note that Merleau-Ponty's major works have the titles : *Structure of Behavior* and *Phenomenology of Perception.*

---

[20]   Ed. Claude Lefort, Paris: Éditions Gallimard, 1969. Trans. John O'Neill (Evanston, Ill.: Northwestern University Press, forthcoming).
[21]   *Themes from the Lectures at the Collège de France, 1952-1960,* trans. John O'Neill (Evanston, Ill.: Northwestern University Press, 1970).
[22]   M. M-P., *Themes,* pp. 124-131, esp. p. 126 on "a philosophy of structure".

I

EXISTENTIAL COMMUNICATION AS PHENOMENOLOGY

1. EXISTENTIAL COMMUNICATION

Communication as a personal experience is, if I may borrow a phrase from R.D. Laing, "that estranged integration we call sanity".[1] The process of communication is normally viewed as a situation in which one person passes on information to a second person with varying degrees of reaction from the latter. Theorists often seize the analogue of the physical sciences to explain this process and human communication becomes just another example of how "information" or "data" is transmitted from one locale to another. The more efficient this process is, the more communication is "effective". The major shortcoming of this approach to communication is that it relegates *meaning* to the physical input or output of the human organism. This is to say, what I mean is only existent in the physical system of transmission. The words I speak or the sentence that I write is my meaning — there is little, and more often no, concern for the *person* who has uttered his ideas. Following the present line of analysis, personal existence can be measured and quantified as a physical object. The presumption here is that man's aesthetic and ethical actions are mere labels or judgments to be placed upon his adherence to or deviation from an agreed upon norm of conduct. In point of fact, what is normal and abnormal is an operational approach to what a person communicates and the sum of a man's utterances come to constitute his history wherein one makes the lightning judgment: "I understand (or don't understand) what he *means*".

In an attempt to bridge the apparent antinomy posed by the fact that man has what is generally called his subjective self and his objective self, or "mind" and "body" if you prefer, R.B. MacLeod has suggested an approach wherein the behavioristic man might be under-

---

[1] R.D. Laing, *The Politics of Experience* (New York: Ballantine Books, 1967), p. 44.

stood in his existential mode. That is, man may be treated as a phenomenon that is definable only in relation to the situation that he finds surrounding him. Such a situation is not to be limited to the rather brief time-space sector of an immediate experience, but should include all those cultural and historical influences that come to constitute "man" as distinct from "homo sapiens".[2]

MacLeod's formulation begins at the behavior level of man in which action is "symbolic" or on an objective level of one thing (object) arbitrarily related to another. In specific terms of communication this might be characterized as the language of mathematics or logic in which the communication has a "meaning" in the experiential world when it is applied to a given function; our modern concept of technology. At this "symbolic level" man's behavior is an abstraction in the sense that it operationally has no situation as a context of meaning.

The second level in which communication can operate, MacLeod suggests, is that of "signification or sign meaning". This level is the bridge between the human being treated as a data-producing thing and man as existential. The use of signs — either a word or action — is a communication technique that allows one to suggest another context for the present sign. This recalled context then allows the generation of a meaning. Nonetheless, this level of communication still views man as an object capable of the proper act of correlation between one set of past data and the present data for which a "high" correlation suggests correct or more probable agreement upon what is "meant".

Perceptual meaning being the third level of communication, MacLeod suggests that it includes at least "expressive or physiognomic meaning". This type of meaning we will refer to as *existential communication*.[3] The basic premise that a definition of existential communication has to rely upon is that it is possible, in varying degrees, for a man to convey his unique humanity to another person. In this context and building on MacLeod's schema, it appears reasonable to assume that the best or most clear meaning would be an utterance or act that simultaneously occurs on all three levels, but which has its origin in the third or perceptual level. This is to say that a communication that *is* what is uttered or acted out means (or defines itself

[2] Sing-nan Fen, "Situation as an Existential Unit of Experience", *Philosophy and Phenomenological Research* XI, no. 4 (June, 1951), pp. 555-560.
[3] R.B. MacLeod, "Phenomenology: A Challenge to Experimental Psychology", in *Behaviorism and Phenomenology*, ed. T.W. Wann (Chicago: University of Chicago Press, 1964), p. 71.

as) that which exists at the time and place of its use. This meaning is known only by perception, yet the perception is itself a joint product of a set of signs that are used in an accepted manner to signify the possibilities of perception. Put simply, perception is the unity of conception (that for which the symbol stands) and sensation (symbol use).

The analysis that we have made beyond MacLeod is in fact an explanation of an existential communication as a phenomenon of personal experience. It is the first step in discussing the method of phenomenology as an approach to analyzing existential communication as it exists and the conditions that allow its emergence. But, the discussion of phenomenological method is a matter for later analysis.

The rigorous insertion of man, in his role as a person among people, into the process of communication bears the obvious mark of a philosophic concern for the ways in which our world is defined.

At no time like the present has scientific knowledge overturned its own *a priori*. Literature has never been as "philosophical" as it has in the twentieth century; never has it reflected as much upon language, truth, and the significance of the act of writing. At no time like the present has political life shown its roots or its web and challenged its own certitudes, first those of conservatism and now those of revolution. Even if philosophers were to weaken, others would be there to call them back to philosophy. Unless this uneasiness consumes itself, and the world destroys itself in experiencing itself, much can be expected of an age which no longer believes in philosophy triumphant but is through its difficulties a permanent appeal to rigor, criticism, universality, and philosophy militant.[4]

This long quotation from Merleau-Ponty is by way of suggesting the urgency with which he felt that philosophy in its examination of man must concentrate upon the man of action in an age of questioning and doubt. And what better key to man than his communication — whether spoken or written ? Obviously, the progress of science has left man waiting for his place in the constitution of meaning : first, on a personal level where life must have a purpose; second, on a social level where individual actions must be harmonized to allow and sustain personal life; and third, on an environmental level where the interactions of men provide the conditions requisite to personal and social existence. An examination of communication on these three levels as interrelated levels is a province of philosophical concern that is genuinely existential in that the unity of fact and value is a necessary pre-condition to meaning.[5]

[4] M. M-P., *Signs*, pp. 157-158.
[5] M. M-P., *Signs*, p. 101.

The realm of existential communication is put rather concisely by Jean Wahl:

Communication has consistently been one of the major problems in the philosophies of existence. Indirect in Kierkegaard, direct and striving in Jaspers, divided into "authentic" and "inauthentic" in Heidegger (the authentic sphere being reversed, it seems for poetic expression), clumsy and failing in Sartre, communication is always there—at least as a problem. Even in the absence of communication, the idea obstinately persists.[6]

Existential philosophy thus utilizes communication in various ways as Wahl has suggested. The concern of the present study is to explain briefly how these various views of existential communication have been synthetically incorporated into the communication theory of Maurice Merleau-Ponty.

1.1. *The Philosophical School of Paris*

Jean Wahl is responsible for first using the phrase "the philosophical school of Paris" in reference to the close association of Jean-Paul Sartre, Simone de Beauvoir, and Maurice Merleau-Ponty. Wahl equated this "school" with existentialism as it existed in France.[7] The affinity of these three French philosophers is drawn from different sources of concern, but our primary intent with them here is to indicate that Merleau-Ponty alone chose to examine communication as an integral part of his phenomenological method. Although the Sartian masterwork, *Being and Nothingness,* is subtitled "An Essay on Phenomenological Ontology", the concern is with Being as a metaphysical problem and communication does not figure in any large measure. Sartre and de Beauvoir alike choose to use language via literature only as a means of exemplifying their philosophical position which is largely a construction from "nothingness".[8]

In contrast to his two associates, Merleau-Ponty views the object of philosophy to be positive in the sense that existence should be a function of phenomenology. In this respect Merleau-Ponty's existentialism is an advance from an original statement of phenomenology in the tradi-

---

[6] Jean Wahl, *A Short History of Existentialism,* trans. F. Williams and S. Maron (New York: The Philosophical Library, 1949), p. 11.

[7] Wahl, *A Short History* ..., p. 2.

[8] See Jean-Paul Sartre, *Being and Nothingness,* trans. H.E. Barnes (New York: The Philosophical Library, 1956); Simone de Beauvoir, *The Ethics of Ambiguity,* trans. B. Frechtman (New York: The Citadel Press, 1964).

tion of Edmund Husserl.[9] In particular, Merleau-Ponty's affinity with the late Husserl suggests that for Merleau-Ponty "the phenomenological attitude to be adopted is not an effort at universalization, but a return to the speaking subject".[10] Merleau-Ponty himself emphasizes this judgment by his remark that "it is absolutely necessary to underline the *philosophical* import of the return to speech".[11]

How Merleau-Ponty arrives at his concern for speaking as a phenomenon of *existential* phenomenology is not a simple matter. Nonetheless, certain clear influences are visible. For example, Martin Heidegger's existentialism is built upon an appreciation of the power of speech. Barrett has suggested that in Heidegger's philosophy of existence there are three general traits : (1) mood or feeling; (2) understanding; and (3) speech.[12] For Heidegger these elements are *existentialia* and together constitute the basic categories of existence.

Heidegger himself, when considering the very question of philosophy's definition, has stated :

We are introduced to and become acquainted with what philosophy is only when we learn how, in what manner, it is. It is in the manner of correspondence which is to the voice of the Being of being.
This correspondence is a speaking. It is in the service of *language*. What this means is difficult for us to understand today, for our current conception of language has undergone strange changes. As a consequence, language appears as an instrument of expression. Accordingly, it is considered more correct to say that language is in the service of thinking rather than that thinking, as correspondence, is in the service of language.[13]

There is a subtle distinction that is drawn by Heidegger between language and speaking which reflects the phenomenological distinction between existential speech and sedimented speech (Heidegger's "idle talk"). This is to say that speaking is the existential risk of commitment that transcends language as a system of symbols only ready for use, but not used. And, it is in this sense that Heidegger argues that "philoso-

---

[9] See, e.g., Alphonse DeWaelhans, "Maurice Merleau-Ponty [obituary]", *Revue Philosophique de Louvain* 59, Troisieme serie, no. 62 (May, 1961), p. 378-380, esp. 379.
[10] Mary Rose Barral, *Merleau-Ponty: The Role of the Body-Subject in Interpersonal Relations* (Pittsburgh: Duquesne University Press, 1965), p. 197.
[11] M. M-P., *Signs,* pp. 92-93.
[12] William Barrett, *Irrational Man* (Garden City: Doubleday Anchor Books, 1962), p. 220. (first published, 1958).
[13] Martin Heidegger, *What is Philosophy?*, trans. J.T. Wilde and W. Kluback (New Haven: College & University Press, 1956), pp. 91-92.

phical research will have to dispense with the 'philosophy of language' if it is to inquire into 'the things themselves'...".[14]

1.2. The Return to Phenomena

Edmund Husserl's famous dictum "Back to the things themselves !" [Zurück zu den Sachen selbst !] is usually taken to be the epigram that explains the philosophic concern of phenomenology. In terms of a philosophy of language, the work of Merleau-Ponty becomes especially significant in that a philosophy of language is taken to be a return to phenomena in the positive and active sense of a philosophy of *speaking* that is the phenomena of meaning *per se*. "The word accumulates expressive power with unusual plasticity and possibility of cross-reference, making it possible to transcend the sign toward the sense".[15]

Phenomenology by its concern with a return to original phenomena is not a limitation of philosophy to science, but rather an attempt to make, in Husserl's phrase, philosophy a "strict science".[16] This idea is formulated within Merleau-Ponty's philosophy of speaking as a return to the speaking subject rather than an examination of language as a symbolic system. In short, Merleau-Ponty's philosophy is not a linguistics — either structural or transformational. The return to the speaking subject is "the rediscovery of the subject in the act of speaking, as contrasted to a science of language which inevitably treats this subject as a thing".[17]

The basic division between the analysis of the speaking subject and language analysis is the difference between living in the meaning of discourse and objectifying words as units of the physical world or sense-data.[18] Although Merleau-Ponty develops a semiology that by itself would constitute a partial linguistics, his construction of the lived-body experience as a unity of perception and speaking clearly places

---

[14] Martin Heidegger, *Being and Time*, trans. J. Macquarrie and E. Robinson, (New York: Harper & Row, 1962), pp. 209-210.

[15] Thomas Langan, *Merleau-Ponty's Critique of Reason* (New Haven: Yale University Press, 1966), p. 124.

[16] Edmund Husserl, "Philosophy as a Strict Science", *Cross Currents* VI, no. 3 (Summer, 1956), pp. 227-246; VI, no. 4 (Fall, 1956), pp. 325-344. Cf., Maurice Natanson, "Phenomenology as a Rigorous Science", *International Philosophical Quarterly* VII, no. 1 (March, 1967), pp. 5-20, and James M. Edie, "Phenomenology as a Rigorous Science", *International Philosophical Quarterly* VII, no. 1 (March, 1967), pp. 21-30.

[17] M. M-P., *Signs*, p. 104.

[18] M. M-P., *Phenomenology*, p. 336.

his philosophy beyond linguistics *per se*. The idea that speech and perception are performed by the embodied person (body-subject) is Merleau-Ponty's major philosophical thesis in his theory of communication.

There would appear to be an antinomy in what has been said about existential communication in that speaking as an existential communication implies a subjective utterance that automatically becomes objective when uttered. This is to suggest that what is indeed existential *per se* cannot be communicated, for the transfer of information or felt experience must be an object that another person can perceive. In short, one might suppose that what is existential cannot be communicated, and what is communicated is not existential.

2. THE APPARENT ANTINOMY OF EXISTENTIAL COMMUNICATION

Communication as a philosophical problem becomes an antinomy only if one confuses phenomenalism and phenomenology as methodologies in determining the nature and preconditions of existentialism. The subtle distinctions that exist between the theories of linguistic phenomenalism and the phenomenology of language are drawn from a basic perception of the relationship that exists between any given subject and object. Whether this relationship is a dualism, a synthesis, or synopsis generally distinguishes a phenomenalism, phenomenology, or existential phenomenology respectively.[19]

2.1. *Phenomenalism*

The philosophic method that is labeled "phenomenalism" is probably more explicitly and more often called "linguistic phenomenalism". Such a phenomenalism operates to define the object/subject dualism (deriving primarily from Rene Descartes) not by a description of the constituents of matter, but by an elucidating of the concept of a material object. The definition of matter proceeds by an explicit specification in terms of "sensa" or specific items of sense data. At best we seize upon a "definition in use" in which the sensa of a given time-space coordinate can be perceived as some sensible unity. It is essential to note that sensa derive not from the physical object but from the

[19] Cf. Don Ihde, "Some Parallels Between Analysis and Phenomenology", *Philosophy and Phenomenological Research* XXVII, no. 4 (June, 1967), pp. 577-586.

statements about the object. Thus, our linguistic task would be to translate the "definition in use" or statements about material objects *into* equivalent sets of statements about the sensa. Obviously, the goal in such a procedure is to arrive at an equivalence between the world of objects and the world of language.

The means of arriving at the subject/object equivalence has taken various forms in the history of phenomenalism. It is beyond the scope of the present analysis to detail each one of these approaches, however an indication of the major tendencies within the phenomenalism movement can be made. First, phenomenalism was associated with logical positivism and operationalism wherein the meaning of material-object statements was held to lie in their mode of verification, that is, in the sensum statements that would verify them. The specific thrust of this approach to the Cartesian dualism will be treated in our discussion of semiology.

Second, phenomenalism gained great momentum in its ties with the study of logic, particularly with Bertrand Russell. Russell's attempt to find an "ideal language" by the application of his theory of types to ordinary language usage greatly encouraged those interested in solving metaphysical problems by language analysis. Russell's belief was that his theory of types as a purely logical formulation could explain the world as man experienced it in his use of language. In brief, Russell's logic was adapted to ordinary language by means of a "translation" where equivalent sensa are used. This "theory of description" as a product of the "theory of types" will also be elaborated when our study takes up semiotic theories of language and experience.[20]

Phenomenalism, in a third instance, appears to be a useful basis of explanation for certain physical phenomena that bear analogous structures to language. This is to say, physics in particular with its concern for unobservable particles finds an analogous relation with language wherein the ambiguity of meaning is similarly "unobservable". The speculation is that an examination of language in its conceptual structure of sensa will be an insight to the logical relation of sensa in the objective world.[21]

The point to be kept in mind concerning linguistic phenomenalism

[20]   For a detailed account of several of the problems raised here, see: Bertrand Russell, *The Basic Writings of Bertrand Russell, 1903-1956*, ed. R.W. Egner & L.E. Denonn (New York: Simon & Schuster, 1961).

[21]   This argument is explained in detail by Bertrand Russell, "Mentalism vs. Materialism", in *Understanding History* (New York: The Philosophical Library, 1957), pp. 105-122.

is that meaning is a function of objective reality as know by a perceiving subject. By this "meaning" is meant a conscious construct
derived from objective encounter. The dualism of subject and object
is prerequisite to a coherent formulation of meaning in either sector —
the personal or the mundane. In short, as Mikel Dufrenne has explained it, "the ambition of logical language is to be sufficient unto
itself and to find its semantics on the same level as its syntactics".[22]

2.2. *Phenomenology*

Whereas phenomenalism as an epistemology limits the scope of meaning to phenomena that (1) are physical phenomena or the totality of
objects of actual or possible perception and (2) mental phenomena as
the totality of objects of introspection, phenomenology is the study
of essences whether in perception or in consciousness. Phenomenology is concerned with essences as a means of knowing existentials.
This point of view reflects the notion of a synthetic being in which
essence is intricately attached of what is existent. A judgment of this
nature presumes that the duality of subject and object can lead to a
pure knowledge of the subject or object only by a concomitant knowledge of its polar opposite. Yet, the requirements of knowing essences
as that phenomenon which is immediately given suggest in phenomenological theory the necessity of dealing with essences on a subjective
level. By subjective is meant the possibility of individual perception
wich may intentionally operate either on a private level or public
level of knowledge. The perception is however a primordial affair of
the individual that may be shared to greater or lesser degrees depending
on the extent of similar perceptions by other persons.

In this fashion Merleau-Ponty summarizes the approach that Husserl
made to phenomena by the use of Hegel's logic of synthesis.

At this point phenomenology, in Husserl's sense, rejoins phenomenology in
the Hegelian sense, which consists in following man through his experiences
without substituting oneself for him but rather in working through them in
such a way as to reveal their sense. The term *phenomenology* ends up bringing
out into the open everything that is implicitly contained at the start.[23]

---

[22] Mikel Dufrenne, *Language and Philosophy*, trans. H.B. Veatch (Bloomington:
Indiana University Press, 1963), p. 63. A specific application of this view can be seen
in Karl Britton, *Communication: A Philosophical Study of Language* (New York:
Harcourt, Brace & Co., 1939), or, in Grace Andrum de Laguna, *Speech: Its Function
and Development* (Bloomington: Indiana University Press, 1963). See M. M-P.,
Themes, p. 94.
[23] M. M-P., *Primacy*, p. 92. Also see: James M. Edie, "Recent Developments in

Phenomenology thus requires that there be a world other than ourselves or "outside" where things and people are exposed to us — an objective world. However, this experienced world is a product of an intentional perception, i.e., a consciousness *of* what is "there", and a perspectival phenomenon which is always incomplete. Meaning in any given case then becomes the synthesis of the subjective and objective experience, or psychological sensation tempered by psychic perception (intentionality).

The synthetic nature of phenomenology is best seen in Spiegelberg's historical presentation of phenomenological method as it has developed over a number of years and through a variety of philosophers. The method consists in seven steps.[24]

2.2.1. *Investigating Particular Phenomena*

This process follows a pattern of three steps in which one proceeds from phenomenological intuition, to analysis, and to description. Phenomenological intuition is a strict adherence to knowledge as it is immediately given in experience. The primary concern of the practitioner is to determine if the immediate experience is actual or not; that is, is the experience an actual perception or merely an imputed concept of a given sensation.

Phenomenological analysis is often wrongly construed to be a bedfellow of "ordinary language analysis" because of the similar concern of many phenomenologists and Logical Empiricists (Positivists) with the analysis of language.[25] However, phenomenologists in their concern

---

Phenomenology", *American Philosophical Quarterly* I, no. 2 (April, 1964), p. 115-128.
[24] Herbert Spiegelberg, *Phenomenological Movement*, II, p. 659ff. Cf., William Earle, "Phenomenology and Existentialism", *Journal of Philosophy* LVII, no. 2 (January 21, 1960), pp. 75-84.
[25] The difference here is well exemplified in Charles Taylor and A.J. Ayer, "Symposium: Phenomenology and Linguistic Analysis", *Proceedings of the Aristotelian Society*, Supp. XXXIII (July 10-12, 1959), pp. 93-124. A specific comparison of methodology is undertaken by Paul G. Kuntz, "Order in Language, Phenomena, and Reality: Notes on Linguistic Analysis, Phenomenology, and Metaphysics", *Monist* XLIX, no. 1 (January, 1965), pp. 107-136, esp. 129-136. A further comparison appears in two articles by John Wild, "On the Nature and aims of Phenomenology", *Philosophy and Phenomenological Research* III, no. 1 (September, 1942), pp. 85-95, and "Is there a World of Ordinary Language?" *The Philosophical Review* LXVII, no. 4 (October, 1958), pp. 460-476. There is a specific comparison of Gilbert Ryle and Maurice Merleau-Ponty in J.H. Jacques, "Exorcizing the Ghost in the Machine", *The Listener* LXXIV, no. 1893 (July 8, 1965), pp. 49-51. Cf., Frank Tillman, "Transcendental

with language utilize it as only one of many expressions of *structure* that are available in perception. This is a fundamental distinction as we shall see later in discussing Merleau-Ponty's theory of communication wherein a base semiology or structure system is equally applicable to perception and speaking.

Phenomenological description is simply the procedure of classifying and naming those perceptions which constitute familiar phenomena; or, with unfamiliar phenomena, the process of negation by which a category is more generally and provisionally assigned in contrast to known phenomena. At times the unfamiliar may best be described by way of analogy or metaphor until analysis allows a more explicit formulation of its structure.[26] It should be noted that phenomenological description is never an absolute process in the sense of arriving at a final definition of phenomena since our source of knowledge is still the perceiving subject whose experience itself is never a final attainment, but an on-going process of synthesis.

2.2.2. *Investigating General Essences (Eidetic Intuiting)*

The process of intuiting general essences is, following Husserl's lead, the procedure of treating individual phenomena as examples or instances of the more general phenomena. The idea is that the *structural nature of the example stands in correspondence to the class* or category of such phenomena in such a manner that a general essence may be intuited of all such phenomena in that particular category. The primary significance of this procedure is that it illustrates the impossibility of seeing particular essences without also coming to know the ground of the structural affinities that a category of phenomena possess. Indeed, such structural affinities are the essence of the phenomena and thus the essence of the particular is a possibility for perception.

2.2.3. *Apprehending Essential Relationships Among Essences*

The determination of relationships falls into two categories : The relationships in a given essence and the relationships between several

Phenomenology and Analytic Philosophy", *International Philosophical Quarterly* VIII, no. 1 (March, 1967), pp. 31-40; and, Stanley Cavell, "Existentialism and Analytic Philosophy", *Daedalus* XCIII, no. 3 (Summer, 1964), pp. 946-974.

[26] James M. Edie, "Expression and Metaphor", *Philosophy and Phenomenological Research* XXIII, no. 4 (June, 1963), pp. 538-561.

essences. In an analysis of the relationships in a particular essence the object is to determine which elements of the essence are essential to its being and which are not. Husserl employed the technique of "free imaginative variation" which is generally practiced by most phenomenologists. The technique involves the omission of certain elements of an essence or the replacement of certain elements by others in a given essence to determine its primary structure that is in fact its "essence".

The results of this procedure fall into three possibilities : (1) The essence is as described — the structure designated by the general name remains unaffected by the omission or substitution of elements; (2) The essence will be fundamentally changed by the omission or substitution — although the *gestalt* or character of the changed essence may still be conceivable as changed; or (3) The essence is eliminated or "destroyed" by the omission or substitution of elements. As Spiegelberg notes, the first possibility is "essential possibility", the second is "relative essential possibility", and the third is a verification of "absolute essential necessity".[27]

2.2.4. *Watching Modes of Appearing*

Phenomenologies are as concerned with the manner in which essences appear as with what essences appear to be. In short, how one comes into contact with essences is a fundamental aspect of determining what one is perceiving. Our perception along this line of analysis follows three possibilities. First, what we perceive may be a synthesis of the side or aspect of an immediate perception with the whole perception of an object. For example, we *recognize a whole* building by just perceiving the front of it.

A second aspect of apprehending how an essence comes to be perceived in its totality is explained by what appears to be perspectival deformations. For example, the rendering of a railroad track progressing off toward the horizon is not explicitly an expression of the essence of what a railroad track is since the perceived rails tend to and fundamentally do appear to converge, although the rails are not convergent in essence. Thus, the deformation of perspective in fact allows us to apprehend the sense of depth that informs us that the rails do in fact progress toward a horizon in the same essential form or structure as is apparent to us from the vantage of immediate perception.

[27] Spiegelberg, *Phenomenological Movement*, II, p. 681.

Appearance is also affected by changes of perspective in which the clarity or distinction of what is perceived allows a greater or lesser degree of recognition. The contrast between what is given as distinct and that which is an indistinct residue allows the given perception to fix on the essential elements of a perception. This is to say that an appearance which can be "focused" in or out will by its harmony or disharmony posit the necessary elements of an essence. An excellent example is the reversible appearances of optical illusions.

2.2.5. *Exploring the Constitution of Phenomena in Consciousness*

The reference to "constitution" implies the notion of a gradual building in our conscious awareness of the elements of a given essence. The purpose of this procedure is not to assemble the facts relevant to a given phenomenon in order to objectively define it. Rather, the purpose of a study of the constitution of a phenomenon is to ascertain the typical structure of the constitution *per se* as it evolves in consciousness by a detailed analysis of the essential sequence of the structure formation. In most cases this is a passive or spontaneous event, but the necessity of analyzing constitutions is not thereby precluded. The very harmonizing of my conscious use of constitution enables me to see the similarity of my perceptions to yours. This notion is effectively exploited in Merleau-Ponty's notion of a "radical gestalt" which will be discussed in more detail in a later section of this study.

2.2.6. *Suspending Belief in the Existence of the Phenomena*

The suspension of belief in the existence of a phenomenon or the explicit doubt (following Descartes) that the phenomenon exists, is what Husserl referred to as "bracketing" [Einklammerung]. This procedure is not to deny the existence of the phenomenon, but merely to concentrate on the "what" of the phenomenon in order to ascertain its essential content. This procedure is in fact what Husserl called the "phenomenological reduction". However, the full meaning for Husserl includes a number of other points in addition to what has already been said. The bracketing must include the systematic cancellation of those acts by which our consciousness comes to constitute the phenomena. The aim of the reduction is to allow an uninhibited intuiting, analysis, and description of the immediate phenomena. Thus, the preconceptions that we possess about the nature of existence, experience, appearance, and so on, are to be put aside before an accurate use of phenomenological method can be undertaken.

One aspect of the reduction should be emphasized at this point. That is, the temporary nature of the reduction as it relates to a given phenomenon must be kept in mind as it is always necessary to come to the *existence* of the phenomena. This whole area of the return to existence figures as the major advance that Merleau-Ponty's use of phenomenological method makes over that of Husserl. In point of fact, the positive possibility of the Cartesian *cogito* is taken up by Merleau-Ponty in what he terms the "radical *cogito*". Here, the return to existence from the essence of the phenomena is explained as the unitary production of the positive ("I can") out of the negative ("I think"). This entire theory will be detailed later.

2.2.7. *Interpreting Concealed Meaning*

This step in the phenomenological method is largely a post-Husserl addition that derives from both the French and German heritage of philosophy. In particular the existential philosophies of Heidegger, Sartre, and Merleau-Ponty lead to a level of phenomenological analysis that is termed *hermeneutics*. Hermeneutic is an attempt to interpret the meaning or "sense" of a given phenomenon. This procedure is generally contrasted with the previous six steps of method detailed above which usually bears the label "descriptive phenomenology".

The object of hermeneutic is to go beyond the meaning that is revealed by phenomenological intuiting, analysis, and description. This is to say, a hermeneutic seeks to discover the meaning that is not immediately manifest to description. In Merleau-Ponty hermeneutic takes the form of a return to the pre-reflective level of consciousness that underlies the conscious level of the lived-body experience of the body-subject — also a subject to be detailed at length in a following section. In general, the use of hermeneutic is an attempt to uncover those pre-conscious structures of meaning that inhere in the conscious presence of phenomena.

The above seven step review of phenomenological method is primarily drawn from Spiegelberg, as we have noted previously. The same analysis has been performed by Schmitt although his review is more critical in its approach and does not include the speculation about a possible phenomenological hermeneutic.[28]

[28]   Richard Schmitt, "Phenomenology", in *The Encyclopedia of Philosophy*, ed. Paul

This review of phenomenological method should allow one to grasp the basic divergence of interest between phenomenalism with its concern for specifying the objective existence of phenomena, as opposed to the phenomenological concern with a subjective approach to the object's essence. Before following the implication of the phenomenological hermeneutic, that an existentialism is the final subject matter of the phenomenological reduction, it will be necessary to specify the nature of existential philosophy as it is viewed in the communication process.

3. COMMUNICATION AS EXISTENTIALISM

Communication is a central force in most of the existential philosophers in the French and German tradition. This process of incorporating communication into the basic explanation of existence has taken four basic forms : (1) Existence as indirect communication; (2) Existence as direct communication; (3) Existence as authentic or inauthentic communication; and (4) Existence as primordial or genetic communication. These theories of communication are typically represented in the respective writings of Kierkegaard, Jaspers, Heidegger, and Merleau-Ponty. Of course, there are other philosopher's who would serve to explicate the respective communication theories. However, the purpose here is not to present a detailed analysis of each communication theory as part of a philosophic movement or of any given philosopher as opposed to another. Rather, the aim is to examine each type of philosophy in a specific application to communication as an existential concept. This in itself will provide a base of understanding from which a detailed analysis of Merleau-Ponty can proceed, inasmuch as his theory of primordial communication tends to incorporate or at least assume various elements of the other theories of communication.

3.1. *Existence as Indirect Communication*

The knowledge of existence, indeed the very proof of existence, can be derived from communication. Yet, this communication in the philosophy of Soren Kierkegaard assumes an "indirect" stance, which is to say, indirect communication is subjective in orientation. Christopherson has summarized this approach as follows :

Edwards, (New York: Macmillan Co. and The Free Press, 1967), pp. 135-151.

Communication of ability is that process whereby the existing individual relates himself to existence in such a way as to preserve his inwardness by directly (through interest, passion, and mood via language symbols, dialectical puzzles, and the like) relating himself in reduplication and double reflection and to others as a situational determinant and mode of disclosure for authentic existence. The beginning and end of communication of ability is authentic existence.[29]

This definition of communication, as Kierkegaard's philosophy suggests, is subjective in the sense that only the knowledge of self existence is assured by communication. And, such knowledge is obtained only indirectly in those communications that take place between persons. This is to say, there is for Kierkegaard no sure knowledge that what is communicated to me is an objective constituent of my being; I may take it as such only indirectly by some other form of verification (such as self experience). Even what I communicate directly becomes an indirect element of existence since another person is always involved in the process and thus verification of what I have communicated can only take place through him. The process of communication comes to rely on the subject's ability to experience and live in a objective world. The reliance, in the final analysis, of the individual upon himself as only a subjective being makes communication a constant source of error. A definition of existence through communication is thus an indirect procedure.

Indirect communication becomes for them [Nietzsche and Kierkegaard] the sole way of communicating genuine truth; indirect communication, as expression, is appropriate to the ambiguity of genuine truth in temporal existence, in which process it must be grasped through sources in every Existenz.[30]

The existential power of indirect communication is further explained by Jasper's remark that "what may be senseless for the understanding can be a necessary form of sense; and that which to the understanding

---

[29] Myrvin F. Christopherson, "Soren Kierkegaard's Dialectic of Communication: An Approach to the Communication of Existential Knowledge", unpublished Ph-D. dissertation, Department of Speech and Theatre, Purdue University, 1965, p. 190. Also, see: Raymond E. Anderson, "Kierkegaard's Theory of Communication", unpublished Ph. D. dissertation, University of Minnesota, 1959. A brief, but accurate presentation of Kierkegaard's concept of communication as "double reflection" appears in David F. Swenson, "The Existential Dialectic of Soren Kierkegaard", *Ethics* XLIX, no. 3 (April, 1939), pp. 309-328, esp. 311-312.
[30] Karl Jaspers, *Reason and Existenz*, trans. William Earle, (New York: The Noonday Press, 1955), p. 27.

seems literal can be a total perversion of the meaning of what is intended".[31]

All discourse for Kierkegaard assumes the burden of bringing forth the inner subjectivity of man. The primacy of the "inner" man is therefore the end of communication, whether used existentially by man to become, or as used to confirm the existence of the subject in its objective or world modality.[32]

3.2. *Existence as Direct Communication*

Kierkegaard's existentialism utilizes indirect communication as a proof that subjectivity, as a primordial originator of being in an objective sense, is the only true mode of existence. Karl Jaspers' philosophy suggests the counterpart to this approach, which is to say existence is a basic product of direct communication. Jaspers' contention is that objective reality assumes the status of "being-an-object" which he calls a "cypher". It is the cypher that allows for direct communication, for the cypher is the object in the modality of transcendence or being-an-object. The cypher is not listened to or cognized, but "only steps forth more clearly in communication".

The characteristic of the cypher separates the signification from that which is signified in it. This separation is false. If we call cyphers a form of communication then the listening to the language *of the* cypher is itself a metaphor for something merely analogous but in itself quite different compared with our mode of listening to Being *in the* cypher.[33]

The view that Jaspers has of the communication affirms that the exchange of meaning between a person in his subjectivity and the objective reality that he encounters is a cypher function. This cypher function or "cypher-status" suggests that objectivity does not exist unless there is a subjective encounter with it, yet the encounter does not allow the immediate experience of objectivity. Rather, what one calls objectivity is the immediate experience of the object in transcendence. The transcendence is the movement of objectivity *qua* objectivity to objectivity-for-me. In other words, the cypher function

---

[31] Jaspers, *Reason and Existenz*, p. 112.
[32] Raymond E. Anderson, "Kierkegaard's Theory of Communication", *Speech Monographs* XXX, no. 1 (March, 1963), pp. 1-41. See: Robert Cumming, "Existence and Communication", *Ethics* LXV, no. 2 (January, 1955), pp. 79-101.
[33] Karl Jaspers, *Truth and Symbol* (from *Von Der Wahrheit*), trans. J.T. Wilde, W. Kluback, and W. Kimmel, (New York: Twayne Publishers, 1959), pp. 40-42.

allows the person to realize an objective world when he takes the cypher as lived reality, not as reality cognized or conceptualized. Even then, subjectivity is affirmed as existential for it is the modality of the experiencing subject that allows the synthesis of objectivity into subjectivity through the transcendence of the object.

Although Jaspers utilizes a theory of direct communication to support his account of existence, there is still a basic reliance on the ability to separate the object from the subject — even if they are synthetically and dialectically functions of each other. In point of fact, the transcendence of objectivity to subjectivity would not be possible in Jaspers' system unless the basic dualism is assumed, at least as a primitive notion. The explicit implications that this theory of communication has for existentialism will be expanded when Jaspers is covered in a later section on his semiology as a development beyond semiotic phenomenalism.

3.3. *Existence as Authentic and In-authentic Communication*

As with Kierkegaard and Jaspers, our treatment of Martin Heidegger must be brief for the moment, although a more detailed analysis will follow as an introduction to Merleau-Ponty's elaborations of his (Heidegger's) position on communication.

In his monumental *Being and Time,* Heidegger draws a clear distinction between what he terms "talk" and "idle talk". In terms of existential communication these two polar uses of language represent an authentic and in-authentic usage. The nature of "talk" or "discourse" is put quite explicitly by Heidegger.

The way in which discourse gets expressed is language. Language is a totality of words—a totality in which discourse has a 'wordly' Being of its own; and as an entity within-the-world, this totality thus becomes something which we may come across as ready-to-hand. Language can be broken up into words-Things which are present-at-hand. Discourse is existentially language, because that entity whose disclosedness it Articulates according to significations, has, as its kind of Being, Being-in-the-world—a Being which has been thrown and submitted to the 'world'.[34]

Before commenting on the authenticity of talk, it will facilitate matters to define "idle talk".

Idle talk is the possibility of understanding everything without previously making the thing one's own. If this were done, idle talk would founder; and

[34] Heidegger, *Being and Time,* p. 204.

it already guards itself against such a danger. Idle talk is something which anyone can rake up, it not only releases one from the task of genuine understanding, but develops an undifferentiated kind of intelligibility, for which nothing is closed off any longer.[35]

The simplest distinction that can be drawn between talk and idle talk as expression of authentic and in-authentic discourse is to suggest that the subject has two modalities of being-in-the-world. First, the subject has original or primordial experience with objectivity. Talk or discourse about this encounter suggests that the articulation constitutes for the subject a Being-in-the-world *with* "an entity within-the-world". This is to say, discourse allows the synthetic transcendence of subjectivity into objectivity by the person's encounter (as subject) with an external objectivity that suggests the person's objectivity. Thus, existence as both subject and object is the primordial or authentic status revealed by talk or discourse.

However, idle talk is more of a probability in our encounters within the world. Discourse tends to encase and pass along not the experience of the primordial encounter, but the *understanding* that is secondary. Idle talk reveals an experience in the absence of perception; it is as an appearance — intelligible, yet lacking complete meaning. Idle talk is thus an in-authentic form of communication that does not convey authentic existence.

The existential distinction that Heidegger is advancing will become more explicit in Merleau-Ponty's theory of authentic or existential speaking and sedimented speaking.

3.4. *Existence as Primordial Communication*

Before indicating the scope of Merleau-Ponty's theory of primordial communication, it will be advantageous to briefly review Jean-Paul Sartre's use of the en-soi/pour-soi [in-itself/for-itself] dualism as it is manifest in the use of language. Sartre conceives of a divided Being in the sense that Being-for-itself [être-pour-soi] is the negation of Being-in-itself [être-en-soi]. Being-for-itself is the lack of Being that requires the use of Nothingness to make itself stand apart from Being-in-itself. Language is a modality in which this dualism operates at a manifest level of consciousness.

---

[35] Heidegger, *Being and Time*, p. 213.

Thus the "meaning" of my expressions always escapes me. I never know exactly if I signify what I wish to signify nor even if I *am* signifying anything. It would be necessary that at the precise instant I should read in the Other what on principle is inconceivable. For lack of knowing what I actually express for the Other, I constitute my language as an incomplete phenomenon of flight outside myself. As soon as I express myself, I can only guess at the meaning of what I express—i.e., the meaning of what I am—since in this perspective to express and to be are one.[36]

Sartre's explanation of existential communication follows Kierkegaard in that he affirms the authentic or primordial communication must be indirect, since a direct encounter can never be known via the other person. But in addition, Sartre's position leads him to say that even the subject cannot know his existence from communication, except insofar as it fails to produce meaning. Communication is thus a recognition of the subject/object duality where the subject is primordial in reference to the object, but there is also a duality of the subject which cannot be known primordially. The existent subject is that response to Nothingness by which the subject affirms his possibility. Yet, the subject never affirms that he *is* by his communication.

In short, Sartre's philosophy of communication asserts a dualism within a dualism. There is a duality of the For-itself or Consciousness and the In-self or Being, and, there is a duality within the For-itself : indirect communication and lack of communication. Communication, then, when it occurs is a synthesis of the dualism at either level and it is a synthesis that necessitates and posits the pre-existence of the dualisms.

Without the commitment of beginning the detailed presentation of Merleau-Ponty's theory of communication here, several fundamental tenets of his theory will explain primordial communication as a philosophy of existence. Merleau-Ponty denies the existence of the Sartrian dualisms. He maintains that we are a presence-at-the-world or being-with-the-world [être-au-monde] in which the pour-soi and en-soi are a unitary *presence*. Second, he denies the dualism of direct and indirect communication by suggesting that direct communication is a primordial or existential communication of our presence-at-the-world. This communication can become "sedimented" in the sense that its meaning *can* be recalled, realizing that such a recollection is no longer primordial and therefore a secondary or indirect communication. This indirect communication is positive in nature by suggesting the essence of the

---

[36]   Sartre, *Being and Nothingness,* p. 373.

primordial communication, rather than negative in the Sartrian sense of suggesting the lack of primordial essence in the recalled communication.

A further point to be made is that for Merleau-Ponty a primordial communication is an authentic communication of existence, whereas a sedimented communication is in-authentic in the sense of not being existential.

The extent and meaning of Merleau-Ponty's theory of communication will become apparent as his phenomenological method and concept of existence as *gesture* are explained in some detail. The actual theory of speaking as existential phenomenology still requires an examination of semiology as a prelude to the parallel systems of perception and speaking.

4. MERLEAU-PONTY'S PHILOSOPHY AS EXISTENTIAL PHENOMENOLOGY

Before an examination of Merleau-Ponty's methodology of phenomenology as a method of knowing existence, it will help to understand his concept of philosophy in general and philosophy as a synoptic discipline which has a place in all fields of knowledge. In short, Merleau-Ponty felt philosophy as philosophy to be "philosophy militant" — a philosophy charged with action in the theoretical and practical life of man.

4.1. *Philosophy qua Philosophy*

"There is not *a* philosophy which contains all philosophies; philosophy as a whole is at certain moments in each philosophy. To take up the celebrated phrase again, philosophy's center is everywhere and its circumference nowhere".[37] As Merleau-Ponty summarizes in these remarks, philosophy is in the midst of "life's contagion".[38] As a vital force in man's being and history, philosophy assumes the role of a certain consciousness that we have of ourselves, nature, and other people.

We shall call "philosophy" the consciousness we must maintain—as our consciousness of the ultimate reality whose functioning our theoretical con-

---

[37] M. M-P., *Signs*, p. 128.
[38] M. M-P., *Signs*, p. 130.

structions retrace but could not possibly replace—of the open and successive community of *alter egos* living, speaking, and thinking in one another's presence and in relation to nature as we sense its presence behind, around, and before us at the limits of our historical field.[39]

Merleau-Ponty's theme in this view of philosophy is that man in the very practice of his affairs, in particular the act of speaking with others, is practicing philosophy. In fact, every level of experience is dependent on the intersubjective exchange that occurs between one subject and another. This primary philosophical consciousness is prerequisite to our understanding of the world in an objective sense. Without this concern for philosophy as philosophy, we would have no awareness of our subjective movement within our world. Because "we are born into reason as into language",[40] our concern is not with the history of man's involvement in the creation and solution of "problems", but in the structural experience that is to us an "interrogative ensemble".[41] In this context, the person's project as a philosopher "is indeed, and always, a break with objectivism and a return from *constructa* to lived experience, from the world to ourselves".[42]

Merleau-Ponty's analysis has one goal in mind and that is to demonstrate that philosophy qua philosophy *is* existential philosophy.

The "subject" is no longer just the epistemological subject but is the human subject who, by means of a continual dialectic, thinks in terms of his situation, forms his categories in contact with his experience, and modifies this situation, and this experience by the meaning he discovers in them. In particular, this subject is no longer alone, is no longer conscious in general or pure being for itself. He is in the midst of other consciousnesses which likewise have a situation; he is for others, and because he undergoes an objectivation and becomes generic subject. *For the first time since Hegel, militant philosophy is reflecting not on subjectivity but on intersubjectivity.*[43]

It is apparent in this brief statement that Merleau-Ponty's concern with intersubjectivity lends itself to a deep concern with communication as the mediating force in both personal and interpersonal expression. Existentialism as a philosophy then makes better sense to Merleau-Ponty if it is conceived as the idea of a universality that men affirm in the dialectic of living encounter, in the reason that is immanent in

---

[39] M. M-P., *Signs*, p. 110.
[40] M. M-P., *Sense*, p. 3.
[41] M. M-P., *Visible*, p. 187. See *Themes*, pp. 39-45.
[42] M. M-P., *Signs*, p. 112.
[43] M. M-P., *Sense*, p. 134.

unreason, and in the freedom that is found in the act of accepting limits.[44]

The practice of philosophy then becomes philosophy *as* philosophy in which man's existence is affirmed. "Philosophy is irreplaceable because it reveals to us both the movement by which lives become truths, and the circularity of that singular being who in a certain sense already *is* everything he *happens to think*".[45] The single movement of the world, time, speech, and history are not to be taken by philosophy as accomplished fact, but must be taken as existential, as the "passage of meaning" in the experience of life.[46]

4.2. *Merleau-Ponty's Method*

Merleau-Ponty's philosophic method is phenomenology in a "radical" form. This is to say that he adheres to the general methodology of the seven procedures (as discussed previously), but that they have a different formulation which in fact suggests the basis for an existentialism. His own definition of phenomenology suggests this conclusion.

Phenomenology is the study of essences; and according to it, all problems amount to finding definitions of essences: the essence of perception, or the essence of consciousness, for example. But phenomenology is also a philosophy which puts essences back into existence and does not expect to arrive at an understanding of man or the world from any starting point other than that of their 'facticity'. It is a transcendental philosophy which places in abeyance the assertions arising out of the natural attitude, the better to understand them; but it is also a philosophy for which the world is always 'already there' before reflection begins—as an inalienable presence; and all its efforts are concentrated upon re-achieving a direct and primitive contact with the world, and endowing that contact with a philosophical status. It is the search for a philosophy which shall be a 'rigorous science', but it also offers an account of space, time and the world as we 'live' them.[47]

Within this brief definition is subtly woven the elements that constitute Merleau-Ponty's theory of existence and methodology for the knowledge thereof. However, the explicit statement of method — and the one often repeated by scholars[48] — is presented as the following

44   M. M-P., *Sense*, p. 70.
45   M. M-P., *Signs*, p. 113.
46   M. M-P., *Praise*, p. 9.
47   M. M-P., *Phenomenology*, p. vii.
48   Colin Smith, *Contemporary French Philosophy* (London: Methuen & Co., Ltd., 1964), p. 56; Spiegelberg, *Phenomenological Movement*, pp. 536-538.

formula : "Reflection must elucidate the unreflective view which super-
sedes, and show the possibility of this latter, in order to comprehend
itself as a beginning".[49] Or as it is more loosely put :

A phenomenology, therefore, has a double purpose. It will gather together
all the concrete experiences of man which are found in history—not only
those of knowledge but also those of life and of civilization. But at the same
time it must discover in this unrolling of facts a spontaneous order, a meaning,
an intrinsic truth, an orientation of such a kind that the different events do
not appear as a mere succession.[50]

Merleau-Ponty's method may, in short, be formulated as a reflection
in two steps : First Reflection — a reflection on the phenomenal field
or *gestalt* as given in lived experience (immediate perception); and,
Second Reflection — a reflection on the conditions necessary for the
perception of the phenomena of the First Reflection (pre-objective
phenomena). In the more familiar terminology of Merleau-Ponty, the
first reflection is the "primacy of perception" while the second reflection is the "radical reflection" or "radical reduction" (or occa-
sionally, the "phenomenological reduction").

To leave the statement of Merleau-Ponty's method at this stage
would be an error since there is a third factor which must be considered,
namely, the "radical *cogito*". Merleau-Ponty's interpretation of the
Cartesian *cogito* is in fact a new and positive (thus "radical") statement
of its function. The radical *cogito* is in fact the presence-at-the-world
in which the *cogito* reveals to me "the movement of my own transcendence in the very act of being immersed in the world by actual
perception".[51] Thus, it is by the use of the radical cogito that Merleau-
Ponty comes to posit the final step of his phenomenological method as
the self-awareness of existence. His philosophy of phenomenlogy is an
existentialism. That is, his phenomenology is a method whereby essential
experience is known as a reflection of the existent.

Phenomenological or existential philosophy is largely an expression of surprise
at this inherence of the self in the world and in others, a description of this
paradox and permeation, and an attempt to make us *see* the bond between
subject and world, between subject and others, rather than to *explain* it as
the classical philosophies did by resorting to absolute spirit.[52]

---

49   M. M-P., *Phenomenology*, p. 213.
50   M. M-P., *Primacy*, p. 52.
51   Barral, *Merleau-Ponty*, p. 244.
52   M. M-P., *Sense*, p. 58.

It must be apparent that Merleau-Ponty's equation of existentialism and phenomenology, of existence and essence, is a basic denial of the Cartesian dualism. For Merleau-Ponty there is no such category as pure subject or pure object, nor is there synthesis of subject and object as subject-object. Rather, Merleau-Ponty posits the primacy of perception through the primacy of the body-subject. This is to say, his existential phenomenology is a "bi-polar phenomenology"[53] in terms of actual perception of phenomena. The body-subject is at once his own body, yet he knows himself in the subjective mode of being conscious and being "in" his body. The subjective modality that is consciousness is in fact the joint presence-at-the-world of the body and its consciousness of action in the world and in relation to others.

Phenomenology in this case is neither a materialism nor a philosophy of mind, but the assertion of the preconditions for both.[54] Phenomenology in this orientation is a "phenomenology of origins".[55] The origin of man's act, the thing perceived, the history experienced, the others encountered. In the experience of perception the body-subject affirms the lived reality that his actions constitute in conjunction with others who undergo the same perceptual experiences.[56] As a body-subject present-at-the-world with other body-subjects equally present-at-the-world, the lived-body experience is a phenomenal existence that is not a synthesis of body and mind, of object and subject, but the lived perception that is a "transitional synthesis".[57] Yet, the transitional synthesis is also misleading for, as was noted before, a synthesis in any form presupposes polar opposites or anti-thetical categories. "Let us say for the moment that we prefer, to the notion of synthesis, that of synopsis, which does not yet point to an explicit positing of diversity".[58] Thus, Merleau-Ponty consistently maintains the unity of the body-subject in the lived-body experience.

Although Merleau-Ponty's method as reflected in the lived-body experience will be detailed in a separate chapter, and although there are certain elements to the method that were not mentioned in this

[53] Spiegelberg, *Phenomenological Movement*, II, p. 535.
[54] M. M-P., *Signs*, p. 165.
[55] M. M-P., *Phenomenology*, p. xviii. See Thomas Busch, "Merleau-Ponty and the Problems of Origins", *Philosophy Today* XI (Summer, 1967), pp. 124-130, esp. 125.
[56] Herbert Spiegelberg, "French Existentialism: Its Social Philosophies", *Kenyon Review* XVI (Summer, 1954), pp. 446-462, esp. 454-461 on Merleau-Ponty.
[57] M. M-P., *Phenomenology*, p. 329.
[58] M. M-P., *Phenomenology*, p. 276n. See *Themes*, pp. 53-61.

section, the following summary of method may prove helpful by way of orientation in this complex area.

Merleau-Ponty's method consists of three steps. First, the primacy of perception is asserted wherein the phenomena of perception function in the synopsis of immanence and transcendence. Within this first step is the determination of the essential *gestalt* of perception or the "radical gestalt". Two primary factors in determining the "primacy of perception" are the *intentionality* of the body-subject in the use of perspective and "constitution" and the use of *temporality* as a function of imaginative variation or projection [Einfühlung]. This entire first reflection entails and adds to the method of "descriptive phenomenology" which is concerned with phenomenological intuiting, analysis, and description.

The second step in the phenomenological method of Merleau-Ponty is "radical reflection" or the use of "bracketing" [epoché] in the reduction of the conditions necessary to the operation and existence of the "radical gestalt". This second reflection involves the hermeneutic or meaning interpretation of the primary perception.

The third part of the methodology is the "radical cogito" which allows one to attain the pre-objective or pre-reflective level of the phenomena. That is, the level of the presence-at-the-world in which there is lived-meaning, where the signified *is* the signification. This level of method is a hermeneutic of essence which *is* existence *as lived*. The primordial expression of this existence-as-lived is present in the human *gesture* which is itself the synoptic paradigm of essence as existence. Indeed, the gesture is the very presence-at-the-world.

4.3. *Gesture : Communicating the Existential Phenomena*

Because the human gesture implies a synergic relation between the one gesturing and the situation gestured about, "the primordial human gesture contains in seed all the characteristics of more sophisticated acts of expression".[59] The human body is the vehicle of human communication by reason of its mere physical existence.

It is through my body that I understand other people, just as it is through my body that I perceive 'things'. The meaning of a gesture thus 'understood' is not behind it, it is intermingled with the structure of the world outlined by the gesture, which I take up on my own account.[60]

[59] Langan, *Critique of Reason*, p. 126. See M. M-P., *Humanism*, pp. 94-96.
[60] M. M-P., *Phenomenology*, p. 186.

Thus, it is the base of the human "physical" or "geographical" body that is a perceiving body allowing the emergence of the existential or "lived" body. Just as perception is the reception of meaning in the lived-body, so gesture is the expression of the lived-body. In fact, it is the gesture that operates within virtual space to create lived space which has primordial meaning.[61] Gesture, then, is not an indication of what meaning should be or what meaning might imply. Gesture is the meaning itself. For example, in a fit of anger that is perceivable by its communicative aspects, "the gesture *does not make me think of anger,* it is anger itself".[62]

The phenomenology of existential communication is clearly apparent in the gesture if we stop for a moment and consider the learning process in which the human ability to communicate is developed.

Thus, to learn never consists in being made capable of repeating the same gesture, but of providing an adapted response to the situation by different means. Nor is the response acquired with regard to an individual situation. It is rather a question of a new aptitude for resolving a series of problems of the same form.[63]

The expressive power of the gesture is its unique position with respect to the situation in which it occurs, yet the singularity of the gesture is its power of creating meaning by its form. This is to say, a gesture has existential meaning when its form *is* its own communication of essences; when the gesture repeats the form of known essences, it is a sedimented meaning — this is a meaning recalled, not created anew.

The gestures and the attitudes of the phenomenal body must have therefore a proper structure, an immanent signification; from the beginning the phenomenal body must be a center of actions which radiate over a "milieu"; it must be a certain silhouette in the physical and in the moral sense; it must be a certain type of behavior. In fact, modern psychology has brought to light this immediate apprehension of structure which is the condition of possibility of all judgments of recognition as well as of all associations of ideas.[64]

The distinctive phenomenal element of the gesture becomes the form it takes. Any communication becomes meaningful when its form or structure is self-explanatory, that is, when the gesture is its own meaning

---

[61] M. M-P., *Structure,* p. 117.
[62] M. M-P., *Phenomenology,* p. 184. See Virgil C. Aldrich, "Expression by Enactment", *Philosophy and Phenomenological Research* XVI, no. 2 (December, 1955), pp. 188-200.
[63] M. M-P., *Structure,* p. 96.
[64] M. M-P., *Structure,* p. 157.

because it is the phenomenal or lived expression of an intended meaning. The structure or "construction is a gesture, which means that the actual lines drawn are the outward expression of an intention".[65]

It is probably obvious at this point, that a gesture is an intentional structure that is "pregnant" with meaning. The structure or form has no specific essence itself, but is a product of the lived-body. This is to say, the gesture is a phenomenal expression of the body-subject as lived. "The form is a visible or sonorous configuration (or even a configuration which is prior to the distinction of the senses) in which the sensory value of each element is determined by its function in the whole and varies with it".[66] In this sense there are no "things" as separate from "people". There are only "physiognomies" that are their own definition or lived-meaning.

It may be apparent now that "words" or language are a gesture of the body-subject and our encounter with them is as our response to a gesture. Indeed, one can feel the anger of the "word" as intimately as the anger of the physical gesture. "Words have a physiognomy because we adopt towards them, as towards each person, a certain form of behaviour which makes its complete appearance the moment each word is given".[67] Such a linguistic gesture is only a sedimented meaning, it has no existential or creative force because it is the "learned" response to communications of a given form.

Gesture as existential communication occurs in the act of human speaking. For Merleau-Ponty, "the act of speaking" is the "true physiognomy" that *is* what it means.[68]

Speech is comparable to a gesture because what it is charged with expressing will be in the same relation to it as the goal is to the gesture which intends it, and our remarks about the functioning of the signifying apparatus will already involve a certain theory of the significations expressed by speech.[69]

The phenomenological investigation of speaking will thus lead to a positing of what is existential by way of its essential presence-at-the-world. Speaking is the lived-body experience that is existential by its use.

---

[65]   M. M-P., *Phenomenology*, p. 386.
[66]   M. M-P., *Structure*, p. 168; this point is well illustrated by Richard P. Blackmur, "Language as Gesture", in *Language as Gesture: Essays in Poetry* (New York: Harcourt, Brace, & Co., 1935-1952), pp. 1-24.
[67]   M. M-P., *Phenomenology*, p. 235. See *Themes*, p. 6.
[68]   M. M-P., *Phenomenology*, p. 181.
[69]   M. M-P., *Signs*, pp. 89-90.

The link between the word and its living meaning is not an external link of association, the meaning inhabits the word, and language 'is not an external accompaniment to intellectual processes'. We are therefore led to recognize a gestural or existential significance in Speech, as we have already said.[70]

The point that Merleau-Ponty is making is a clear distinction between words as gestures of sedimented meaning and spoken words that are an existential meaning.

All words are the carriers of their own meaning and their form allows them to be their own meaning.[71] But this mere form in the absence of use is a sediment, it requires use to be unique — to create meaning by making what is essential the very presence of that which exists.

If I am a certain project from birth, the given and the created are indistinguishable in me, and it is therefore impossible to name a single gesture which is merely hereditary or innate, a single gesture which is not spontaneous—but also impossible to name a single gesture which is absolutely new in regard to that way of being in the world which, from the very beginning, is myself.[72]

What then is the line of distinction between existential and sedimented communication as it emerges in human speaking ? Speaking is existential when the act in the context of the lived-body experience not only signifies the meaning inherent in the linguistic gesture, but also signifies the pre-reflective meaning that allows the speaking to be a primordial communication of immanent meaning.

... The spoken word is significant not only through speaking, but also through accent, intonation, gesture and facial expression, and as these additional meanings no longer reveal the speaker's thoughts but the source of his thoughts and his fundamental manner of being ....[73]

Thus it is that speaking which creates its own gestalt or structure of meaning is existential communication. The meaning of the spoken word is a gesture which is its own meaning. In this sense, "the gesture which is inseparable from the living expression" is *speaking*.[74]

This entire analysis is put summarily by Merleau-Ponty in the following manner.

---

70 M. M-P., *Phenomenology*, p. 193.
71 M. M-P., *Sense*, p. 175.
72 M. M-P., *Sense*, p. 21.
73 M. M-P., *Phenomenology*, p. 151.
74 M. M-P., *Phenomenology*, p. 151.

The meaning of language, like that of gestures, thus does not lie in the elements composing it. The meaning is their common intention, and the spoken phrase is understood only if the hearer, following the "verbal chain", goes beyond each of its links in the direction that they all designate together.[75]

Merleau-Ponty takes speaking to be existential communication when it performs the basic reduction inherent in a phenomenological or lived experience. That is, speaking is existential when its primordiality is apparent in the joint presence of meaning and the conditions of that meaning — if you will — when the existential and genetic element is co-present with the essential and constitutive element of meaning. It is not a large or difficult move to the next step of this philosophical orientation, which is to suggest that a phenomenology of speaking can indeed be the beginning of an ontological phenomenology.

For this crystallization which is partly given to us ready-made is in other respects never terminated, and thereby we can see how the world comes about. It takes form under the domination of certain structural laws: events let general powers show through, powers such as the gaze or the word, which operate according to an identifiable style, according to "if ... then ..." relationships, according to a logic in action whose philosophical status must be defined if we wish to get out of the confusion in which the ready-made notions of thought, subject, and object throw us, and if we wish to know finally what the world is and what being is.[76]

In short, Merleau-Ponty's philosophic description of speaking is an "incarnate logic" which forms the basis and matter of human communication. Speaking is no less than the genetic act which becomes constituted as language and as the speech which binds person to person and self with self in a common, lived-world.

[75] M. M-P., *Primacy*, p. 8.
[76] M. M-P., *Visible*, p. 100.

II

EXISTENTIAL PHENOMENOLOGY AS SEMIOLOGY

Within Merleau-Ponty's philosophy there is an implicit methodology of knowing existence that is equally applicable to a theory of perception and to a theory of communication. This unitary base, for what is essentially a psychology and an existential "rhetoric", is a theory of semiology that incorporates the principles of perception to formulate meaningful structures and simultaneously provides the meaning inherent in the structure. In short, the semiology is existential as it denominates the existent, and, it is phenomenological in that it arrives at the existential through a study of the essential.

The process by which a semiology becomes an existential phenomenology of speaking must begin with an explanation of phenomenalism in semiology, for it is the dualism in a linguistic phenomenalism as semiology that is over-come by Merleau-Ponty's formulations. In sum, we must examine the familiar Cartesian dualism that separates "mind" as an active agency of thinking from the "body" as a passive agency of extension as it (the dualism) is manifest in the various philosophers who best represent the typical approach to a semiotic phenomenalism. Such a semiotic is dependent on the inability of the semiotic to breach the dualism through either a synthetic or synoptic union.

1. THE CARTESIAN DUALISM: SEMIOTIC PHENOMENALISM

Semiology is in its simplest form the study of signs. However the simplicity of this definition can be misleading in direct proportion to the number of definitions that one can imagine for the term "sign". Obviously, the definition of a sign is dependent on certain other considerations, not the least important of which is the application of the sign system in a given area of knowledge. This element of context was a major factor that emerged when Ferdinand de Saussure ventured to define semiology in terms of its application in human interaction.

A *science that studies the life of signs within society* is conceivable; it would be a part of social psychology and subsequently of general psychology; I shall call it *semiology* (from the Greek *semion* 'sign'). Semiology would show what constitutes signs, what laws govern them.[1]

As Saussure's definition indicates, semiology as a separate branch of studies is defined by the laws or operational restrictions that govern their function. Within semiotic phenomenalism there is agreement that the sign and its functional use or signification are objective entities. The nature of objects as signs varies slightly with the various philosophies of phenomenal semiotic, but there is no question that the mind/body dualism is assumed throughout.

1.1. *The Semiology of Charles Sanders Peirce*

In defining the fundamental notions of his semiology, Peirce limited the notion of a "sign" to any denotation of "an Object perceptible, or only imaginable, or even unimaginable in one sense...".[2] The indication of this definition is that the sign function is to signify or perform the process of *naming* an object. The sign does not stand in a one-to-one correlation with the object, but is the form or structure of the object which is assumed to be its essential content. In short, the sign is an "abstraction" out of the object of those essential *sensa* that constitute what is recognized as "objectivity" by an experiencing subject.

Peirce's approach to semiology clearly places the study of signs in the category of logic as the formulation of procedural rules for abstraction and categorization according to class characteristics. There is little or no concern with the "meaning" of semiotic in the subjective sense of a value implication resultant from a semiotic function. This is to say, there is a "material validity" for Peirce's semiology only in terms of structure. Whatever content is assigned to this structural function must be determined by a subsystem of the semiotic in which the structural consistency and structural self-validation must stand as

---

[1]   Ferdinand de Saussure, *Course in General Linguistics,* ed. C. Bally and A. Sechehaye in collaboration with A. Riedlinger, trans. Wade Baskin, (New York: McGraw-Hill Book Co., 1966), p. 16. (First published in 1959).
[2]   Charles Sanders Peirce, *Collected Papers of Charles S. Peirce,* ed. C. Hartshorns and Paul Weiss (Cambridge, Mass.: Harvard University Press, 1931), II, p. 136.

meaningful abstractions of similar objects. This present analysis is apparent in Peirce's definition of semiotic.

Logic, in its general sense, is, as I believe I have shown, only another name for *semiotic*, the quasi-necessary, or formal, doctrine of signs. By describing the doctrine as 'quasi-necessary', or formal, I mean that we observe the characters of such signs as we know, and from such an observation, by a process which I will not object to naming Abstraction, we are led to statements, eminently falliable, and therefore in one sense by no means necessary, as to what *must be* the character of all signs used by a 'scientific' intelligence, that is to say, by an intelligence capable of learning by experience.[3]

In the formulation of his semiotic, Peirce established an elaborate set of relational functions for the sign that specify the precise sense in which a sign is to be used. In addition, the function of the sign in giving meaning is a concomitant condition of the object signified. This is to say that

... an analysis of the essence of a sign, (stretching that word to its widest limits, as *anything which, being determined by an object, determines an interpretation to determination, through it, by the same object*), leads to a proof that every sign is determined by its object, either first, by partaking in the characters of the object, when I call the sign an *Icon*; secondly, by being really and in its individual existence connected with the individual object, when I call the sign an *Index*; thirdly, by more or less approximate certainty that it will be interpreted as denoting the object, in consequence of a habit (which term I use as including a natural disposition), when I call the sign a *Symbol*.[4]

Peirce is now in a position to indicate how his semiology will function within the subject/object dualism to provide meaning to given essences as existential objects. What is suggested here is that Peirce is like the General Semanticists in separating semiology into a "pure grammar", a "logic proper", and a "pure rhetoric". However, Peirce is more specific in explaining how signs function in these three areas. For Peirce every object appears to a subject as a *representamen* that is composed of the "ground", the "object", and the "interpretant". That is, a perception that operates as a sign-gestalt or signification is the result of a perceiving subject who recognizes the object within a context which indicates the usage meaning. The minimum conditions of recognizing the sign of the object is the province of pure grammar. The conditions of the object which allow a sign to function for objects of

---

[3] Peirce, *Collected Papers,* II, p. 134.
[4] Peirce, *Collected Papers,* IV, pp. 413-414.

a given class is the province of logic and if this function is fulfilled one arrives at a definition of truth.[5]

Pure rhetoric has for its task the formulation of those rules by which one sign can evoke another sign. In particular, pure rhetoric must be concerned with the process of signs in which one sign as a thought causes another sign as a thought to emerge. This project is clearly an attempt to make the objective formulations of a pure grammar and logic of objective essence compatible by identity with subjective existence. It is not an attempt at synthesis or even synopsis, but rather a theory of coherence in which the subject and object have compatible and necessary functions of meaning in relation to each other. Form or structure and content in either a subjective or objective sense are functions of each other's composition. In short, objective essence is a coherent variation of existential subjectivism and subjective essence is verifiable as a coherent function of an existential object. Peirce assumes a coherence theory of truth in which "truth" is a property primarily applicable to any extensive body of consistent propositions. Such a truth theory, as specifically expressed in Peirce's breakdown of semiological applications, also assumes that any one proposition in the system is valid by virtue of its part in the system.

The semiotic of Charles Peirce is therefore a construction of phenomenological meaning based upon the explicit nature of a subject/object dualism wherein signs signify objects or conditions of objects as experienced (whether actually perceived or imaginatively sensed). Semiotic is thus a propositional function that could not exist without the dualism.

1.2. *The Semiology of Charles W. Morris*

The original statement of Morris' semiology appeared in his "Foundations of the Theory of Signs"[6] which indicated his affinity of thought with Charles Peirce. At least the basic assumption of a subject/object dualism was carried on by Morris' theory. However, the evolution of semiology in the writings of Morris suggests that a more accurate statement of his belief will be found in the presentations of applied sem-

---

[5] Peirce, *Collected Papers,* II, pp. 135-136.
[6] *International Encyclopedia of Unified Science,* I, no. 2 (Chicago: University of Chicago Press, 1938), p. 1ff. Reprinted in *Writings on the General Theory of Signs* (The Hague: Mouton, 1972).

iology which he has made. *Signs, Language, and Behavior*[7] and *Signification and Significance : A Study of the Relation of Signs and Values*[8] both represent the application of semiology as a method to human behavior. In this union there is the implicit belief that semiology is the means by which science can be applied to human behavior or man's value world as a way of specifying knowledge. In fact, semiology is "a science among the sciences and an instrument of the sciences".[9] On the other hand, "the language of the philosopher constitutes a proper object of investigation for the semiotician" because "the language of philosophy is made up of those types of discourse dominated by the systemic uses of signs in its greatest comprehension".[10]

Its [semiotic] attempt to gain scientific knowledge concerning signifying, the relation of the modes of signifying, the criteria of truth and adequacy, the nature of signs in the specialized types of discourse, and the individual and social contexts in which signs function will inevitably influence the beliefs, appraisals, and prescriptions of the philosopher. In this sense the philosophy of the future will be semiotically oriented.[11]

How prophetic Morris was in seeing the beginning of semiology as it began to develop into philosophy's modern concern with language and logic as the possible key to man's ontology. And, it is in this sense that the range of semiotic is without limit. This is to say, semiology is a method that can stand as the "primitive notions" by which any area of human endeavor may be explained.

Semiotic has for its goal a general theory of signs in all their forms and manifestations, whether in animals or men, whether normal or pathological, whether linguistic or non-linguistic, whether personal or social. Semiotic is thus an interdisciplinary enterprise.[12]

What then is the semiology of Charles Morris? For him a sign is best defined as "a variable whose values are all concrete particulars — 'tokens' or 'sign-vehicles' ". Further, "It is functionally related to other variables through the relations of connotation, denotation, expressive-

---

7   New York: Prentice-Hall, Inc., 1946. Reprinted in *Writings on the General Theory of Signs*.
8   Cambridge: M.I.T. Press, 1964. The first chapter is reprinted in *Writings on the General Theory of Signs*.
9   Morris, "Foundations of the Theory of Signs", p. 2.
10 Morris, *Signs, Language, and Behavior*, pp. 233-234.
11 Morris, *Signs, Language, and Behavior*, p. 238.
12 Morris, *Signification and Significance*, p. 1.

ness, and such other dimensions or modes of meaning as it is desirable to distinguish".[13]

Within the specific area of the semiology of language, Morris distinguishes three dimensions of meaning for signs. First, there is the dimension of the "prelinguistic sign" in which the determinants of non-verbal signs are manifest. In the child it is the overt, non-verbal behavior that communicates, whereas in the adult it is less overt, but essential behavior that marks the *intent* of verbal behavior.

"Linguistic signs" are those which are in a "language considered as a system of interpersonal signs restricted in their possibility of combination".[14] And last, there are the "postlinguistic signs" which are entities of meaning that owe their signification to language usage, but which are not themselves constituent elements of the language.

Before the implications of the various levels of the Morris linguistic semiology are taken up, it may be well to indicate the basic division that is made by him with respect to the application of linguistic semiology in human behavior.

The following definitions represent a slight modification of those that originally appeared in the "Foundations of the Theory of Signs".

Pragmatics is that portion of semiotic which deals with the origin, uses, and effects of signs within the behavior in which they occur; *semantics* deals with the signification of signs in all modes of signifying; *syntactics* deals with combinations of signs without regard for their specific significations or their relation to the behavior in which they occur.[15]

One example that Morris offers to help illustrate the scope of each of these areas of semiotic is the specification of Aristotle's work within the above categories. That is, the *Organon* represents a study of the semantics and syntactics of the language of science. The *Rhetoric* exemplifies the range of pragmatics, while the *Poetics* in dealing with aesthetic discourse illustrates semantics and pragmatics.[16]

The relational power of a linguistic semiology that utilizes pre-, post-, and mediating signs within human behavior to specify pragmatics, semantics, and syntactics is a structure of reality that requires a dualism of subject and object.

---

[13]   John W. Blyth, "What is a Sign?" *Philosophy and Phenomenological Research* XIII, no. 1 (September, 1952), p. 39.
[14]   Morris, *Signification and Significance*, p. 58.
[15]   Morris, *Signs, Language, and Behavior*, p. 219.
[16]   Morris, *Signs, Language, and Behavior*, p. 286.

Semiotic can release the individual to play his part in his own unique way in the transmission and the transformation of the sign structure upon which the complex individual and the complex society depend for their existence and for their continued growth.[17]

Within Morris' phenomenalism, it is apparent that the subject/object dualism is exploited to explain the ambiguity that exists with a given set of signs in different contexts of use. This is to suggest that the prelinguistic sign can function as a variable of behavior, meaning, or structure in either a subject or object. The same analysis holds for linguistic signs and postlinguistic signs. In short, a sign may have a function with pragmatics that is subjective, which in turn, requires that the same sign in objective terms must be a function of semantics or syntactics or both. For this reason it becomes possible to separate form or structure from content. One can also separate act from intent. In these abilities lies the hope of a scientific analysis of behavior — but it is a hope that clearly relies upon the ability of the analyst to separate subject from object in any given action that is "human behavior".

Much of what Morris has advocated has been adopted and promoted by C.J. Ducasse in a separation of the notions of sign, signal, and symbol.[18] We mention Ducasse only by way of tieing in the theoretical formulation of Morris as they reflect the General Semantics of Ogden and Richards whom we will consider in a moment. Yet, it should be noted that the Morris-Ducasse formulation has provoked John Wild to advance a theory of "realistic semiology" as a clarifying proposal for the paradox of dualism.[19] By paradox, we mean to suggest the difficulties of specifying meaning in a semiology that uses signs in both a subjective and objective sense.

Wild's progression from the Morris theory of semiology is reflected in the following characterization that he (Wild) gives of semiotic.

The single words and verbal combinations which make up ordinary discourse are *signs*. Hence an adequate theory of signs is required for any understanding of logic and the abstract, technical symbols it employs. All knowledge, in fact, would seem to involve the interpretation of signs and symbols. So far as this

---

[17] Morris, *Signs, Language, and Behavior*, p. 214.

[18] C.J. Ducasse, "Symbols, Signs, and Signals", *Journal of Symbolic Logic* IV, no. 2 (1939), p. 43ff. See by the same author "Some Comments on C.W. Morris 'Foundations of the Theory of Signs'", *Philosophy and Phenomenological Research* III, no. 1 (1942-43), pp. 43-54.

[19] John Wild, "An Introduction to the Phenomenology of Signs", *Philosophy and Phenomenological Research* VIII, no. 2 (December, 1947), pp. 217-233.

is true, epistemology itself would seem to rest fundamentally on a theory of signs.[20]

A "realistic theory of signs" must therefore be composed of a statement of "sign relation" and a statement of "sign classifications". Sign relations involve the manifestation of a single object, for "nothing can signify itself".[21] Hence, "a sign is anything capable of manifesting something other than itself as an object to the knowing faculty".[22] Sign relations are simply those links established between a subject or knowing faculty and an object manifest to the senses. If it were put succinctly, a sign *is the agency of relation* between a subject and object.

As mere relations in the "realistic theory", signs have certain classifications. There are *natural signs* that exist in nature independently of anyone's interpretation. And, there are *arbitrary signs* which are not connected with what they signify, thus exist only in interpretation. There is a further division of signs. Natural signs are both *formal* and *instrumental*. Formal signs are a direct, complete reference to an object — it is an intrinsic relation. The natural sign can also be instrumental in which case the whole object of reference is not specified by the sign. There is potentially more in the object's being than is signified.

Arbitrary signs are likewise divided into subcategories. That is, there are *signs proper* that refer to some reality in conjunction with a concept about that reality. A second class of arbitrary signs is the *signal*. Signals indicate some object to be known, not some act to be performed.[23]

Obviously Wild's "phenomenology of the sign" is in fact a phenomenalism applied to semiology; there are no elements of existentialism here. There can be a synthesis of subject and object in some operations of semiotic, as the use of "signs proper", but this function requires the basic dualism of subject and object that is phenomenalism.

1.3. *The Semiology of C.K. Ogden and I.A. Richards*

Although the publication of *The Meaning of Meaning : A Study of the Influences of Language upon Thought and of the Science of Symbolism*

---

20   Wild, "An Introduction ...", p. 217.
21   Wild, "An Introduction ...", p. 229.
22   Wild, "An Introduction ...", p. 229.
23   Wild, "An Introduction ...", p. 232.

by Ogden and Richards in 1923 is the traditional mark of a renewed interest in semiology, our analysis of them is last because their theory is the most blatantly phenomenalistic.[24] For them semiology is limited almost entirely to what Morris called "semantics". But before reviewing their theory of semiology, it might be advantageous to define what they mean by a "sign" and its function.

A sign is something which has once been a member of a context or configuration that worked in the mind as a whole. When it reappears its effects are as though the rest of the context were present. In analysing complex events of refering we have to break them up artificially into the sign-situations out of which they arise; not forgetting meanwhile how interdependent the parts of any interpretation of a complex sign are.[25]

A sign then is an object of experience by the subject which functions to create meaning through a simulation of structure and content in analogous situations. There is an implicit suggestion here that the sign *per se* has no meaning or reference but is the agency of an object not itself. Taken to the next step, we might assume that a combination of signs or a sign-situation contains no meaning except insofar as it points to an object not itself. In point of fact, this very thesis is the foundation of the so-called "semantic triangle" of Ogden and Richards.

The triangle is an interrelationship of three elements : a Thought or Reference, a Symbol, and a Referent. Obviously, the referent is any entity that is objective, while the symbol and thought, respectively, are the physical and intellectual aspects of the subject. Meaning within this triadic relation has a distinct hierarchy wherein there are scientific, poetic, and rhetorical statements or formulations of meaning in a subject/predicate relation.

A *scientific* statement is the expression of a direct causal relation between a thought (reference) and a symbol. In this case the mind conceptualizes of the signs that assume an objectivity in place of the actual referent or object. The relation between the thought and the symbol is a subjective procedure that allows one to symbolically insert an object in opposition to a subject based on past experience. Thus, the symbolic use of sense-data tends to confirm the data-as-sensed and as it could be sensed, given the same conditions of knowing.

A poetic or *emotive statement* is a sign relationship in which there

[24] New York: Harcourt, Brace, and Co., Inc., 1923.
[25] I.A. Richards, *Principles of Literary Criticism* (New York: Harcourt, Brace & World, Inc., 1925), p. 90. This definition is used in preference to that in *The Meaning of Meaning* because of its succinct brevity.

is an indirect causal relation between a thought or reference and the referent or object. This relationship is indirect because it is a subjective response to the object. Whereas with a scientific statement there is a subjective creation of the object — hence a complete meaning. The emotive statement is a relation of signs in which an object is specified by the experience of encountering it. The signs are limited to signifying the given situation, hence the reversion to analogy, metaphor, and the like when the sign relations do not suggest a reference or known thought. There is an inability to form a direct causal relation between experience and thought, between perception and conception.

The third possibility of meaning in the semantic triangle is the *rhetorical statement* which is a mixture of scientific and emotive relationships. Sign relations are partially direct causation and partially indirect causation. In this situation the subject/object relation vacillates between signification and response to signification. On the one hand, there is denotation and on the other, connotation. Signs exist as objective. In a rhetorical statement they are mixed. Thus in the mixed statements there are imputed relations between the symbol and the referent that can operate within the subject/object dualism to create meanings that can be accurate or totally misleading.

Hence, the Ogden and Richards theory of semiology is a fundamental statement of phenomenalism. There is a subject/object dualism and there is a dualism in the behavior of the subject which is mental or intellectual action paired with physical or bodily action. Within linguistic semiology in particular there is a separation between concept and perception or sound-image as a sign of objectivity to be experienced by the subject. There is in this theory of semiology a fine presentation of phenomenalism *as* human behavior manifest in discourse.[26]

1.4. *The Semiology of Bertrand Russell*

Before an explicit examination of Russell's semiology insofar as one is manifest in his philosophy of language, we might temper our outlook with a representative look at semiology in scientific philosophy. A typical approach is that of Hans Reichenbach. For him there is no dualism of subject and object except insofar as the subjective is an outgrowth or partial expression of the objective. For example, "we may also say that the word 'mind' is an abbreviation denoting a bodily

[26]   Ogden and Richards, *The Meaning of Meaning*, p. 14ff.

state that shows certain kinds of reactions". Hence, "The belief in the independent existence of a mind is a fallacy evolving from the misunderstanding of abstract terms".[27] In this context, his statements about semiology are an express phenomenalism that recognizes "subjective" signs as those which are yet to be objectively verified.

What is this cognitive content? It is not something that is added to the sign system; it is a property of the sign system. Signs are physical things, such as ink mounds on paper, or sound waves, which are used in a correspondence relation to physical things; the correspondence, which does not rest upon any similarity, is based on a convention.

A sign combination which can either be shown to be true or be shown to be false is called meaningful. This concept is important because we are often concerned with sign combinations whose truth or falsity cannot be determined at present, but can be determined at some later time.[28]

Reichenbach goes on to argue that modern science is a documentation of this view that the *verifiability theory of meaning* is correct as a semiology of both experience and language. And, it is within this frame of reference that Bertrand Russell advances his theory of types and theory of descriptions as equally valid in logic and mathematics as in language.

Since our interest in Russell is primarily his approach to semiology, his analysis of words and meaning[29] will be our chief concern. For Russell a meaning is the relation that exists between a word and a thing designated by that word. In this relation the word can be considered as a physical thing apart from its meaning, that is, apart from its referent for which it is the sign perceived. These words as physical entities may be either spoken or written. But, in either event the particular instance of the word consists of a series of movements. In writing the movement is only potential, while in speaking it is actual.

---

[27] Hans Reichenbach, *The Rise of Scientific Philosophy* (Berkeley and Los Angeles: University of California Press, 1963), p. 272.

[28] Reichenbach, *The Rise of Scientific Philosophy*, p. 256. This explanation of "cognitive meaning" is balanced by a theory of "instrumental meaning" which involves imperatives that are neither true or false. Such instrumental meanings are often associated with acts of volition that do have a cognitive correlate that makes them a function in degree of cognitive meaning. This point is elaborated in Chapter 17 of the work cited in this note. See Hans Reichenbach, *Elements of Logic* (New York: Macmillan Co., 1947), p. 17ff. Here, there is a distinction between cognitive and instrumental meaning in more detail.

[29] Bertrand Russell, *The Analysis of Mind* (Baltimore: Penguin Books, 1962), pp. 21-101, 158-202.

In this frame of reference a single word becomes a class or a "family"[30] of similar series of movements.

Thus, by observation and analysis the meaning of a word emerges as that which distinguishes the word from other sets of similar movements. This is a common phenomena in the use of language where metalanguage develops to explain how the meaning of words functions in relation to other words. It is therefore possible to have speech about speech and to write about writing. The essence of language, consequently, lies in the fixed associations between words and their referents in order that something now sensible — a spoken word — may call up the idea of *something* else — a referent. In this schema it is assumed that the sensible or sensa is a sign with "pointing" ability or a symbol. Meaning thus functions as the object which stimulates the occurrence of the idea.

The characteristics of meaning can be exemplified in the process of *naming* where there is a distinction between proper names and general names. That is, in a proper name is manifest a particular individual or entity (thing, person, animal, etc.) which is a series of occurrences bound together by causal laws. This process which is designated as a whole system of *particular occurrences* is the proper name. In distinction to proper names are general names which are the means of designating a whole *system* or *group* of occurrences of similar individuals or entities. The general name is a designation of a class or collection of particulars with proper names.

The process of "understanding" a word is manifest when a person uses a word in suitable circumstances to specify his idea or when the hearing of a word causes suitable behavior in him. It should be noted that to understand a word, it is not necessary to know what it means. Russell suggests by this announcement that the correct use of a word is not a thought out act, rather, the word is used and then if necessary the meaning is distilled out by observation and analysis.

What has just been covered above is a loose explanation of Russell's application of the Theory of Types to language and the resulting Theory of Descriptions. It is necessary at this juncture to specify what each of these theories asserts in the field of language analysis, since they represent the specific application of the semiotic of logic and mathematics to language in an attempt to formulate an "ideal language" where there is pure meaning in sign functions.

[30]   Bertrand Russell, *An Inquiry into Meaning and Truth* (New York: 1940), Chapter 4, "Language".

1.4.1. *Applying the Theory of Types to Ordinary Language*

The application of a logic to language implies many difficulties if the application, in fact, seeks to make meaning objective in a one-to-one correlation of object to symbol. Yet, the theory of types as applied to language attempts to overcome two specific problems : (1) The contradictions inherent in reducing all statements to a subject-predicate form; and, (2) The contradictions present in the use of formal logic relations in the analysis of ordinary language.[31]

Russell suggests that the above two problems can be easily solved with the theory of types as presented in the *Principia Mathematica*.[32] However, the analysis which Russell started soon showed that the theory of types is a solution only for the second problem (above) and that the first problem required his "theory of descriptions".

The theory of types as applied to language can be explained in the following manner. There must be a restriction of the kinds of symbols which may be inserted into a given context. A proper name with meaning would be such a symbol. Thus all entities which are designated by symbols all of which can be inserted into some one context are said to belong to the *same type*. A segregation of entities into a logical heirarchy of types results, whose members are individuals, functions of individuals, functions of functions, and so on. Of course there are also resulting extensional hierarchies of classes and relations. For the resulting problems that can occur in a given type, Russell suggests that the theory of types be applied within the type, thus creating a "branching theory of types". Such an approach to ordinary language can indeed solve its syntactical problems insofar as it postulates a "pure" logic for language.[33]

Applying the above stated theory of types to a given language has this result : it is impossible to substitute one word for another in a

---

[31]   Max Black, "Russell's Philosophy of Language", in *The Philosophy of Bertrand Russell*, Volume V of *The Library of Living Philosophers*, ed. Paul A. Schilpp (Evanston, Ill.: Northwestern University Press, 1944), pp. 229-255.

[32]   By Bertrand Russell in collaboration with A.N. Whitehead, 3 vols. (London and New York, 1910-1913), second edition, 1925-1927. See Bertrand Russell, *Logic and Language*, ed. R.C. Marsh (London: George Allen and Unwin, 1956). This work is a reprinting of various articles including the important article by Russell "The Philosophy of Logical Atomism", *The Monist* XXVII (1918), pp. 495-527; XXIX (1919), pp. 32-63, 190-222, 345-380. Cf. B. Russell, "Logical Atomism", *Contemporary British Philosophy* I (1924), also reprinted in Marsh.

[33]   Bertrand Russell, "On Propositions: What They Are and How They Mean", *Proceedings of the Aristotelian Society*, Supp. II (1919), pp. 1-43.

single context. The word has a "pure" object status. How is this possible ? The theory of types in ordinary language requires the assertion that grammatically impeccable sentences in ordinary language often prove to be "crypto-nonsense" generated by a propensity for substituting in the same context words which agree in grammatical form while differing in logical form. This is to say, a word or symbol may form part of a significant proposition — in this sense have a meaning — without being always able to be substituted for another word or symbol in the same or some other proposition without producing nonsense.

Thus, Russell asserts that a set of criteria which would specify which substitutions of words are legitimate is needed. Here the theory of types applies : words that can replace one another in all contexts belong to the same type.

1.4.2. *Applying the Theory of Descriptions*

The purpose of the theory of descriptions is to suppress invalid trains of inference, against which the theory of types provides no protection.

By a "description" I mean a phrase such as "The present President of the United States", in which a person or thing is designated, not by name, but by some property which is supposed or known to be particular to him or it.[34]

According to this theory a phrase having the form "the so-and-so" if rightly analyzed allows the "so-and-so" to disappear. The point is that definite descriptions are quite unlike proper names. Contrary to appearances, descriptions do not name any object and thus have no meaning in isolation. If Russell's assumption is not correct, what is the object (meaning) of such definite descriptions as "the present King of France" or "the round square" ? Thus the theory of descriptions is an *instrument* whereby meaningless phrases that function in the subject-predicate form can be eliminated by analysis, in turn allowing for the efficient operation of the theory of forms.

These formulations by Russell suggest in straight forward terms the requirements of an "ideal language" where every symbol will be a logically "proper name" denoting objects of acquaintance. In short, there will be one word for every simple object. For complex structures there would be a combination of words.

[34] Bertrand Russell, *A History of Western Philosophy* (New York: Simon and Schuster, 1945), p. 831.

Russell's theory of language as a function of logical analogy presupposes the ability to transform or eliminate those subjective characteristics of language which have no object signification from usage. Hence, Russell attempts to solve the problems inherent in the subject/object dualism by the theory of descriptions which eliminates the "subject" from the dualism, thus creating only subjects in an objective world. Nonetheless, Russell acknowledges the basic premise that the world of ordinary language exists on the level of a subject/object dualism which is, he says, precisely why there is confusion in meaning in language.

Now that phenomenalism as a linguistic semiology has been reviewed in its more characteristic modes, the semiotic of existentialism can be presented. This approach attempts to synthesize the object into the subject in language, which is the reverse of the phenomenalistic procedures as we just examined them.

2. DUALISTIC SYNTHESIS: SEMIOTIC EXISTENTIALISM

Merleau-Ponty in commenting on Karl Jaspers' work in psychology before turning to philosophy suggests that Jaspers was greatly influenced by the phenomenology of Edmund Husserl.[35] What Merleau-Ponty wishes to convey in this remark is the fact that existentialists such as Jaspers utilized the concept of synthesis as it developed in the phenomenology of Hegel and Husserl with a specific application to ontology. The philosophic project here is to find the transcendent subject that is the final statement of existence. The dualism of subject and object is utilized to affirm the primacy of subjectivity.

2.1. *The Semiology of Karl Jaspers*

Jaspers discusses a four step methodology by which one can "seize methodically in every presence what is essentially real".[36] This procedure is in fact the means of finding existence (subjectivity) through the affirmation of objectivity. Objectivity is thus the progressive result of man's research, illumination, reflection, and affirmation.

Research consists in the methodology of science as a means of experiencing the empirically real. One is trained to see and to observe.

---

35 M. M-P., *Primacy*, p. 47.
36 Jaspers, *Truth and Symbol*, p. 70.

"... I try to raise whatever I experience into consciousness, to transform it into knowledge, and to experience it as something new and better".[37] The second step above research is "illumination". *Illumination* is the coming into "full consciousness" through the exercise of thought. Such thought is not the structuring of an objective world, but the potentiality of man in that world.

The third level of objectivity consists in "reflection" which is the search for a fundamental knowledge in the "totality of the sciences, and in the categories and methods of which thinking in all these directions makes use".[38] The end of this three step process of research, illumination, and reflection is the "affirmation" of being as so experienced in the contact of subject with object — of person with world. "Authentic being becomes realized in the cypher", this is *affirmation*. Thus, in the cypher is existence — finally an object of being for the subject. Jaspers does, indeed, announce an existential semiotic.

The dualistic synthesis of Jaspers' existential semiotic is apparent in the very nature of the *cypher*.

The cypher is the object which is least of all only object, but rather in its being-an-object is already no longer an object like all other specific objects. As a cypher the object is, as it were, in suspension. In the very definiteness of what is objective, which is only its element, the cypher is lost. For it is itself not a definable object but that which encompasses both the subject and the object in what is objective. For this reason the cyphers are not still another new objective domain. They are not an objective conclusion. They are rather hidden in all objectivity. Everything that is, can be a cypher. It becomes a cypher through a transformation of the mode of being-an-object in the act of transcendence.[39]

The character of the cypher is one of direct communication, as was noted earlier in Chapter I. Thus the cypher cannot itself be considered a communication, because the cypher already *is* before it can be presented. "For this reason the character of the cypher is only encircled but not reached if, in metaphor, we call it speech".[40]

It may be advantageous to examine the difference between a cypher and symbol as Jaspers uses them. The cypher we just discussed. The symbol is "the complete presentness of Being. In it is the strongest, most penetrating mode of being present of whatever is".[41] The symbol is thus

[37] Jaspers, *Truth and Symbol*, p. 70.
[38] Jaspers, *Truth and Symbol*, p. 71.
[39] Jaspers, *Truth and Symbol*, pp. 38-39.
[40] Jaspers, *Truth and Symbol*, p. 41.
[41] Jaspers, *Truth and Symbol*, p. 41.

the subjective counterpart of the cypher and in the semiology of Jaspers the symbol is of critical importance. "The symbol is *communication* [Sprache]".[42]

Put simply, the symbol is one manifestation of the cypher in which Being is perceptible as *being-as-a-symbol*. The cypher at this level is the subject which knows its own existence and is thus objective to itself, yet it is the cypher that is manifest to others and to the world as a symbol of that which is cypher. In this modality cyphers can be known (have meaning) according to the *form* of the relation which they suggest or according to the *contents* of the interpreting.[43]

One more consideration is necessary and that is the notion of *being-as-a-sign*. Jaspers parenthetically defines the sign in its mode of being as "the sign, and what is encountered in the sign, are essentially different, without similarity, without comparability, a mere referral".[44] The import of this definition as it relates to the cypher and the symbol is suggested in the following explanation by Jaspers.

Being is revealed through the symbol. The symbol is suspended when I grasp essential reality in it. If it becomes fixed and definite and turns into an object in the world, then it loses its essential reality. It collapses into a sign, into a signification, into a metaphor. There are such symbols in incalculable numbers which can be arranged according to multiple points of view. They constitute the world of cyphers which, as an object of consideration, bears the same relation to its origin as does the herbarium to living plants, or as does a collection of bones to live bodies. As soon as we talk about the symbols, we have completed this transformation. Only when in thinking we proceed from the symbols in them [the cyphers], are we dealing with the essential reality which speaks out of them.[45]

Jasper's point of view is that existence (which he commonly speaks of as an objectivity or cypher-status) is essentially a subjective Being that is manifest in an original manner as symbol which can become "sedimented" into signs and their resultant signification. The subjective Being in its modality before it is known or before it is manifest as symbol or sign is in fact *cypher*.

The conclusion of this semiology is that the dualism of subject and object (as we have used them) is presumed as a necessary condition of existence insofar as that existence is to be known or is to have meaning. As was noted when this analysis began, there is a process of coming

---

[42] Jaspers, *Truth and Symbol*, pp. 39-40.
[43] Jaspers, *Truth and Symbol*, pp. 61-62.
[44] Jaspers, *Truth and Symbol*, p. 62.
[45] Jaspers, *Truth and Symbol*, p. 49.

to the knowledge of the cypher. Indeed, the method allows the movement from essences — as sign or symbol — to the existential force of being which is cypher.

The operant vitality of the semiology that Jaspers advances is dependent in large measure upon his theory of communication which is the assumption of "truth as communicability". It is necessary to examine Jaspers' theory of communication because it is the fundamental exposition of the dualism that is synthesized in the semiology of the cypher.

For Jaspers the existential modality of Being involves three levels of existence : (1) empirical existence; (2) consciousness as such; and (3) spirit. Empirical existence is first of all a synthesis of Self and Other. "I am, first of all, an empirical existent".[46] As myself I become an empirical object by my fact of being in existence, yet as soon as I become an object of investigation I am absorbed into the being of the world — the being of Other. "In this fashion we are apprehended only as one sort of being among others, not yet as properly human".[47] Thus, on the empirical level one can exist only as body and as an object in Nature.

The second mode of the *Encompassing,* which is what Jaspers calls the synthetic unity of existence, is *consciousness as such.*

Only what appears to our consciousness as experiencable, as an object, has being for us. What does not appear to conscious, what can in no wise touch our cognition, is as good as nothing for us. Hence, everything which exists for us must take on that form in which it can be thought or experienced by consciousness. It must in some fashion appear in the form of an object; it must become present through some temporal act of consciousness; it must become articulated and thereby communicable through its thinkability.[48]

In this modality consciousness has two meanings. First, consciousness is an element that we possess as living "existents" and as such are not yet or are no longer "encompassing". This level of consciousness is the unconscious ground of what we consciously experience. Second, there is that consciousness that is termed a "consciousness as such". Because as existent individual persons we possess a single consciousness, we are collectively only so many more or less singular, yet similar consciousnesses which is to say we are a consciousness as

[46]   Jaspers, *Reason and Existenz,* p. 54.
[47]   Jaspers, *Reason and Existenz,* p. 55.
[48]   Jaspers, *Reason and Existenz,* pp. 55-56.

such.[49] Thus, there is an actuality of living consciousness in its temporal process and there is a consciousness in general as the "site" of a timeless meaning. Yet, this duality of consciousness is not absolute.

Rather it is an abstraction which can be transcended through the clarification of the Encompassing. The actual existence of this timeless meaning insofar as it is something produced, something temporal, which grasps and moves itself, is a new sense of the Encompassing, and this is called spirit.[50]

At this point it is appropriate to turn to the three levels of truth as communicability insofar as they are direct reflections of the Encompassing. This is to say that truth is communication as the Encompassing. "Truth therefore cannot be separated from communicability. It only appears in time as a reality-through-communication. Abstracted from communication, truth hardens into an unreality".[51]

Communication in the Encompassing has three basic forms, as might be guessed; (1) communication in empirical existence; (2) communication in consciousness as such; and (3) communication in spirit. The communication in empirical existence is the attempt to advance knowledge beyond what is already known to science; it must be the will to preserve and develop without limit. "To achieve these goals; the Encompassing of empirical existence demands the communication of a community which can preserve life".[52] Jaspers is advocating what Aristotle suggested as the role of a "rhetoric" in the ethics and politics of a society.

Compromise is the truth which does not forget that every standpoint, no matter how right it seems, can also be refuted through the very fact of process. Accordingly, for the continuity of a living community the art of conversation must be developed.[53]

The communication of consciousness as such, the second type of communication, "is the communication of a self-identical consciousness dispersed into the multiplicities of its empirical existence".[54] Consciousness as such is therefore that which is between a "point-consciousness" (which is indifferently replaceable and which is valid for everybody because it exists in the knowable dichotomies of subject-object, form-matter, and the like) and the consciousness as multiplicity.

[49] Jaspers, *Reason and Existenz*, p. 56.
[50] Jaspers, *Reason and Existenz*, p. 57.
[51] Jaspers, *Reason and Existenz*, p. 79.
[52] Jaspers, *Reason and Existenz*, p. 80.
[53] Jaspers, *Reason and Existenz*, p. 82.
[54] Jaspers, *Reason and Existenz*, p. 82.

The last aspect of communication in the truth of encompassing is that of spirit. "The communication of the spirit is the emergence of the Idea of a whole out of the communal substance".[55] To the extent that a communication does not possess the vitality of this whole or community, it is "indifferent and trivial".

Communication at the higher level of spirit has two modalities of use in the existence of Being, that is, existential and rational communication. Before quoting Jaspers to illustrate and define his concept of existential communication it should be noted that rational communication is existential communication. That is, reason penetrates everything. Rational communication is in existential or authentic communication in the following manner.

Reason, having its substance in Existenz, arises from the authentic communication of one nature with another, and it arises in such a fashion that empirical existence, consciousness as such, and spirit are, so to speak, the body of its appearance. Not for an instant is reason without these, and they are all moved and changed by it.[56]

But before this level of rational communication can be achieved there must be existential communication.

In contrast to the communication of identical and indifferently replaceable points of consciousness as such, this existential communication is between irreplaceable individuals. In contrast to the struggle for existence over power, superiority, an annihilation, here the struggle over the content of Existenz is without the will to power in the same sense; it is a struggle where every advance of the individual comes only if the other advances too, and every destruction of the other is my own. In contrast to spiritual community, where there is security in the comprehensive Idea, it does not overlook the crack in Being for us, and it is open for Transcendence. It expresses the inevitability of struggle in temporal existence and the inability of truth to be completed by unceasingly pushing the movement of communication forward as the authentic appearance of truth. To be self and to be true are nothing else than to be in communication unconditionally.[57]

This excessive quotation is a rather comprehensive summary of the levels and modalities of communication as they express the semiology of being that Jaspers presents in the cypher as symbol and sign. The dualism of the semiology between cypher and symbol/sign is the dualism between existential and rational communication that is respec-

[55] Jaspers, *Reason and Existenz*, p. 82.
[56] Jaspers, *Reason and Existenz*, p. 92.
[57] Jaspers, *Reason and Existenz*, p. 91.

tively synthesized in being-as-a-symbol (cypher) and the will-to-com-
municate. Jaspers' theory is an existential semiotic that is a dualistic
synthesis of communication as truth.

2.2. *The Semiology of Martin Heidegger*

In Chapter I, Heidegger's theory of communication was explained insofar as a distinction between *talk* and *idle talk* indicated existential
authenticity and inauthenticity. As with Jaspers, the communication
theory of Heidegger is fundamentally linked to a semiotic of subjective
and objective phenomena.

In explaining the relation of the existing subject to the world as
existent, Heidegger formulates the agency of knowing that relationship.
This agency is the existential modality of *reference* and *sign*.

The word 'sign' designates many kinds of things: not only may it stand for
different *kinds* of signs, but Being-a-sign-for can itself be formalized as a universal kind of relation, so that the sign-structure itself provides an ontological
clue for 'characterizing' any entity whatsoever.
But signs, in the first instance, are themselves items of equipment whose specific
character as equipment consists in *showing* or *indicating*.[58]

One should not be misled by this rendering of the "sign" by Heidegger,
for the sign is not an object which by its existence allows the subject
to perceive it as a reference for a given meaning.

A sign is not a Thing which stands to another Thing in the relationship of
indicating; it is rather *an item of equipment which explicitly raises a totality
of equipment into our circumspection so that together with it the worldly character
of the ready-to-hand announces itself.*[59]

This definition suggests that Heidegger views the sign as an *agency*
of value in the sense that the sign gives rise to the meaning of a reference made in the world by an existing personage. "A sign to mark
something indicates what one is 'at' at anytime. Signs always indicate
primarily 'wherein' one lives, where one's concern dwells, what sort of
involvment there is with something".[60] Thus, the concept of reference
or "assignment" is the meaning generated by the perception of signs.

For clarity, it is well to note that the sign is not a relation between
the subject and object where that relation is thought to be a reference

---

58   Heidegger, *Being and Time*, pp. 107-108.
59   Heidegger, *Being and Time*, p. 110.
60   Heidegger, *Being and Time*, p. 111.

stimulated by the perception of signs. Rather, the sign is a modality of existence that is both objective and subjective. The sign's subjective character is manifest in its power to indicate or to show what is "ready-to-hand" as an objectiveness of itself; that is, the sign is self-indicating of existence. The sign is a subjectivity or way of being that is knowable and it takes on objectivity or reference by its encounter with other signs or with its distinctness in a sign-structure. The nature of sign possibility is explained by Heidegger in this way.

The Being-ready-to-hand of signs in our everyday dealings, and the conspicuousness which belongs to signs and which may be produced for various purposes and in various ways, do not merely serve to document the inconspicuous constitutive for what is most closely ready-to-hand; the sign itself gets its conspicuousness from the inconspicuousness of the equipmental totality which is ready-to-hand and 'obvious' in its everydayness.[61]

It is clear, now, that the sign is a "pure" agency that is characterized by its ability to synthetically function as the subjectiveness and objectiveness of the act of referring. "A sign points *at* what is indicated. Such indicating is a relation, but not an agreement of the sign with what is indicated".[62] With this concept of agency in mind, Heidegger offers the following definition of the sign/reference relation as it operates in the function of a semiotic.

The relation between sign and reference is threefold. 1. Indicating, as a way whereby the 'towards-which' of a serviceability can become concrete, is founded upon the equipment-structure as such, upon the 'in-order-to' (assignment). 2. The indicating which the sign does is an equipmental character of something ready-to-hand, and as such it belongs to a totality of equipment, to a context of assignments or references. 3. The sign is not only ready-to-hand with other equipment, but in its readiness-to-hand the environment becomes in each case explicitly accessible for circumspection. *A sign is something ontically ready-to-hand, which functions both as this definite equipment and as something indicative of* [*was ... anzeight*] *the ontological structure of readiness-to-hand, of referential totalities, and of worldhood.*[63]

It now remains to make the specific connection between this theory of existential semiotic and the theory of authentic-inauthentic communication (talk and idle talk). Being-in-the-world as Dasein is presented through signs in both an authentic, existential modality that is revealed in talk; and, it is presented through signs in an unauthentic,

[61] Heidegger, *Being and Time*, p. 112.
[62] Heidegger, *Being and Time*, p. 258.
[63] Heidegger, *Being and Time*, pp. 113-114.

essential modality that is apparent in idle talk. The semiology of idle talk is explained quite explicitly by Heidegger.

In this concern—that is, in the Being-in-the-world of Dasein itself—a supply of 'signs' is presented. Signs, as equipment take over the giving of directions in a way which is explicit and easily manipulable. They keep explicitly open those regions which have been used circumspectively—the particular "whithers" to which something belongs or goes, or gets brought or fetched.[64]

On the other hand, signs can be authentic in talk which is constitutive of the existential modality of Being-in-the-world.

If Dasein *is*, it already has, as directing and deserving, its own discovered region. Both directionality and de-severance, as modes of Being-in-the-world, are guided beforehand *by the circumspection* of concern.[65]

And, this circumspection of concern is the authentic sign as it is self-manifesting in "talk".

Heidegger's semiology leads to the conclusion that idle talk is the synthesis of being as subject which comes to be object in the experienced world. This is to say that for primitive man the sign can be a substitute for what it indicates and can even come to be meaning in which the "sign itself always *is* what it indicates".[66] This is the obvious situation of idle talk that leads to an inauthentic conception of existence. In contrast, the semiotic of talk indicates that the reference or assignment is not itself a sign, but that reference is an *involvement with* an entity *in* something.[67] In this sense talk is an original use of signs that are referential, but not references, and, idle talk is the use of signs that are references, but which lack an original reference in the absence of the original sign-structure.

Heidegger's semiology thus exemplifies a dualistic synthesis in which authentic communication is a subjective semiotic that becomes objective in the inauthentic usage. The movement of reference and sign are a synthesis or a convergence in idle talk while they are a dualism and divergence in talk.

---

[64] Heidegger, *Being and Time*, p. 143.
[65] Heidegger, *Being and Time*. This point has been accurately explained by Thomas N. Munson, "Heidegger's Recent Thought on Language", *Philosophy and Phenomenological Research* XXI, no. 3 (March, 1961), pp. 361-372, esp. 364-365.
[66] Heidegger, *Being and Time*, p. 113.
[67] Heidegger, *Being and Time*, p. 115. M. M.-P., *Themes*, p. 121.

2.3. *The Semiology of Jean-Paul Sartre*

Sartre says very little about language and communication in his writings, and then the formulation is "clumsy and failing".[68] And his formulations on semiology are equally obscure. Yet, there are sufficient references to suggest the nature of a semiology were it to be developed in detail. According to Sartre, the "sign" is "a consciousness".[69] In this rather simple definition there is the implication that semiotic functions are only a subjective relation between an object and its perception. This idea is suggested by Sartre in his description of the process of reading. The act of reading involves the perception of the physical "strokes" that are our language for which a meaning emerges. "These strokes are no longer of importance to me, I no longer perceive them : what I have really done is to assume a certain attitude of consciousness which envisions another object through them".[70] The function of semiotic is thus to create the object for a conscious subject by establishing the link between a symbol and its referent in which the symbol disappears to the extent that the object is primary in consciousness.

The material on which my intention was directed, becoming transformed by that intention, now forms an integral part of my actual attitude; it is the material of my act, it is a *sign*. In the case of the sign, as in that of the image, we have an intention which envisions an object, a material which it transforms, an envisioned object which is not present.[71]

At this point, he separates the notion of sign and symbol in the process of expression. There are four points of separation. First, there is no relation between a sign and its object; what relation does come to exist is a matter of convention developed through the associations of habit. In contrast, the image and its object resemble each other and form either an imaginary or perceptual synthesis which is meaning. Second, the sign is like a beacon : "it presents itself, awakens a meaning, and this meaning never returns to the word [sign] but goes to the thing and the word [sign] is dropped".[72] In direct contrast, the image is an intentionality that constantly returns to the "image-portrait". Each

---

[68] Wahl, *Short History of Existentialism*, p. 11.
[69] Jean-Paul Sartre, *The Psychology of Imagination*, anon. trans., (New York: The Citadel Press, 1966), p. 35. First published in 1948.
[70] Sartre, *The Psychology of Imagination*, p. 28.
[71] Sartre, *The Psychology of Imagination*, p. 28.
[72] Sartre, *The Psychology of Imagination*, p. 30.

detail of the image is a correspondent detail of the object; the parts of the image are the parts of the object.

The third area of comparison for signs and images is the existence of the sign and symbol as objects. The sign has no "positional determination"; it can be "envisioned" but its existence cannot be affirmed.[73] The image is just the opposite — it always has positional determination, even when it does not posit the existence of its object. Thus, the fourth distinction is a logical consequence of the first three comparisons. The sign "does not deliver its object. It is constituted as a sign by an empty intention".[74] The creation of meaning thus becomes the synthetic act of joining the sign to a perception. However, the image is not a synthetic function — it is its own meaning in consciousness. This consciousness is, nonetheless, of an existent object.

In short, there is a direct correlation between Sartre's theory of communication and his semiology. In his communication theory, as has been previously noted, there is a dualism of consciousness (For-itself) which is manifest in the semiotic as "sign" and "image". And, there is the dualism of Consciousness and Being that is manifest in the semiology as sign and object, a synthetic product, *and* as image and object, an analytic product.[75] The operation of the synthetic product is necessary to the analytic, thus demonstrating that in communication theory and in semiotic, Sartre relies on a dualistic synthesis to examine existence.

3. SEMIOTIC AS EXISTENTIAL PHENOMENOLOGY

The reason for reserving the discussion of semiology as it functions in existential phenomenology is explained in the positive statement of such a semiology. Existential phenomenology posits the *sign as given,* not as the synthetic product of a phenomenalism (or objective principium) or the synthetic product of an existentialism *per se* (or subjective principium).

---

[73] Sartre, *The Psychology of Imagination*, p. 31.
[74] Sartre, *The Psychology of Imagination*, pp. 32-33.
[75] Jean-Paul Sartre, *The Emotions: Outline of a Theory,* trans. B. Frechtman (New York: The Philosophical Library, 1948), pp. 44-45.

3.1. *Semiology as Problematic*

The basic problem that semiology raises and that problem to which phenomenalism and existentialism have both responded with synthetic approaches was first formulated by Edmund Husserl as a phenomenological question. In attempting to clarify and correct a "fundamental error" with respect to the definition of *perception* Husserl suggests that semiotics as those discussed previously as a phenomenalism are in error.

The thought that the transcendence of the thing is that of an *image* or sign has proved misleading here. The image-theory is often zealously attacked and a sign-theory substituted for it. But the one and the other alike are not only incorrect but nonsensical. The spatial thing which we see is, despite all its transcendence, perceived, we are consciously aware of it as given in its *embodied form*. We are not given an image or a sign *in its place*. We must not substitute the consciousness of a sign or an image for a perception.
Between *perception* on the one hand and, on the other, *the presentation of a symbol in the form of an image or meaning* there is an unbridgeable and essential difference.
Through acts of immediate intuition we must intuit a "self". No apprehensions at a higher level are built up on the basis of these apprehending acts of intuition; nothing is therefore known *for which* the intuited might serve as a "sign" or "image".[76]

Before beginning a concise statement of the problem, it is necessary to cite one more passage from Husserl to indicate the direction that a phenomenological semiotic must take.

An image or sign points to something that lies beyond it, which, could it but pass over into another form of presentation, into that of a dator intuition, might "itself" be apprehended. A sign and copy does not "announce" in its self the self that is signified (or copied). But the physical thing is nothing foreign to that which appears in a sensory body, but something that manifests itself in it *alone* indeed in a primordial way, a way that is also *a priori* in that it rests on essential grounds which cannot be annulled.[77]

The import of Husserl's discussion of perception and its competitive theories of sign and image suggests that any objective reality is given *per se* and that such an object can be perceived as is, but that there is no sign or image to be perceived. Two answers to this problem have

---

[76]   Edmund Husserl, *Ideas: General Introduction to Pure Phenomenology*, trans. W.R.B. Gibson (New York: Collier Books, 1962), p. 123. First published in 1913 as *Ideen zu einer reinen Phänomenologie und phänomenologischen Philosophie*.
[77]   Husserl, *Ideas: General Introduction to Pure Phenomenology*, p. 145.

already been reviewed. Phenomenalism merely assigns the function of the sign as being identical with the physical object, while an image is an abstraction from the object. The second suggested answer to Husserl comes via existentialism where the sign is a subjective agency that allows the subjective awareness of self to become known as an objective condition of the subject — the synthesis of subject and agency allows for existence as precedent to essential manifestation of the self.

A third approach to the problem, and the one that is utilized in the existential phenomenology of Merleau-Ponty, is suggested in the work of the linguist, Ferdinand de Saussure.

Our definition of the linguistic sign poses an important question of terminology. I call the combination of a concept and a sound-image a *sign*, but in current usage the term generally designates only a sound-image, a word, for example (*arbor*, etc.). One tends to forget that *arbor* is called a sign only because it carries the concept 'tree', with the result that the idea of the sensory part implies the idea of the whole.

Ambiguity would disappear if three notions involved here were designated by three names, each suggesting and opposing the others. I propose to retain the word *sign* [*signe*] to designate the whole and to replace *concept* and *sound-image* respectively by *signified* [*signifié*] and *signifier* [*signifiant*]; the last two terms have the advantage of indicating the opposition that separates them from each other and from the whole of which they are parts.[78]

From this definition, two general laws or characteristics of the "sign" are possible. First, the joint association of the signified and the signifier in the sign necessitates that in the agency of use "the linguistic sign is arbitrary".[79] And second, the nature of the *signifier* is linear in that it represents a single span that is measured in one dimension.[80] That one dimension is *time*.

It should be noted that by *signifier* De Saussure means what is commonly called the "symbol".[81] Thus, the various levels of language become functions of a semiology that takes signs as unitary designations of idea and symbol. This approach to the original problem of perception raised in Husserl's work meets the conditions of a satisfactory answer. The sign becomes the object of *perception*. Whether a physical object or a word, the sign can be perceived or used as an existential unit. The ontological ramifications of this position will be

[78]   De Saussure, *Course in General Linguistics*, p. 67.
[79]   De Saussure, *Course in General Linguistics*, p. 67.
[80]   De Saussure, *Course in General Linguistics*, p. 70.
[81]   De Saussure, *Course in General Linguistics*, p. 68.

dealt with in the analysis of Merleau-Ponty's semiology. However, for the moment, the implication of this semiotic for perception should be examined.

3.2. *The Semiology of Roland Barthes*

Barthes correctly interprets De Saussure to mean that linguistics is only a part of semiology when semiology is the base method of perceiving a world of signs and consequent significations.

Semiology therefore aims to take in any system of signs, whatever their substance and limits; images, gestures, musical sounds, objects, and the complex associations of all these, which form the content of ritual, convention or public entertainment: these constitute, if not *language*, at least systems of signification.[82]

The impact of Barthes' approach is to include all that is perceptible into a one or another system of signs for which meaning is a concomitant function. In this context, the agency of any semiology becomes closely bound to language.

Finally, and in more general terms, it appears increasingly more difficult to conceive a system of images and objects whose *signifieds* can exist independently of language: to perceive what a substance signifies is inevitably to fall back on the individuation of a language: there is no meaning which is not designated, and the world of signifieds is none other than that of language.[83]

Barthes assumes in this approach to semiology that language is the perspective of perception that yields meaning. Yet, the specific modality of language *as* perception is spoken language or *speaking*. This is in fact the basis of Barthes' semiotic.

We shall therefore postulate that there exists a general category *language/ speech*, which embraces all the systems of signs; since there are no better ones, we shall keep the terms *language* and *speech*, even when they are applied to communications whose substance is not verbal.[84]

This postulation recognizes the fundamental contribution of Merleau-Ponty's separation of "speaking speech" and "spoken speech" which is

---

[82]   Roland Barthes, *Elements of Semiology*, trans. A. Lavers and C. Smith (New York: Hill and Wang, 1968), p. 9. (First published in 1964). [This translation contains minor errors.]
[83]   Barthes, *Elements of Semiology*, pp. 10-11.
[84]   Barthes, *Elements of Semiology*, p. 25.

elaborated beyond De Saussure's formulation to suggest that any *process* presupposes a *system*. This formulation recognizes a basic opposition between "event" and "structure". It is in the event or situation that a single instance of usage reflects the structure of the system. Thus, in speaking there is a paradigm that reflects the structure of the system, namely, language. This analysis will be expanded in our consideration of Merleau-Ponty's theory of communication in a later chapter.

Barthes suggests that the multifarious group of signs, symbols, signals, indexes, and so on demand a schemata whereby varying definitions of each can be compared and a sensible agreement reached on the nature of variations in semiological systems. His suggestion is that distinctions be based on alternatives — the presence/absence of elements — of *relata*. These guidelines are : (1) "the relation implies, or does not imply, the mental representation of one of the *relata*"; (2) "the relation implies, or does not imply, an analogy between the *relata*"; (3) "the link between the two *relata* (the stimulus and its response) is immediate or is not"; (4) "the *relata* exactly coincide or, on the contrary, one overruns the other"; (5) "the relation implies, or does not imply, an existential connection with the user".[85]

While this schemata lends clarity to semiology in a general sense, the notion of sign in linguistics does not give rise to any competition between neighboring terms. In this respect, Barthes confirms De Saussure in the unitary presence of the linguistic sign.[86] But in contrast to the linguistic sign, Barthes' major concern is the *semiological sign*. This semiological sign follows the linguistic sign in *form* (it is a compound : signifier and signified), but there is a difference in *substance*.

While the substance of the linguistic sign is to "signify", that of the semiological sign is to "signify" in a derivative way some utilitarian or functional use — it is a *sign-function*.[87] The semiological sign, Barthes suggests, can thus become the basis of an entire system of meaning, for example, a garment system, a car system, a furniture system, and so on.[88] Each system could be subdivided insofar as it is a separate means of communication. Within this context the semiological sign system has three characteristics : matter (substance), language (form), and usage (signifying). In contrast, as was noted earlier, lin-

---

[85] Barthes, *Elements of Semiology*, p. 36.
[86] Barthes, *Elements of Semiology*, p. 38.
[87] Barthes, *Elements of Semiology*, p. 41.
[88] Barthes, *Elements of Semiology*, pp. 25-30.

guistic signs are characterized only by form and matter, as the union of matter and form *is* usage.

The import of Barthes' semiology is confirmed in the applications that anthropology has made in correlations between language/speech and other functional semiotics. "Spoken language is the completest form of communication, and every other form is embodied in it to a greater or lesser degree".[89] "Further, if we return to language as it is spoken (not written) as a specialized communication system, we can learn something of how other less elaborated systems work".[90] The primacy of speaking in semiology is affirmed by Merleau-Ponty in the role of existential phenomenology which must exceed the limits of a phenomenal reason.

On a deeper level, anthropology's concern is neither to prove that the primitive is wrong nor to side with him against us, but to set itself up on a ground where we shall both be intelligible without any reduction or rash transposition. This is what we do when we take the symbolic function as the source of all reason and unreason. For the number and richness of significations man has at his disposal always exceed the circle of definite objects which warrant the name "signified", because the symbolic function must always be ahead of its object and finds reality only by anticipating it in imagination. Thus our task is to broaden our reasoning to make it capable of grasping what, in ourselves and in others, precedes and exceeds reason.
This attempt rejoins that of other "semiological" sciences, and in general, of the other sciences.[91]

The pragmatic confirmation of Merleau-Ponty's extension of speech semiotic to the functional systems of social life have been corroborated by the work of his friend and colleague at the Collège de France, Claude Lévi-Strauss.

The tremendous change brought about by the theory of communication consists precisely in the discovery of methods to deal with objects — signs — which can be subjected to a rigorous study despite the fact that they are altogether much more numerous than those of classical mechanics and much less than those of thermodynamics.
Therefore, the present condition of social-structure studies can be summarized as follows: Phenomena are found to be of the same kind as those which, in

[89]   J.L. Aranguren, *Human Communication,* trans. F. Partridge, (New York: McGraw-Hill Book Co., 1967), p. 88.
[90]   Edward T. Hall, *The Silent Language* (Greenwich, Conn.: Fawcett Publications, Inc., 1959), p. 96. Also, see Harold W. Scheffler, "Structuralism in Anthropology", *Yale French Studies* nos. 36-37 (October, 1966), pp. 66-88, esp. 70-71. See M.M-P., *Themes,* pp. 39-45.
[91]   M. M-P., *Signs,* p. 122.

strategics and communication theory, were made the subject of a rigorous approach.[92]

The full impact of a semiology such as that of Bathes is to demonstrate that the model of linguistic semiotic contains within it an existential presence of structure and substance in perception that can have varying degrees of meaning in other systems of signs or can be a conjunctive semiology with language as spoken. Thus, our analysis may now turn to Merleau-Ponty's concept of semiology as it is a structure and matter that is equally applicable to perception and speaking as elements of the process of existential communication.

3.3. *The Semiology of Maurice Merleau-Ponty*

Merleau-Ponty's phenomenology is a complex statement of an existentialism that is fundamentally different from phenomenalism, as we have discussed it, and from existentialism *per se*. The genesis of his theory lies in a unique theory of semiology that lends itself to phenomenological method and existential ontology. Merleau-Ponty's study of psychology and philosophy led to his formulation of an *existential phenomenology* that is founded on the premise that human existence is a synoptic presence — there is no duality of subject and object or of mind and body.[93] This unity of being is the human perceived-perceiving synergism that is indivisible.

Phenomenology is here the recognition that the theoretically *complete*, full world of the physical explanation is not so, and that therefore it is necessary to consider as ultimate, inexplicable, and *hence as a world by itself* the whole of our experience of sensible being and man. A world by itself: i.e., it is necessary to translate into *perceptual logic* what science and positive psychology treat as fragments of the In Itself *absque praemissis*.

$$\begin{cases} \text{touching} - \text{touching oneself} \\ \text{(the things} \\ \text{the lived body [\textit{le corps propre}])} \end{cases}$$

[92] Claude Lévi-Strauss, *Structural Anthropology*, trans. C. Jacobson and B.G. Schoepf (Garden City, New York: Doubleday & Co., 1967), pp. 308-309. First published in 1958. Also, see R.C. Poole, "Indirect Communication. 2. Merleau-Ponty and Lévi-Strauss", *New Black Friars* XLVII, no. 555 (1966), pp. 594-604; and, David M. Levin, "On Lévi-Strauss and Existentialism", *American Scholar* XXXVIII, no. 1 (Winter, 1968-9), pp. 69-82. Cf., Maurice Merleau-Ponty, "De Mauss à Claude Levi-Strauss", *La Nouvelle Revue Française* VII, no. 82 (October, 1959), pp. 615-631. [Trans. in *Signs*, pp. 114-125.]
[93] Alfred Schutz, "Language, Language Disturbances, and the Texture of Consciousness," *Social Research* XVII, no. 3 (September, 1950), pp. 380-382.

$\left\{\begin{array}{l}\text{seeing — seeing oneself} \\ \text{hearing — } \textit{hearing oneself} \text{ (Radio)} \\ \text{understanding — speaking} \\ \text{hearing — singing} \\ \text{Unity by } \textit{nervure} \text{ [nervure = synoptic presence; R.L.L.]} \\ \text{pre-objective } [94]\end{array}\right.$

This definition of phenomenology and the "polarity" of terms following it are not intended to express a duality, but on the contrary to show the spectrum of unitary function in human existence. In particular, the last notation suggests the synergism of pre-objective being in the bodily presence of a human being. In short, Merleau-Ponty is suggesting some of the scope of a "perceptual logic" which is in fact an existential semiotic capable of having all of human reality "translated" into it. How this translation occurs is the present concern; it requires a statement of Merleau-Ponty's semiology, his formulation of immanence and transcendence, and his premise of meaning as "man speaking".

3.3.1. *Semiology as Semiotic in Merleau-Ponty*

The expression *semiology as semiotic* is intended to designate the existential nature of a theory of signs that is in fact a phenomenological approach to perception in any modality. What the perceptual logic means is a condition of what is perceived, whether it be a physical presence or an uttered word.

Phenomenology is not considered as the function of the mind but the power to translate and enlighten, to make transparent and to express in language the darkness of pre-reflexive reality. Phenomenology, therefore, puts aside that function or activity of the mind that translates this same reality into serviceable symbols.[95]

This is to say that Merleau-Ponty's phenomenological method does not posit a division in the function of perception between what might be termed a mental sign and its physical representative or a symbol.[96]

---

[94]   M. M-P., *Visible*, p. 256. See *Themes*, p. 111.

[95]   Manuel Virasoro, "Merleau-Ponty and the World of Perception", trans. M. Correa, *Philosophy Today* III, no. 1 (Spring, 1959), p. 71. Originally published as "Merleau-Ponty y el mundo el nivel da la percepcion", *Ciencia y Fe,* Ano XIII, no. 2 (Abril-Junio, 1957), pp. 147-157.

[96]   This analysis is flatly denied by Eugene F. Kaelin who asserts that M. M-P. separates sign and symbol in his phenomenology of communication. E.F.K., *An Existential Aesthetic: The Theories of Sartre and Merleau-Ponty* (Madison: The Uni-

This method was utilized by Jaspers' in his existentialism, but it is not a hermeneutic phenomenology. The basis for this analysis will be apparent in a moment in Merleau-Ponty's semiotic theory. In short, "phenomenology is not falling back into phenomenalism but the maintenance of contact with 'the thing itself' ".[97] This point is made definitive by Merleau-Ponty.

Yet today as in the past there is only one single marvel — a considerable one it is true — which is that man speaks or calculates. In other words, the marvel is that he has constituted for himself these prodigious organs of algorithm and language which do not wear out, but on the contrary grow through use, being capable of indefinite labor, of returning more than has been invested in them, and yet relating themselves unceasingly to things. But we have no rigorous theory of symbolism.[98]

Merleau-Ponty's semiology assumes in the form of language an expression of the synoptic presence of subject and object. The distinction that De Saussure made between a "synchronic linguistics of speech" and a "diachronic linguistics of language" is eliminated by Merleau-Ponty and the phenomenology of language in its synoptic presence as speech is asserted with full ontological implication. "At first the 'subjective' point of view envelops the 'objective' point of view; synchrony envelops diachrony. The past of language began by being present". And then, "in another connection, diachrony envelops synchrony. If language allows random elements when it is considered according to a longitudinal section, the system of synchrony must at every moment allow fissures where brute events can insert themselves".[99]

The purpose of the phenomenological method is to get behind the artifical constructions of objective and subjective phenomena to the very basis of existence, to the basic semiotic by which meaning is generated and constituted as a perceptible entity.

Probably the chief gain from phenomenology is to have united extreme subjectivism and extreme objectivism in its notion of the world or rationality. Rationality is precisely measured by the experiences in which it is disclosed.

---

versity of Wisconsin Press, 1966), p. 188. Kaelin apparently confuses M. M-P.'s phenomenology with an existential phenomenalism, e.g., that of Karl Jaspers. The existential phenomenalism which appears in Kaelin's analysis is illustrated in a parallel analysis by Roderick M. Chisholm, "Intentionality and the Theory of Signs", *Philosophical Studies* III, no. 4 (June, 1952), pp. 56-63.

[97] M. M-P., *Primacy*, p. 41.
[98] M. M-P., *Signs*, p. 194.
[99] M. M-P., *Signs*, p. 86.

To say there exists rationality is to say that perspectives blend, perceptions confirm each other, a meaning emerges.[100]

Merleau-Ponty's analysis on this point is formulated in a proposition that is reflected throughout his semiology, that is, that "it is by considering language that we would best see how we are to and how we are not to return to the things themselves".[101]

The linguistic relations among men should help us understand the more general order of symbolic relations and of institutions, which assure the exchange not only of thoughts but of all types of values, the co-existence of men within a culture and, beyond it, within a single history.[102]

One of the chief elements in any semiology and in particular a linguistic semiology is structure or the systemic nature of the semiotic as it is manifest in its different modalities. This is to say that semiotic systems find their meaning as a correlation of structure and content in a comparison with language structure and content. What is meant in one structure often suggests what is meant in a similar structure. The meaning of a semiotic system "can be compared to the meaning of a spoken language, which is not transmitted in conceptual terms in the minds of those who speak, or in some ideal model of language, but which is, rather, the focal point of a series of verbal operations which converge almost by chance".[103]

The object of Merleau-Ponty's semiology is thus a system that establishes equivalence in human behavior that can have a known meaning.[104] Such a semiotic system is a phenomenology that attempts to obtain an understanding of the essential relationships existent in phenomena as a means of determining their existential modalities. Semiology as an existential phenomenology begins "as soon as certain elements of the world take on the value dimensions to which from then on we relate all the others and in whose language we express them".[105]

---

100   M. M-P., *Phenomenology*, p. xix.
101   M. M-P., *Visible*, p. 125.
102   M. M-P., *Primacy*, pp. 9-10. Also, see André Martinet "Structure and Language", *Yale French Studies*, nos. 36-37 (October, 1966), pp. 10-18.
103   M. M-P., *Primacy*, p. 200.
104   M. M-P., *Primacy*, p. 182.
105   M. M-P., *Signs*, p. 54.

3.3.2. *Signs and Signification*

Merleau-Ponty does not advance a strict definition of either the sign or signification in the customary sense of the word "define". Rather, his explanation of what he sees in the semiology of De Saussure and what advances are to be made from that semiology come to constitute a new statement of semiology. This is by way of saying that Merleau-Ponty accepts the view of De Saussure that "signs" are composed of signifiers or sound-images and signifieds or concepts. Yet this must be explained, for Merleau-Ponty does not accept any dualism such as concept and sound-image.

The true sign represents the signified, not according to an empirical association, but inasmuch as its relation to other signs is the same as the relation of the object signified by it to other objects. It is because of this that we can decipher unknown languages.
With symbolic forms, a conduct appears, which expresses the stimulus for itself, which is open to truth and to the proper value of things, which tends to the adequation of the signifying and signified, of the intention and that which it intends. Here behavior no longer *has* only one signification, it *is* itself signification.[106]

Thus, the sign is always a sign in use, if you will, the *sign is a gesture*. But just as the gesture is known within the context of its use, so the sign is known only through the context of other signs. Meaning as present in signs is not in signs themselves (as signifier and signified), but meaning *is* the signs. Signs are the perceived-perceiving, the speech-speaking, the thought-thinking, — in short — the phenomenal existence which is man.

... What we have learned from Saussure is that, taken singly, signs do not signify anything, that each one of them does not so much express a meaning as mark a divergence of meaning between itself and other signs.
... This sort of circle, according to which language, in the presence of those who are learning it, precedes itself, teaches itself, and suggests its own deciphering, is perhaps the marvel which defines language.[107]

Merleau-Ponty's analysis indicates that the "meaning of a sign" is simultaneous with the knowledge of its differentiation from other signs.[108] Even the absence of a sign *is a sign*.[109] Thus, the perception

---

106 M. M-P., *Structure*, pp. 121-122. See Maurice Lagueux, "Merleau-Ponty et la linguistique de Saussure", *Dialogue* IV, no. 3 (1965), pp. 351-364, esp. 361.
107 M. M-P., *Signs*, p. 39.
108 M. M-P., *Signs*, p. 40.
109 M. M-P., *Signs*, p. 44.

of a single sign is not possible for such a perception always includes what is *not* perceived which has sign meaning. This definition of a sign becomes clear when it is put under the pressure of an analytic division. Barthes has suggested how such an analysis might work, but before it is presented it may help to cite a passage in which Merleau-Ponty presents the same extrication with a lack of analytic specification.

> The acquisition of language appeared to us [in a previous lecture course] to be the acquisition of an open system of expression. That is, such a system is capable of expressing, not some finite number of cognitions or ideas, but rather an indeterminate number of cognitions or ideas to come. The system that is speech is learned by the child, not at all by a genuine intellectual operation (as though by means of intelligence the child understood the principles of speech, its morphology, and its syntax). Rather, what is involved is a kind of *habituation*, a use of language as a tool or instrument. The employment of language, which is an effect and also one of the most active stimuli of intellectual development, does not appear to be founded on the exercise of pure intelligence but instead on a more obscure operation — namely, the child's assimilation of the linguistic system of his environment in a way that is comparable to the acquisition of any habit whatever: the learning of a structure of conduct.[110]

Merleau-Ponty has presented here, in effect, what is called by Barthes a system of metalanguage functions or semiotic functions that give rise to language specifications in structure and content.

Barthes suggests a schema in which there is a primary base of meaning in language, or specifically in a sign, in which the signifier and signified are unitary — this is the sign of De Saussure and the sign of Merleau-Ponty that is marked by differences from other signs — as *real meaning*. The secondary level of signs is a denotation construction which is a metalanguage *per se*. Herein the signifier is separated from the signified, yet they exist in a one-to-one relationship where one means only what the other is. The tertiary level of sign meaning is connotation wherein the signifier is unitary in its application with no clear signifier, if any, indicated. This usage is denominated as the province of "rhetoric" by Barthes. Also at this third level, the signified operates singularly without any clear signifier in view and this function is generally equal to an ideology.[111]

The importance of this schema is that meaning at any level beyond the first is dependent on that which immediately precedes it. Thus

[110] M. M-P., *Primacy*, p. 99.
[111] Barthes, *Elements of Semiology*, pp. 92-93.

denotation is dependent on a primordial meaning and connotation is dependent on the denotation. Also, the meaning elements in the signifier and signified which are different at each level are the divergences in signs of which Merleau-Ponty speaks. For example, a sign used only in a "rhetorical" connotation is a signifier or sound-image devoid of a signified or concept. However, its use has a meaning when the given sign (the signifier) is either coupled in perception with silence (a sign) — thus creating no meaning, or coupled with the object of a previous perception (a sign in which the signified is linked to another signifier). When this second alternative (a previous experience) is taken, the signifier assumes the meaning of the second signifier through the agency of the signified. Thus, the sign which is used in the agency of connotation is a connotation simply because each perception of it has a denotative meaning for the perceiver. In turn, each denotation has meaning only because the signified *or* signifier draws from the "real system" a signified or signifier that *is inseparable* respectively from its signifier or signified.

The genius of Merleau-Ponty is that he formulated *the basis of sign meaning on the differences* that are apparent in any set of perceived signs. That is, connotation in either form (rhetorical or ideological) is immediately perceived because of its character as a sign in relation to other signs. A connotation is a sign with only a signifier (rhetorical) or a signified (ideological) and is immediately known by its related sign — the absence of its counterpart (respectively a signified or signifier). Or, the connotation is immediately known by its substitution of a counterpart foreign to it (the counterpart belonging to a separate denotation). The possibilities of explanation are infinite, thus for the reader who finds this analysis hard going one gets the flavor of this semiotic agency in figures of speech where signifiers take on "abnormal" signifieds thus causing meaning to be formed within the context of the signifier which belongs to the borrowed signified. To illustrate : "The ice cream is like a rock". The signifier "ice cream" is being used "rhetorically" and assumes the signified (e.g., hardness) of the signifier "rock". The sign meaning of "ice cream" is then in terms of the essence of a "rock" which is to say that existential perception of the utterance "ice cream" is known through the essential agency of the sign reference "rock".

It should be apparent that this semiological analysis is a phenomenology that looks to essential signs to know existence and it must be equally obvious that such a semiotic can apply to any agency of existence. Yet, it is particularly suited to language which bears this semiotic structure and since language is an expression of perceived reality. It is not difficult to see the implication for an ontology through the agency of speaking from a phenomenology of perception. This is to say, "Merleau-Ponty's philosophy is an analysis of the given".[112] It is an analysis in which "his primary task is to *describe* the real and not to *construct* it; and hence he insists that perception must be kept distinct from synthetic products such as judgment, action, and predication".[113] "There appears here a new kind of analysis which no longer consists in isolating elements but in understanding the character of a whole and its immanent law".[114]

By postulating that semiotic meaning emerges from the combination of signs, Merleau-Ponty introduces the concept of immanence and transcendence. This topic will form a special consideration in a moment, however we are only concerned with the immanent signification or meaning that results from the grouping of signs. In suggesting that the sign is a gesture, there is the corollary notion that a sign is immanent in being the present of its past and the present of an oncoming future of signification. That is, "this meaning arising at the edge of signs, this immanence of the whole in the parts, is found in the history of culture".[115] And in turn, this immanence may in usage become the meaning of the future — a transcendence, a new signification.

A language sometimes remains a long time pregnant with transformations which are to come; and the enumeration of the means of expression in a language does not have any meaning, since those which fall into disuse continue to lead a diminished life in the language and since the place of those which are to replace them is sometimes already marked out — even if in the form of a gap, a need, or a tendency.[116]

In short, the only semiological "constants" appear to be the divergences that appear in the immanent usage and those differences that appear

---

[112]   Raymond Bayer, "Merleau-Ponty's Existentialism", *University of Buffalo Studies* (Monographs), XIX, no. 3 (1951), p. 95.

[113]   Bayer, "Merleau-Ponty's Existentialism", p. 97. Cf. James M. Edie, "Transcendental Phenomenology and Existentialism", *Philosophy and Phenomenological Research* XXV, no. 1 (September, 1964), pp. 52-63.

[114]   M. M-P., *Structure*, p. 65. This thesis which runs through our own analysis of M. M-P.'s semiology of language is confirmed in a similar analysis of the semiotic of music, *Structure*, pp. 87-88, 121-122. After spelling out the semiotic of music (as we did language), M. M-P. says "The physiology of language has need of a coordination of this kind." (p. 87) Apparently, this task was to be taken up in *The Visible and the Invisible*.

[115]   M. M-P., *Signs*, p. 41.

[116]   M. M-P., *Signs*, p. 41.

through a transcendence of a formerly immanent signification. Thus it is clear why Merleau-Ponty prefers to use the term *synoptic* in preference to synthesis; because, the sign meaning is the synoptic result of immanence and transcendence. There is never a synthetic product simply because there is no finality of meaning in any given perception. As the gesture, the sign is its own meaning because it is an essential manifestation of an existent that is in constant modification and constitution.

On this point of the meaning or signification of a gesture as semiotic, Barral suggests there is a critical question to be answered. "The question of the 'natural' and 'conventional' sign is relevant here : is the gesture a 'natural' sign and language a 'conventional one ?"[117] She indicates that Merleau-Ponty's discussion of signs leaves the question unanswered with the vague suggestion that language is not composed of conventional signs and that gesture is not a natural sign convention. Yet, Merleau-Ponty does appear, to our reading, to suggest that there are no conventional signs that function in a pure symbol-referent agency and that natural signs exist independently of any reduction of conventional signs. He further maintains that natural signs are not constitutive of gesture or language because the sign is never a correspondence between specific signs and "states of mind".[118]

Merleau-Ponty's suggestion, by elimination, is that signs operate as a conventional agency but without the perfect one-to-one correspondence. The sign is a primordial meaning, it is not a relationship between thought and object. When the sign does become "sedimented" into culture it takes on the vicarious nature of an experience-meaning recalled by a new experience.

Behavior creates meanings [significations] which are transcendent to the anatomical apparatus, and yet immanent to the behavior as such, since it communicates itself and is understood. It is impossible to draw up an inventory of this irrational power which creates meanings and conveys them. Speaking is merely one particular case of it.

What is true, however — and justifies the view that we ordinarily take of language, as being in a peculiar category — is that, alone of all expressive processes, speaking is able to settle into a sediment and constitute an acquisition for inter-subjective use. This fact cannot be explained by pointing out that speech can be recorded on paper, whereas gestures or forms of behavior are transmitted only by direct imitation.[119]

[117] Barral, *Merleau-Ponty*, p. 189.
[118] M. M-P., *Phenomenology*, pp. 188-189.
[119] M. M-P., *Phenomenology*, pp. 189-190.

With this introduction to the nature of signs and signification, a specific definition of the sign as a phenomenon of speech that is existential (creates meaning by being genetically meaningful *per se*) can be offered.

Meaning [signification] is usually thought to transcend signs in principle (just as thought is supposed to transcend the sound or sights which indicate it), and to be immanent in signs in the sense that each one of them, having *its* meaning once and for all, could not conceivably slip any opacity between itself and us, or even give us food for thought. Signs are supposed to be no more than monitors which notify the hearer that he must consider such and such of his thoughts. But meaning does not actually dwell in the verbal chain or distinguish itself from the verbal chain in this way. Since the sign has meaning only in so far as it is profiled against other signs, its meaning is entirely involved in language. Speech always comes into play against a background of speech; it is always only a fold in the immense fabric of language. To understand it, we do not have to consult some inner lexicon which gives us the pure thoughts covered up by the words or forms we are perceiving; we only have to lend ourselves to its life, to its movement of differentiation and articulation, and to its eloquent gestures. There is thus an opaqueness of language. Nowhere does it stop and leave a place for pure meaning; it is always limited only by more language, and meaning appears within it only set in a context of words. Like a charade, language is understood only through the interaction of signs, each of which, taken separately, is equivocal or banal, and makes sense only by being combined with others.[120]

3.3.3. *Immanence and Transcendence in Semiology*

"We hope to share the experience of a relationship, but the only honest beginning, or even end, may be to share the experience of its absence".[121] If signs and significations are to be a meaning of a synergic presence, then the limitations of the present and the absent, the immanent and the transcendent, must be converted to a primordiality (a living logic, a "pregnant" meaning).

But if the sign is only a certain deviation between signs, and the signification a similar deviation between significations, thought and speech overlap one another like two reliefs. As pure differences, they are indiscernible. Expression is a matter of reorganizing things-said, affecting them with a new index of curvature, and bending them to a certain enhancement of meaning. There was that which is of itself comprehensible and sayable — notably that which more mysteriously summons all things from the depths of language before hand as nameable. There is that which is to be said, and which is as yet no more than a precise uneasiness in the world of things-said. Expression is a

120   M. M-P., *Signs,* p. 42.
121   Laing, *The Politics of Experience,* p. 56.

matter of acting in such a way that the two gather one another in or cross one another. I would never take a step if my faraway view of the goal did not find in my body a natural art of transforming it into an approaching view. My thought could not advance a step if the horizon of meaning it opens up did not become, through speech, what is called in the theater a *real* décor.[122]

Merleau-Ponty indicates that meaning is inherent in the semiotic presentation, that what is given and what is not given in the signs present is a synoptic knowledge that is process in the act of becoming. "Likewise it is true that the things are forever distinct from every 'object of thought' or every 'state of consciousness', transcendent, and at the same time that the consciousness that knows them is defined by its presence to itself, its immanence, the strict identity of appearing and being in it".[123] In terms of the linguistic semiotic that is the paradigm of all semiotics, the act of speaking becomes not a designating or pointing process but the perception proper of that which is existentially present to the perceiving subject.

The word and speaking must somehow cease to be a way of designating things or thoughts and become the presence of that thought in the phenomenal world, and, moreover, not its clothing but its token or its body. There must be, as psychologists say, a 'linguistic concept' *(Sprachbergriff)* or a verbal concept *(Wortbegriff)*, a 'central inner experience, specifically verbal, thanks to which the sound, heard, uttered, real or written, becomes a linguistic fact'.
We find here, beneath the conceptual signification of the words, an existential meaning which is not only rendered by them, but which inhabits them, and is inseparable from them.[124]

Thus, there is an integral presence of being that is the phenomenal "body" that is jointly the subject of existence and the object of essential becoming. The presence is the synopsis of signs-existent and significations-becoming which is the human synergism : the lived-body, the *body-subject.*

I thus cannot conceive a perceptible place in which I am not present. But even in the places in which I find myself are never completely given to me; the things which I see are things for me only under the condition that they always recede beyond their immediately given aspects. Thus there is a paradox of immanence and transcendence in perception. Immanence, because the perceived object cannot be foreign to him who perceives; transcendence, because it always contains something more than what is actually given. And these two elements of

---

[122]   M. M-P., *Signs,* p. 19.
[123]   M. M-P., *Visible,* p. 56.
[124]   M. M-P., *Phenomenology,* p. 182.

perception are not, properly speaking, contradictory. For if we reflect on this notion of perspective, if we reproduce the perceptual experience in our thought we see that the kind of evidence proper to the perceived, the appearance of "something" requires both this presence and this absence.[125]

"This ambiguity is not some imperfection of consciousness or existence, but the definition of them".[126] In direct relation to the semiology that allows for perception, "there is no deciphering, no mediate inference from the sign to what is signified, because the alleged signs are not given to me separately from what they signify".[127]

The present analysis rests heavily upon the concept of the *syntagm* which in linguistics refers to the meaning inherent in recurrent linguistic signs. For example, the words "radical student" derive their meaning as signs which signify by their relation to each other. The meaning takes on another perspective when the signs are seen as "student radical". Yet, in either case a syntagm is present that is a synoptic meaning which is a product of what "student" is and is not in relation to what "radical" is and is not when the two words are coupled. The recurrent *form* of such a syntagm as our examples (adjective-to-noun) becomes a rule by usage that is called *syntax*.

In relation to Merleau-Ponty's semiology the immanence of signs (which are their own signification) is the perceived meaning that is on a syntactical level, while the transcendent meaning functions as a *syntagm*. Here, the syntax implies a form whereas the syntagm implies a content. Both concepts and what they mean are dependent on each other; this is the paradox of immanence and transcendence. It should be noted that the "content" quality of the syntagm as we are using the term is the synoptic result of the signs form and content *as perceived*. It is the lived-body experience that is an existential perception. This is to say, the lived-body, the body-subject, and other such phrases as unit terms are syntagms that illustrate in a semiotic what Merleau-Ponty calls the elimination of the subject/object split. The phenomena that are existent and known (perceived) by their essential presence are a synergic syntagm or synopsis of immanence and transcendence whose union combines more meaning than is present in either presence or absence by itself.[128]

[125]   M. M-P., *Primacy*, p. 16.
[126]   M. M-P., *Phenomenology*, p. 332.
[127]   M. M-P., *Primacy*, p. 15.
[128]   For a detailed explanation of this subject, see: Barthes, *Elements of Semiology*, pp. 58-62.

The majoι lesson of the ambiguity of immanence and transcendence in perception is that its expression through a semiotic is not the transmission of the perception, but rather the communication of intention.

This transcendence of signification over perception, of speaking over perspective, is what makes the reflection on point of view as such possible: I am not immersed in the world to such an extent that I lose the aloofness of signifying, or intending, aloofness that is the principle of speech.[129]

Thus, the principle of semiotic as a knowledge of perception through language or of language through perception is a recognition of semiology as intentional phenomena expressed in-themselves and for-themselves.

To achieve meaning is not to bestow it directly; the word has the admirable property of making its sonority transparent, of fading away bodily in giving rise to the act which confers the sense. In short, the word becomes a sign.[130]

In quoting Ricoeur, the direction of Merleau-Ponty's semiology is specified as a dialectic of immanence and transcendence in which speech is the synoptic meaning of intentional perception. "To understand is to experience the harmony between what we aim at and what is given, between the intention and the performance — and the body is our anchorage in a world".[131]

3.3.4. *Meaning in Semiology*

"In trying to describe the phenomenon of speech and the specific act of meaning, we shall have the opportunity to leave behind us, once and for all, the traditional subject-object dichotomy".[132] This introductory statement will allow us to draw together the various elements of Merleau-Ponty's semiology. This is to say, meaning is the end product of the process of speaking as a semiotic record of perception by the body-subject within the lived-body experience of understanding the world in which and of which he *is*.

But for the subject who is actually speaking, who is no longer an *observer* confronting language as an *object*, his language is undoubtedly a distinct reality. There are regions where he can make himself understood and others where he

---

[129] Paul Ricoeur, *Fallible Man*, trans. C. Kelbley, (Chicago: Henry Regnery Co., 1965), p. 48.
[130] Ricoeur, *Fallible Man*, pp. 43-45. See Ricoeur, "Structure — Word — Event", *Philosophy Today* XII, no. 2 (Summer, 1968), pp. 114-129.
[131] M. M-P., *Phenomenology*, p. 144.
[132] M. M-P., *Phenomenology*, p. 174.

cannot. For him it means something to be speaking French. The circumstances may be more or less precise, more or less rigorous, more or less complex, depending on the culture of the speaker. But for him there is always a moment, a boundary, beyond which he no longer understands and is no longer understood.

Reflection on language now consists not in returning to a transcendental subject, disengaged from all actual linguistic situations, but to a speaking subject who has no access to any truth, not to any thought with a claim to universality, except through the practice of his language in a definite linguistic situation.[133]

Merleau-Ponty argues that meaning is the act of speaking, the act of using the semiotic that allows the expression of perception in speaking. The perception of lived-reality is the use of signs to understand, to grasp the signification that is the sign process.

What we *mean* is not before us, outside all speech, as sheer signification. It is only the excess of what we live over what has already been said. With our apparatus of expression we set ourselves up in a situation the apparatus is sensitive to, we confront it with the situation, and our statements are only the final balance of these exchanges.[134]

The dialectic of perception and speaking that is semiotic in the philosophy of Merleau-Ponty is a "gesture". In the gesture is the concept of meaning as the perceptible act that speaks; the gesture is a process of signs that are their own signification whether existential as a "speaking" or whether essential as a "perception". Thus, "to the extent that what I say has meaning, I am a different 'other' for myself when I am speaking; and to the extent that I understand, I no longer know who is speaking and who is listening".[135]

Language is not the process of replacing one meaning with another meaning, but is the substitution of equivalent meanings that point to the same perceptions that recur in lived-experience. Thus the vehicle of speaking a language is the presentation of a structure that is already present in the old and which explains the past by marking the divergence of the present.[136] "When one goes from the order of events

---

[133]   M. M-P., *Primacy*, p. 82.
[134]   M. M-P., *Signs*, p. 83.
[135]   M. M-P., *Signs*, p. 97. "The chiasm, reversibility, is the idea that every perception is doubled with a counterperception (Kant's real opposition), is an act with two faces, one no longer knows who speaks and who listens. Speaking-listening, seeing-being seen, perceiving-being perceived circularity (it is because of it that it seems to us that perception forms itself *in the things themselves*) — *Activity = passivity*". M. M-P., *Visible*, pp. 264-265.
[136]   M. M-P., *Signs*, p. 81.

to the order of expression, one does not change the world; the same circumstances which were previously submitted to now become a signifying system".[137] In this analysis Merleau-Ponty is following a principle introduced by Heidegger, namely, that the intentional transfer from perception to speaking is the translation of experience into lived-reality. "That which can be Articulated in interpretation, and thus even more primordially in discourse, is what we have called 'meaning' ".[138]

"But is the meaning of our actions to be found in our *intentions* or in the effect they have on others ?"[139] In answering this question, Merleau-Ponty formulates the union between the existent body-subject as an experiencing self who is his own meaning and the encounter of the body-subject with others who see in us a different meaning. This approach to meaning takes firm hold of the idea of a private meaning to self and a public meaning for others. Merleau-Ponty contends that when the perception of others takes place, the meaning of the body-subject becomes a synoptic presence of self in others. In short, the rhetorical question posed by Merleau-Ponty is answered not by asserting the primacy of intentional acts or the primacy of reacting to others, but by showing the intentionality of the body-subject as other. This is to say, the act of expression (speaking) is not a singular existential gesture, but an assemblage of gestures or a communication that is the essential manifestation of divergent existential perceptions made synoptic in the act of expression.

It is simply that all our actions have general meanings, especially as seen from the outside by others, and all these meanings are assumed in our actions because others are the permanent coordinates of our lives. Once we are aware of the existence of others, we commit ourselves to being, among other things, what they think of us, since we recognize in them the exorbitant power to *see us.*[140]

In the present analysis of meaning as a semiology that is the agency of perception and expression — the dialectic of the lived-body experience — it becomes increasingly clear that in semiotic "every action, every human enterprise is a crystallization of time, a cipher of transcendence".[141] In short, meaning as semiology becomes *living,* the exis-

---

[137] M. M-P., *Signs,* p. 69.
[138] Heidegger, *Being and Time,* p. 204.
[139] M. M-P., *Sense,* p. 36.
[140] M. M-P., *Sense,* p. 37.
[141] M. M-P., *Visible,* p. 208. "In short, it is man, burst forth in a single spurt, transcending his presence in being, to reach towards his presence in the other, transcending

tence that is the essential becoming of the body-subject. And, it is the confident awareness of self existence that becomes the basis of the will to communicate, the ground of speaking what is perceived — a selfhood that is the singularity that participates in the universality that we know in the signs that *are* the body-subject as self and as other, namely, *man*.

Without even presuming that I know everything myself, it is certain at least that, among other things, I am a knowing; this attribute assuredly belongs to me, even if I have others. I cannot imagine that the world irrupts into me or I into it: the world can present itself to this knowing which I am by offering it a meaning only in the form of a thought of the world. The secret of the world we are seeking must necessarily be contained in my contact with it. Inasmuch as I live it, I possess the meaning of everything I live, otherwise I would not live; and I can seek no light concerning the world except by consulting, by making explicit my frequenting of the world, by comprehending it from within.[142]

Merleau-Ponty posits the existence of man as the sense of perception — a semiology of meaning from within — as the ground on which is manifest the figure of speaking — a semiology of meaning from without — which is "the external existence of the sense" or its essence. This is the meaning of semiology in the existential phenomenology of Maurice Merleau-Ponty.

---

the past to reach towards the future, transcending each thing and his selfness to reach towards the sign." Jean-Paul Sartre, "Merleau-Ponty" in *Situations,* trans. B. Eisler, (Greenwich, Conn.: Fawcett Publications, Inc., 1965), p. 211. Originally published in 1964 as *Situations IV*.

[142]   M. M-P., *Visible*, p. 32. See this point developed in terms of Martin Heidegger's philosophy, which was probably noted by M. M-P. in his reading of Heidegger, in Cyril Welch, "A Phenomenological Analysis of the Occurrence of Meaning in Experience", unpublished Ph. D. dissertation Pennsylvania State University, 1964, p. 156.

III

PERCEPTION : THE LIVED-BODY EXPERIENCE

Merleau-Ponty's theory of semiology is manifest in one of its functional applications which is the phenomenology of perception or as he designates it : the "primacy of perception" in the lived-body experience. The genesis of the lived-body must be followed through the development of sensation and intellection as the unitary presence that is perception. To borrow a concept from Merleau-Ponty, perception must be the meeting of intent and act in one vital experience — the Yogi must meet the Commissar.[1] This is to say, there must be a union of the philosophy of the interior and the exterior respectively. There must be a development of that *presence* which is the act and intent of primordial perception.

Such an approach to reality is present in the method and in the philosophy of life that is Merleau-Ponty. As Sartre remarks, "First he [Merleau-Ponty] reflected upon the singularity of his life, then, turning back to his historical existence, he had discovered the one and the other were made from the same cloth".[2] It is precisely this movement of self back to historical existence that is reflected in the phenomenological method of Merleau-Ponty. Such a method involves the progression from a theory of perception to a statement of the perceived *gestalt* and the existential import of that *gestalt* as exercised in the radical *cogito*. In short, this chapter deals with Merleau-Ponty's method of knowing existence in the essence of lived-space and lived-time. The next chapter will deal with the expression of that knowledge as a means of existing in a world of essences.

Everything changes when a phenomenological or existential philosophy assigns itself the task, not of explaining the world or of discovering its "conditions of possibility", but rather of formulating an experience of the world, a contact with the world which precedes all thought *about* the world. After this, whatever

---

[1] M. M-P., *Primacy*, p. 219; *Humanism*, pp. 161-163.
[2] Sartre, *Situations*, p. 164.

is metaphysical in man cannot be credited to something outside his empirical being — to God, to Consciousness. Man is metaphysical in his very being, in his loves, in his hates, in his individual and collective history. And metaphysics is no longer the occupation of a few hours per month, as Descartes said; it is present, as Pascal thought, in the heart's slightest movement.[3]

In the above quotation it is apparent that Merleau-Ponty attempts to achieve a knowledge of existence through the methodology of phenomenology. The dualism of a world as object and subject, the dualism of mind (consciousness) and body are both rejected by the existential phenomenology that seeks the lived-body experience that is existential and is knowable through phenomenological inquiry. "In many ways Merleau-Ponty's philosophy is a genuine synthesis of the best in existentialism and phenomenology; the term existential phenomenology probably applies better to Merleau-Ponty's thought than to the thought of any other philosopher".[4]

In short, the phenomenological method of Merleau-Ponty involves three steps : (1) description or the "primacy of perception"; (2) reduction [reflection] or radical reflection as *gestalt*; and (3) intentionality or radical *cogito*.[5]

1. THE PRIMACY OF PERCEPTION (DESCRIPTION)

In order to establish Merleau-Ponty's theory that perception is the inclusive methodology of examining the existence inherent in essences, it is necessary to progress through several stages of analysis. From sensation as an experience of the body-subject in his objective and subjective encounters with reality (which constitute the respective modalities of being as existential and essential presence) to perception as the synopsis of temporality and spatiality, in an integral statement of method.

1.1. *Sensation*

The basis of sensation for human beings is a modality of existence in which the body encounters objects that are defined or have meaning by their relation to the body. This relationship is explainable within the semiological structure which Merleau-Ponty develops.

---

[3] M. M-P., *Sense,* pp. 27-28.
[4] Alden L. Fischer, "Introduction", in *The Essential Writings of Merleau-Ponty* (New York: Harcourt, Brace & World, 1969), p. 7.
[5] M. M-P., *Phenomenology,* pp. viii, xi, xvii.

The passing of the sense-data before our eyes or under our hands is, at it were, a language which teaches itself, and in which the meaning is secreted by the very structure of the signs, and this is why it can literally be said that our senses question things and that things reply to them. 'The sensible appearance is what reveals (Kundgibt), and expresses as such what it is not itself.' We understand the thing as we understand a new kind of behaviour, not, that is, through any intellectual operation of subsumption, but by taking up on our own account the mode of existence which the observable signs adumbrate before us. A form of behaviour outlines a certain manner of treating the world. In the same way, in the interaction of things, each one is characterized by a kind of *a priori* to which it remains faithful in all its encounters with the outside world. The meaning of a thing inhabits that thing as the soul inhabits the body: it is not behind appearances.[6]

What Merleau-Ponty is describing at the level of sensation is a "synaesthetic perception" in which the body functions to build structures of experience that have meaning. Yet, the person is unaware of this process because our scientific orientations shift the "centre of gravity of experience" so that we have unlearned how to use our senses in favor of an artificial intellectualism that is the deduction of experience.[7] This is to say, our experience of sensation has a phenomenal existence itself that is manipulated by cognitive alterations to fit meaning structures not actually representative of the felt sensation. "The thickness of the body, far from rivaling that of the world, is on the contrary the sole means I have to go unto the heart of the things, by making myself a world and by making them flesh".[8]

Before sensation in its role as a modality of perception can be discussed, it is necessary to examine intellection or the concept of a constitutive consciousness that is a subjective response to objective experience.

1.2. *Intellection*

In making our analysis focus on sensation and intellection, there should be no implication of a mind/body dualism. Both sensation and intellection are synergic elements of one process of knowing.

Consciousness does not begin to exist until it sets limits to an object, and even the phantoms of 'internal experience' are possible only as things borrowed from

---

[6] M. M-P., *Phenomenology*, p. 319.
[7] M. M-P., *Phenomenology*, p. 229.
[8] M. M-P., *Visible*, p. 135.

external experience. Therefore consciousness has no private life, and the only obstacle it encounters is chaos, which is nothing.[9]

The force of Merleau-Ponty's analysis is that if one considers the consciousness of man as a constitutive force of specifying objects, then there is no function to consciousness as the limits imposed are on an *already* existent object. In a strict sense, the isolated intellection of a conscious mind cannot be constitutive of objective experience, but only define the perimeter of possible objectivity. Hence, "To be a consciousness or rather *to be an experience* is to hold inner communication with the world, the body and other people, to be with them instead of being beside them".[10]

The unitary motion of the process of knowing as sensation and consciousness thereof is the modality of perception.

Sensation as it is brought to use by experience is no longer some inert substance or abstract moment, but one of our surfaces of contact with being, a structure of consciousness, and in place of one single space, as the universal condition of all qualities, we have with each one of the latter, a particular manner of being in space and, in a sense, of making space. It is neither contradictory nor impossible that each sense should constitute a small world within the larger one, and it is even in virtue of its peculiarity that it is necessary to the whole and opens upon the whole.[11]

Intellection is the coordinating force of sensed objectivity which in turn allows a knowledge of the subject's position in that objectivity as being-an-experience. The nature of the experience that is at once sensation and intellection is explained in large part by the phenomena that we designate as "mind".

The brute and prior experience of the world I thought I found already there by opening my eyes is only the symbol of a being that is for itself as soon as it is because appearing and therefore appearing to itself is its whole being — that is the being we call mind.[12]

By adhering to this method of examining experience one goes through an analysis of behavior in order to "introduce consciousness, not as a psychological reality or as cause, but as structure".[13]

With this groundwork prepared, Merleau-Ponty is situated to advance

[9]   M. M-P., *Phenomenology*, pp. 27-28.
[10] M. M-P., *Phenomenology*, p. 96.
[11] M. M-P., *Phenomenology*, pp. 221-222.
[12] M. M-P., *Visible*, p. 30.
[13] M. M-P., *Structures*, p. 5.

his conception of consciousness as unified with action — but not in a synthetic modality. "In the final analysis, consciousness is defined by the possession of an object of thought or by transcendence to itself; action is defined by a series of events external to each other. They are juxtaposed; they are not tied together".[14] The analysis here explicates the semiotic of Merleau-Ponty in the sense that consciousness or the signified is intimately related to action (behavior) or the signifier in any determinate set of signs. Thus any analysis of the signs must view the functional aspects of the signs as perceived, which is to say, as signifiers in relation to signifieds or vice versa. It is in this sense that perception is known as sensation and intellection as two interrelated aspects of the same phenomena. And, in the same vein an analysis of sensation and intellection is necessarily an inquiry into its opposite number within the context of the whole, i.e., perception.

... Consciousness is a network of significative intentions which are sometimes clear to themselves and sometimes, on the contrary, lived rather than known. Such a conception will permit us to link consciousness with action by enlarging our idea of action. Human action can be reduced to vital action only if one considers the intellectual analysis by which it passes for a more ingenious *means* of achieving animal ends. But it is this completely external relation of end and means which becomes impossible from the point of view which we are adopting. It imposes itself as long as consciousness is defined by the possession of certain "representations", for then the consciousness of act is necessarily reduced to representation of its goal on the one hand and possibly to that of the bodily mechanisms which assure its execution under these conditions.[15]

The point that Merleau-Ponty is making is quite succinct : "The mental ... is reducible to the structure of behavior".[16] The assumption in this theory is that the behavior that is visible from the outside by another person is at the same time visible from the inside by the actor, hence "another person is in principle accessible to me as I am to myself; and we are both objects laid out before an impersonal consciousness".[17] Eldridge Cleaver has stated the perception described by Merleau-Ponty in this way : "The price of hating other human beings is loving oneself less".[18]

To follow Merleau-Ponty's construction of the real world as ex-

---

[14]   M. M-P., *Structures*, p. 164.
[15]   M. M-P., *Structures*, p. 173.
[16]   M. M-P., *Structures*, pp. 221-222.
[17]   M. M-P., *Structures*, p. 222.
[18]   Eldridge Cleaver, "On Becoming", in *Soul on Ice* (New York: Delta Publishing Co., 1968), p. 17.

perienced does not void the limits of convention by which the "normal" and the "abnormal" are separated.

Phenomenology permits psychoanalysis to recognize "psychic reality" without equivocation, the "intrasubjective" essence of morbid formations, the fantastic operation that reconstructs a world on the margin of, and counter to, the true world, a lived history beneath the effective history — a world called illness.[19]

In point of fact, the world of the mentally ill is a construction of the lived experience of the individual as the sole constituent of reality without regard for the encounter with others or for the perception of other persons who see in the ill behavior the disparity of structure and content in the lived experience. The psychoanalyst R.D. Laing affirms this point of view in his discussion of the abnormal in human behavior.

As we experience the world, so we act. We conduct ourselves in the light of our view of what is the case and what is not the case. That is, each person is a more or less naive ontologist. Each person has views of what is and what is not.[20]

Thus, the action and perception of the mentally ill is manifest in the approach that they take in the lived-experience.

In order to extricate Merleau-Ponty's theory of perception from his various works, it is necessary to clarify two concepts in addition to sensation and intellection, viz., the notion of "seeing" and the experience of the Other.

1.3. *Seeing*

The use of the verb "see" by phenomenologists is intended to indicate the knowledge or perception of the lived-experience or the "things themselves". Nonetheless, psychologists and philosophers use the term more often in the cognitive sense of understanding (intellection) as a pure act of consciousness. The phenomenologist contends that to "see" is to be able to describe phenomena in their lived-presence, in their signification as signs. There should be no prejudice introduced into inquiry by an artificial and analytical separation of the signs into their signifiers and signifieds.[21]

---

[19]   Fisher, *Essential Writings of Merleau-Ponty*, p. 81.
[20]   Laing, *The Politics of Experience*, p. 142.
[21]   Kurt Koffka, *Principles of Gestalt Psychology* (New York: Harcourt, Brace & World, Inc., 1963), p. 180. (First published in 1935.)

Seeing is that strange way of rendering ourselves present while keeping our distance and, without participating, transforming others into visible things. He who sees believes himself invisible: for his acts remain in the flattering entourage of his intentions, and he deprives others of his alibi, reducing them to a few words, a few gestures.[22]

This is to say, "since it is a non-coincidence I coincide with here, experience is susceptible to being extended beyond the particular being I am. My perception of my duration is an apprenticeship in a general way of *seeing*".[23]

Merleau-Ponty explains that seeing is the act of perception taken as a vehicle of knowing not an object, but a lived-object. This is to argue that an object is perceived through an intentional act of a living person.

The lived object is not rediscovered or constructed on the basis of the contributions of the senses; rather, it presents itself to us from the start as the center from which these contributions radiate. We *see* the depth, the smoothness, the softness, the hardness of objects; Cézanne even claimed that we see their odor.[24]

Perception is neither sensation or intellection but that lived-experience that is present with the act of experiencing and not in need of cognitive analysis to allow for meaning. To see is to know and feel what is meant because the signification is the sign.

It [vision] is a thinking that deciphers strictly the signs given within the body. Resemblance is the result of perception, not its mainspring. More surely still, the mental image, the clairvoyance which renders present to us what is absent, is nothing like an insight penetrating into the heart of Being. It is still a thought relying upon bodily indices, this time insufficient, which are made to say more than they mean. Nothing is left of the oneiric world of analogy ....[25]

Vision as the phenomenological act of seeing has two basic characters of application. First, there is the vision upon which the perceiving subject reflects : "I cannot think it except *as* thought, the mind's inspection, judgment, a reading of signs".[26] And second, there is the actual vision that occurs as an "honorary or instituted thought, squeezed into a body — its own body" of which we have no cognitive awareness

22   M. M-P., *Signs*, p. 311.
23   M. M-P., *Signs*, p. 184. See *Themes*, pp. 27-32.
24   M. M-P., *Sense*, p. 15.
25   M. M-P., *Primacy*, pp. 171-172.
26   M. M-P., *Primacy*, pp. 176-177.

but the lived awareness of its action which is "the autonomous order of the compound of soul and body".[27] There is the relegation of the thought of seeing to the vision in act.

Now perhaps we have a better sense of what is meant by that little verb "to see". Vision is not a certain mode of thought or presence to self; it is the means given me for being absent from myself, for being present at the fission of Being from the inside — the fission at whose termination, and not before, I come back to myself.[28]

In short, "vision alone makes us learn that beings that are different, 'exterior', foreign to one another, are yet absolutely *together,* are 'simultaneity' ".[29]

In Merleau-Ponty's doctrine of vision as a means of phenomenological description is co-present the doctrine of the immanence and transcendence of signs which allows the vision to simultaneously be and have meaning. In the paradox of seeing what is present and yet absent, there is the *presence of* immanence and transcendence.

... What we see is always in certain respects not seen: there must be hidden sides of things, and things 'behind us', if there is to be a 'front' of things, and things 'in front of' us, in short, perception. The limits of the visual field are a necessary stage in the organization of the world, and not an objective outline.[30]

The assumption is usually that it is not possible to see what is not there, thus limiting vision to a concept of sensory impression that rests only on signification. In fact, vision rests on motivation in the sense that signification is taken as sign present and as sign absent.[31] It should therefore be possible to examine the reality of the visible and invisible world through a phenomenological method that recognizes the existence of elements through their simultaneous presence and absence.[32]

There is a danger that one may take Merleau-Ponty's description of the lived-body experience as "seeing" through the modality of the visible and the invisible as a metaphor for sensation and intellection. There is no metaphor intended or implied. Actually, Merleau-Ponty specifically points out why a metaphorical comprehension of this

[27] M. M-P., *Primacy,* p. 177.
[28] M. M-P., *Primacy,* p. 186.
[29] M. M-P., *Primacy,* p. 187.
[30] M. M-P., *Phenomenology,* p. 277.
[31] M. M-P., *Phenomenology,* p. 262.
[32] M. M-P., *Visible,* p. 27; *Themes,* pp. 33-36.

method would be inappropriate. First, thought involves a quasilocality that has to be described, i.e., a locality that is elastic in being and not an inherence in a point of space and time. Time is not an analogy for the "mind", but a negative indication that mind is not present here in the operation of description. There is only "a locality by investment, and, when all that is said, there is a theater of apparition of the other".[33]

Second, the originating locality that is the visible and the invisible which is the thing or the direction of the thing is not "identifiable in objective space either, not a relation *in* ob-jective space —— A *direction* is not *in* space : it is in filigree across it —— It is therefore transposable to thought".[34] The argument here is that the mind as the point of perception and intellection is not an objective site, yet it is in an environment which it circumvents "as my locality for myself is the point that all the vanishing lines of my landscape designate to me, and which is itself *invisible*".[35]

The fundamental relationship of the visible and the invisible as the immanent and transcendent aspects of seeing is "an openness upon the world" (ouverture au monde).[36] And in this openness one cannot reduce the act of perception to the thought of perceiving as the valid rendering of immanence. To do so is to solidify description into the visible and thus eliminate the possibility of discovering the meaning that is "first held captive in the thing and in the world itself".[37] In short, any reversion to dualistic analysis destroys the lived dialectic of the perception and renders it a mere sensation or intellection as artificial reality.

There is no vision without thought. But *it is not enough* to think in order to see. Vision is a conditioned thought; it is born 'as occasioned' by what happens in the body; it is 'incited' to think by the body. It does not *choose* either to be or not to be or to think this thing or that. It has to carry in its heart that heaviness, that dependence which cannot come to it by some intrusion from outside. Such bodily events are 'instituted by nature' in order to bring us to see this thing or that. The thinking that belongs to vision functions according to a program and a law which it has not given itself. It does not possess its own premises; it is not a thought altogether present and actual; there is in its center a mystery of passivity.[38]

33   M. M-P., *Themes*, pp. 221-222.
34   M. M-P., *Themes*, p. 222.
35   M. M-P., *Themes*, p. 222. See Colin Smith, "The Notion of Object in the Phenomenology of Merleau-Ponty", *Philosophy* XXXIX, no. 148 (April, 1964), pp. 110-119.
36   M. M-P., *Themes*, p. 35.
37   M. M-P., *Themes*, p. 36.
38   M. M-P., *Primacy*, p. 175.

In short, the perception engaged by the body does not result from the body's perspective in allowing certain thoughts of the perceived thing. "My conviction that I see the thing itself does not *result* from the perceptual exploration, it is not a word to designate the proximal vision; on the contrary it is what gives me the notion of the 'proximal', of the 'best' point of observation, and of the 'thing itself' ".[39]

This analysis can be exemplified in the relation between vision, language and an object. "Words do not *look like* the things they designate; and a picture is not a *trompe-l'œil*".[40] This is to say that words allow one to see the best perspective in which to find meaning that is the object designated. Words are a perspective of the perception itself which allows for the unity of the visible and the invisible by suggesting a direction in the dialectic which becomes a *presence* of meaning. The same is true for the painter in a reverse sense.

The painter lives in fascination. The actions most proper to him — those gestures, those paths which he alone can trace and which will be revelations to others (because the others lack what he lacks or in the same way) — to him they seem to emanate from the things themselves, like patterns of the constellations.
Inevitably the roles between him and the visible are reversed. That is why so many painters have said that things look at them.[41]

In short, the relationship that is "seeing" is intimately connected with the concept of Other in relation to the body-subject in the lived-body experience or an openness upon the world. The dialectic that is visible and invisible, that is present and absent, that is immanence and transcendence, is the phenomena of Other as self and as myself.

1.4. *Other*

Hegel postulated that the Other is a necessary condition of the self as being. "For it is the existence of the pure self *qua* self; in speech the self-existent singleness of self-consciousness comes as such into existence, so that its particular individuality is something for others".[42] This is to say that an individual gains existential meaning in the exercise of the agency of speech (as an essential agency) which allows self perception and perception by others. "I discover myself in the other, just as

---

[39] M. M-P., *Visible,* p. 37.
[40] M. M-P., *Sense,* p. 17.
[41] M. M-P., *Primacy,* p. 167.
[42] Hegel, *The Phenomenology of Mind,* p. 530.

I discover consciousness of life in consciousness of death, because I am from the start this mixture of life and death, solitude and communication, which is heading toward its resolution".[43]

Merleau-Ponty follows Husserl's definition of the Other as the union of self knowledge and knowledge for others outside myself. "The 'Other', according to his own constituted sense, points to me myself; the other is a 'mirroring' of my own self and yet not a mirroring proper, an analogue of my own self and yet again not an analogue in the usual sense".[44]

He who "posits" the other man is a perceiving subject, the other person's body is a perceived thing, and the other person himself is "posited" as "perceiving". It is never a matter of anything but cooperation. I see that this man over there sees, as I touch my left hand while it is touching my right.[45]

The exact nature of the Other as a function of perception and description involves four steps of method according to Merleau-Ponty.

The problem of the experience of others poses itself, as it were, in a system of four terms: (1) myself, my "psyche", (2) the image I have of my body by means of the sense of touch or of synesthesia, which, to be brief, we shall call the "introceptive image" of my own body; (3) the body of the other as seen by me, which we shall call the "visual body"; and (4) a fourth (hypothetical) term which I must re-constitute and guess at — the "psyche" of the other, the other's feeling of his own existence — to the extent that I can imagine or suppose it across the appearances of the other through his visual body.[46]

One should not be misled by this delineation of factors, since Merleau-Ponty's intent is not to suppose an intersubjective dualism, but rather to verify the unity of the perceiving person who encounters another. The purpose of such a methodology is to recognize within the self a junction of the for-itself and the in-itself — "unless I have an exterior others have no interior".[47] This is to say that a plurality of consciousness and perception is not possible if I view myself as an absolute consciousness and perception.

In approaching the Other in the manner suggested by Merleau-Ponty it quickly becomes apparent that "the experience of my body and the

---

[43]   M. M-P., *Sense*, p. 68.
[44]   Edmund Husserl, *Cartesian Mediations: An Introduction to Phenomenology*, trans. D. Cairns (The Hague: Martinus Nijhoff, 1969), p. 94.
[45]   M. M-P., *Signs*, p. 170. See *Humanism*, pp. 108-110.
[46]   M. M-P., *Primacy*, p. 115.
[47]   M. M-P., *Phenomenology*, p. 373. See *Themes*, pp. 106-107.

body of the other form a totality and constitute a 'form' ".[48] With the emergence of structure as convergence and divergence between myself and the other there is the understanding of "seeing".

... I know unquestionably that that man over there *sees*, that my sensible world is also his, because *I am present at his seeing*, it *is visible* in his eyes' grasp of the scene. And when I say I see *that* he sees, there is no longer here (as there is in "I think that he thinks") the interlocking of two propositions but the mutual unfocusing of a "main" and a "subordinate" viewing.[49]

With this context before us, an examination of each of the four "terms" that allow an understanding of the Other through self will clarify the dialectic of "seeing".

1.4.1. *Myself, My "Psyche"*

This first term in which the self is known prior to the experience of self-as-other or prior to knowing the other is a primordial self aware-ness. It is the *cogito* as radical *cogito* — a point that will be developed in detail later in this chapter. Yet, this knowledge of "myself" is an existence that Merleau-Ponty designates by the term *flesh,* that which is not knowable as a dualism in form or act.

What we are calling flesh, this interiorly worked over mass, has no name in philosophy. As the formative medium of the object and the subject, it is not the atom of being, the hard in itself that resides in a unique place and moment: one can indeed say of my body that it is not *elsewhere,* but one cannot say that it is *here* or *now* in the sense that objects are; and yet my vision does not soar over them, it is not the being that is wholly knowing, for it has its own inertia, its ties. We must not think the flesh starting from substances, from body and spirit — for then it would be the union of contradictories — but we must think it, as we said, as an element, as the concrete emblem of a general manner of being.[50]

The individual that is the psyche itself is a mass of sensations. Such sensations occur within my body and are knowable only by me; they are sensations that you and I cannot share as a concrete reality. Only I am conscious of the mass of sensations and you can never come to know them.[51] Merleau-Ponty specifies this notion by saying that "the invisible is *there* without being an *object,* it is pure transcendence,

---

48   M. M-P., *Primacy,* p. 120.
49   M. M-P., *Signs,* p. 169.
50   M. M-P., *Visible,* p. 147. See *Humanism,* pp. 115-117.
51   M. M-P., *Primacy,* p. 114.

without ontic mask. And the 'visibles' themselves, in the last analysis, they too are only centered on a nucleus of absence".[52]

1.4.2. *Introceptive Image*

The introceptive image is the product of the sensing self; it is the image of the lived-body as witnessed from the interior, that is the psyche, that is only myself. "This subject which experiences itself as constituted at the moment it functions as constituting is my body".[53] In due course, "everything happens as if the functions of intentionality and the intentional object were paradoxically interchanged".[54] One comes to know by perception that the body functions as the psyche in a sensational modality that is beyond the psyche. "I am snapped up by a second myself outside me; I perceive an other".[55]

The power of the realization that there is another myself exterior to me and a public figure on display for others is seen most accurately in the experience of seeing oneself in a mirror. In the mirror experience there is the literal perception of psyche looking at body, yet the understanding that the image and the psyche are one.

The experience of the introceptive image as experienced in seeing oneself in the mirror is first witnessed in the behavior of the child.

The child's problem is not so much one of understanding that the visual and the tactile images of the body — both located at points in space — in reality comprise only one, as it is of understanding that the image in the mirror is *his* image, that it is what others see of him, the appearance he presents to other subjects; and the synthesis is less a synthesis of intellection than it is a synthesis of coexistence with others.[56]

The experience is always there, even in the mature adult.

In the same way the image in the mirror, even for the adult, when considered in direct unreflective experience, is not simply a physical phenomenon: it is mysteriously inhabited by me; it is something of myself.[57]

Although the mirror experience is primarily visual, the same class of experience is present for the person who hears his voice on an audio tape the first time or most dramatically for the person who hears and

---

[52]   M. M-P., *Visible*, p. 229.
[53]   M. M-P., *Signs*, p. 94. See *Themes*, pp. 46-52.
[54]   M. M-P., *Signs*, p. 94.
[55]   M. M-P., *Signs*, p. 94.
[56]   M. M-P., *Primacy*, p. 140.
[57]   M. M-P., *Primacy*, p. 132.

sees himself on video tape for the first time. The introceptive image becomes that Other — a consciousness seen from the outside.[58]

1.4.3. *Visual Body*

The visual body is the body of the other as seen by me. In this third step one comes to the first encounter with the Other as another person, but only on the sensed level of perceiving his corporeal existence as being similar to our own. "If one starts from the visible and the vision, the sensible and the sensing, one acquires a wholly new idea of the 'subjectivity' : there are no longer 'syntheses', there is a contact with being through its modulations, or its reliefs".[59] This is to say that my sense of body and that of another's body come to constitute a common form or structure that is knowable by contrast and comparison. In this analysis of likeness and dissimilarity of corporeal perception there are two ways in which to view the other. The applications of each will be explored as they relate to the "visual body".

Nevertheless there are two ways in which we can consider the image — one, a reflective, analytic way according to which the image is nothing but an appearance in a visible world and has nothing to do with me; the other, a global and direct one, of the kind which we use in immediate life when we do not reflect and which gives us the image as something which *solicits* our belief.[60]

In this statement of approach, Merleau-Ponty indicates that our perception of others can be analytic and designate others as mere *objects* or our view can constitute them as *bodies* insofar as we know our own corporeal existence. This bifurcation does not exist in a formal sense because our bodily existence is such that objectivity quickly gives way to self perception in the other.

Already the other body has ceased to be a mere fragment of the world, and become the theatre of a certain process of elaboration, and, as it were, a certain

[58]   M. M-P., *Sense,* p. 45. For a detailed account of the "introceptive image" consult Remy Kwant, "The Human Body as the Self-Awareness of Being (An Inquiry into the Last Phase of Merleau-Ponty's Philosophical Life)", *Review of Existential Psychology and Psychiatry* III, no. 2 (Spring, 1968), pp. 117-134. Originally published in *Humanitas* II, no. 1 (1966), pp. 43-62. The direction and content of this article are further detailed in R. Kwant, *From Phenomenology to Metaphysics: An Inquiry into the Last Period of Merleau-Ponty's Philosophical Life* (Pittsburgh, Pa.: Duquesne University Press, 1966).
[59]   M. M-P., *Visible,* p. 269. See *Themes,* p. 9.
[60]   M. M-P., *Primacy,* p. 130. Sartre argues that such a dual choice is not available and that there is only being-as-object, *Being and Nothingness,* p. 365.

'view' of the world. There is taking place over there a certain manipulation of things hitherto my property. Someone is making use of my familiar objects. But who can it be? I say that it is another person, a second myself, and this I know in the first place because this living body has the same structure as mine. I experience my own body as the power of adopting certain forms of behavior and a certain world, and I am given to myself merely as a certain hold upon the world: now, it is precisely my body which perceives the body of another person, and discovers in that other body a miraculous prolongation of my own intentions, a familiar way of dealing with the world. Henceforth, as the parts of my body together comprise a system, so my body and the other person's are one whole, two sides of one and the same phenomenon, and the anonymous existence of which my body is the ever-renewed trace henceforth inhabits both bodies simultaneously.[61]

A simple confirmation of Merleau-Ponty's analysis is offered in a consideration of human emotion as jealousy. "I would not covet, in right and principle, what others have if I did not sympathize with them, if I did not consider others as 'other myselves' ".[62]

In short, the visual body is the medium through which the individual body-subject comes to an awareness of others whose bodily existence bears analogy to his own. "... We recognize a certain common structure in each person's voice, face, gestures and bearing and that each person is nothing more or less to us than this structure or way of being in the world".[63] And it is in this context that Merleau-Ponty has rightly commented that "to live in public affairs is *to live according to others*".[64]

1.4.4. *"Psyche" of the Other*

Merleau-Ponty has called this a hypothetical term of the other since it can only be guessed at by me — I can never know the reality of the other as he knows his own real presence. In the same way, he cannot know me completely. This is to say, "other minds are given to us only as incarnate, as belonging to faces and gestures".[65] The presence of another's psyche to me as his bodily situation is best illustrated in the sexuality of the person.

---

[61]   M. M-P., *Phenomenology*, pp. 353-354. "But this dilemma, which is given as part of the human lot, is not one for me as pure consciousness: it is still I who cause the other to be for me, and who cause us both to be as members of mankind." *Ibid.* p. 435.
[62]   M. M-P., *Primacy*, p. 143.
[63]   M. M-P., *Sense*, p. 53.
[64]   M. M-P., *Signs*, p. 205. See *Humanism*, p. 34.
[65]   M. M-P., *Sense*, p. 16.

As aggression does not aim at a thing but a person, the intertwine of the sexual and the aggressive signifies that sexuality has, so to speak, an interior (that it is lined throughout with a person-to-person relationship), and that the sexual is our way (since we are flesh, our carnal way) of living our relationships with others. Since sexuality is relationship to other persons, and not just to another body, it is going to weave the circular system of projections and introjections between other persons and myself, illuminating the unlimited series of reflecting reflections which are the reasons why I am the other person and he is myself.[66]

This general direction of sexuality as a presence of the psyche of another purely through bodily perception is illustrated in nymphomania which is often labeled as a form of telepathy.

This visibility of my body (for me — but also universal and, eminently, for the other) is what is responsible for what is called telepathy. For a minute indication of the other's behavior suffices to activate this danger of visibility. For example, a woman feels her body desired and looked at by imperceptible signs, and without herself looking at those who look at her.[67]

An equally sufficient illustration of the felt presence of the psyche of another through his bodily presence alone is found in transitivism. Here the subject himself attributes to others what belongs to him, which is to say his psychic presence to his corporeal presence is imputed to another as the other's psychic modality.[68]

Before passing on to the act of speaking as a means of knowing (with degrees of potential verification) the psyche of the Other, the operation of immanence and transcendence must be indicated in a non-verbal presence of bodies.

A perceiving body that I see is also a certain absence that is hollowed out and tactfully dealt with behind that body by its behavior. But absence is itself rooted in presence; it is through his body that the other person's soul is soul in my eyes. 'Negatives' also count in the sensible world, which is decidedly the universal one.[69]

Merleau-Ponty is suggesting that absence and presence of our knowledge of the other's "hypothetical" psyche is linked to the presence and absence of the body to our psyche.

---

[66]   M. M-P., *Signs,* p. 230. For a full explanation of sexuality as the visual and gestural presence of the body-subject, see Joseph J. Kockelmans, "Merleau-Ponty on Sexuality", *Journal of Existentialism* VI, no. 21 (Fall, 1965), pp. 9-29.

[67]   M. M-P., *Visible,* p. 245.

[68]   M. M-P., *Primacy,* p. 148.

[69]   M. M-P., *Signs,* p. 172.

The other, not as a "consciousness", but as an inhabitant of a body, and consequently of the world. [sic] Where is the other in this body that I see? He is (like the meaning of the sentence) immanent in his body (one cannot detach him from it to pose him apart) and yet, more than the sum of the signs or the significations conveyed by them. He is that of which they are always the partial and non-exhaustive image — and who nonetheless is attested wholly in them. Always in process of an unfinished incarnation — Beyond the objective body as the sense of the painting is beyond the canvas.[70]

This is to say, the immanence of the body which is its presence always holds out the possibility of transcendence which is its absence. Further, the possibility of transcendence is not just at the corporeal level but at the level of the psyche. The possibility of the psyche taking on the perspective of the body is manifestly present in the act of speech which is the act of the body presenting the psyche. It is at this juncture that one sees the vitality of the gesture as an essential or bodily presence that is self transcending to a psychic presence between the Other and myself. There is the possibility for knowing what the Other means.

Merleau-Ponty's doctrine of immanence and transcendence relies on the understanding that one has both an empirical being and a transcendental or existential being and that these beings are the "observe and reverse of one another".[71] Because of the personal realization that this immanence and transcendence is intrapersonal, there is through analogy or variance the possibility that the Other's experience is like mine. In this knowledge of the possible Other there are two levels of potentiality : the corporeal and the intercorporeal. The *distinction of degree* is marked out most fundamentally in the use and non-use of speech in the intercorporeal setting.

I remain the sole *ipse*; the other, as long as he does not speak, remains an inhabitant of my world, but he reminds me very imperiously that the *ipse* is a nothing, that this anonymity does not form the spectacle for itself, that it forms it for X, for all those presumptively who might wish to take part in it.[72]

This is to say that the other and I are the possibility of one another and can know each other as the like body of myself. And, the presence of the other moves from a possibility, from the potential X, to the constituted other through the action that is gesture, facial movement, bodily position, and *speech* to an experienced actuality. This process

---

[70]   M. M-P., *Visible,* pp. 209-210.
[71]   M. M-P., *Visible,* p. 61.
[72]   M. M-P., *Visible,* p. 59.

is the lived experience that "each one of us [is] pregnant with the others and confirmed by them in his body".[73]

The reality of the other comes strikingly before us in the interpersonal relation of aggression that is marked in the personality of the sociopath and his victim.

In the same moment that I am about to be afraid that I make others afraid; it is the same aggression that I repel and send back upon others; it is the same terror which threatens me that I spread abroad — I live my fear in the fear I inspire. But by a counter-shock, the suffering that I cause rends me along with my victim; and so cruelty is no solution but must always be begun again. There is a circuit between the self and others, a Communion of Black Saints.
A sentence is never anything but a statement, a collection of significations which as a matter of principle could not possibly be equivalent to the unique savor that each person has for himself. And yet when the victim admits defeat, the cruel man perceives another life beating through those words; he finds himself before *another himself*.[74]

The force of Merleau-Ponty's analysis is that the psyche of the other, incarnate in his bodily presence, assumes a new dimension when the other begins to speak. The words of the other become a public record within my corporeal presence that attests to the intent of the other — his psyche made known through his body.

There is, then, a taking up of others' thought through speech, a reflection in others, an ability to think *according to others* which enriches our own thoughts. Here the meaning of words must be finally induced by the words themselves, or more exactly, their conceptual signification must be formed by a kind of deduction from a *gestural signification*, which is immanent in speech.[75]

With speech as a vehicle for knowing the psyche of the Other there is an accompanying threat to the other that his private existence may become a public phenomenon through speech. This felt threat is generally a *post hoc* experience in that the speaking of the other (or of me for the other) lingers on in my psyche. The Other becomes part of me, in my psyche, which is the threat of possession — even of my body, for the psyche and the body are co-possessive.[76] This phenomena is a *rhetoric of risk* in which "privacy is a means of establishing a world, and what genuine argument to persuade does is to publicize that

[73] M. M-P., *Signs*, p. 181.
[74] M. M-P., *Signs*, p. 212. See *Humanism*, p. 35n.
[75] M. M-P., *Phenomenology*, p. 179.
[76] M. M-P., *Phenomenology*, pp. 354-355.

privacy".[77] The risk is the knowledge that myself and the other are variations of one another in our reflective encounter of psyche and bodily image. What one must be aware of is the separation of myself and the other, not as subject and object, but as corporality and corporality with the possibility of psychic reflection that is a claim to immediacy (i.e., the lived-body experience).

Even if each of us has his own archetype of the other, the very fact that he is open to participation, that he is a sort of cipher or symbol of the other, obliges us to pose the problem of the other, not as a problem of access to another nihilation, but as a problem of initiation to a symbolics and a typicality of the others of which the *being for itself* and the *being for the other* are reflective variants and not the essential forms.[78]

1.5. Perception

Perception is the intentional encounter with a presence which is a synoptic spatiality and temporality. The nature of perception requires that one first be introduced to the separate concepts of spatiality and temporality as they are viewed in a phenomenological sense. That is, both space and time exist as essential elements in which the existential elements are synoptic unions of space and time.

1.5.1. Spatiality

Merleau-Ponty indicates that there is a *virtual space* which is the possible act of man within *actual space*. The virtual space is recognized as the spatial values that a point would receive in terms of any other corporeal position possible for us to assume. With this structure at hand a "cultural space" is built up in which Others and myself participate in the same or similar spatiality of situations.

A system of correspondence is established between our spatial situation and that of others, and each one comes to symbolize all the others. This insertion of our factual situation as a particular case within the system of other possible situations begins as soon as we *designate* a point in space with our finger. For this pointing gesture, which animals do not understand, supposes that we

---

[77] Maurice Natanson, "The Claims of Immediacy", in *Philosophy, Rhetoric, and Argumentation,* ed. M. Natanson and H.W. Johnstone, Jr. (University Park: The Pennsylvania State University Press, 1965), p. 19. Cf., Hannah Arendt, "The Disclosure of the Agent in Speech and Action", in *The Human Condition* (Garden City, New York: Doubleday Anchor Books, 1959), pp. 155-161.
[78] M. M-P., *Visible,* p. 82n.

are already installed in virtual space — at the end of the line prolonging our finger in a centrifugal and cultural space.[79]

The use of the body in virtual space is not a conception since the gesture is a function of our body. Yet, there is the fundamental theory of the mind (psyche) in the body which is manifest in the reciprocal exchange that is made with the instruments of the body; there is an existence which is virtual space. The value of such virtual space is recognized in ourselves and others by the correspondence of bodily movement manifesting psychic intent.

Sensation as it is brought to use by experience is no longer some inert substance or abstract moment, but one of our surfaces of contact with being, a structure of consciousness, and in place of one single space, as the universal condition of all qualities, we have with each one of the latter, a particular manner of being in space and, in a sense, of making space.[80]

It is in this frame of reference that Merleau-Ponty is led to conclude that "being is synonymous with being situated".[81]

Space, therefore, is to be defined not as "the setting (real or logical) in which things are arranged, but the means whereby the positing of things becomes possible".[82] The best insight to space as a positing of elements is the dimension of depth that is a direct positing from width and height. Depth is the most existential of all dimensions because it is not impressed on the object itself, "it quite clearly belongs to the perspective and not to things".[83] This phenomenon is apparent in a example that was cited previously, namely, the perception of railroad tracks moving away toward the horizon. The perception of depth is a product of width and height in relation to one another. The convergence of the rails at the horizon is necessary to their divergence before us.

We have said that space is existential; we might just as well have said that existence is spatial, that is, that through an inner necessity it opens on to an 'outside', so that one can speak of a mental space and a 'world of meanings and objects of thought which are constituted in terms of those meanings'.[84]

In this vein Merleau-Ponty evolves virtual space to constitute a "topological space" as a model of being. This is to say, topological space is

[79] M. M-P., *Primacy*, p. 7. See *Structure*, p. 91.
[80] M. M-P., *Primacy*, p. 7.
[81] M. M-P., *Phenomenology*, p. 221. See *Themes*, p. 77.
[82] M. M-P., *Phenomenology*, p. 243.
[83] M. M-P., *Phenomenology*, p. 256.
[84] M. M-P., *Phenomenology*, p. 295.

the encounter of a "perpetual residue" of virtual space. The content and structure of virtual space point to a topology of existence underlying the essential potential of virtual space.[85] In fact, the specification of the lived space that is the structure to be found in the virtual space, that has itself the structure of topological space, is the task of anthropology.[86]

1.5.2. Temporality

Time is a simultaneous condition of space because time is a genesis of being and movement within lived-space allowing for relations between the elements that are in it. "Time is, therefore, not a real process, not an actual succession that I am content to record. It arises from *my* relation to things". In consequence "within the things themselves, the future and the past are in a kind of eternal state of pre-existence and survival" in relation to my presence.[87]

Time for the body-subject is a "network of intentionalities"[88] that are a product of spatial position. In fact, the notion of virtual space allows for the concepts of past and future. "Correspondingly it is necessary for the subject not to be himself situated in it, in order to be able to be present in intention to the past as to the future"[89] This is to argue that there is no natural time in object existence because time is the empirical manifestation of the intentional subject, the body-subject.[90]

Things co-exist in space because they are *present* to the same perceiving subject and enveloped in one and the same temporal wave. But the unity and individuality of each temporal wave is possible only if it is wedged in between the preceding and the following one, and if the same temporal pulsation which produces it still retains its predecessor and anticipates its successor. It is objective time which is made up of successive moments. The lived present holds a past and a future within its thickness.[91]

Merleau-Ponty argues that "time presupposes a view of time"[92] which means that as a product of intentional space "my body takes possession

---

85   M. M-P., *Visible*, pp. 210-211.
86   M. M-P., *Signs*, p. 119.
87   M. M-P., *Phenomenology*, p. 412.
88   M. M-P., *Phenomenology*, p. 417.
89   M. M-P., *Phenomenology*, p. 414.
90   M. M-P., *Phenomenology*, p. 453.
91   M. M-P., *Phenomenology*, p. 275.
92   M. M-P., *Phenomenology*, p. 411.

of time; it brings into existence a past and a future for a present; it is not a thing, but creates time instead of submitting to it".[93] Time becomes an affecting of self in the sense that the movement to the future is the transition from one present to another in which the "affecting agent and affected recipient are one".[94] Thus, it is in this sense that phenomenologists speak of the lived-body experience of the perceiving-perceived or the speaking-speech.

We are saying that time *is* someone, or that temporal dimensions, in so far as they perpetually overlap, bear each other out and ever confine themselves to making explicit what was implied in each, being collectively expressive of that one single explosion or thrust which is subjectivity itself. We must understand time as the subject and the subject as time.[95]

Temporality in Merleau-Ponty's conception assumes that the thing and the world around it exist only through the experience that one has of them. There is a "concatenation of our perspectives, yet they transcend all perspectives because this chain is temporal and incomplete".[96]

The present mediates between the For Oneself and the For Others, between individuality and generality. True reflection presents me to myself not as idle and inaccessible subjectivity, but as identical with my presence in the world and to others, as I am now realizing it: I am all that I see, I am an intersubjective field, not despite my body and this situation, but, on the contrary, by being this body and this situation, and through them, all the rest.[97]

The primordiality of time as the present is observed most profoundly in the act of speaking in which the body-subject presents himself as public man born of private man. "Communication exists between the moments of my personal time, as between my time and that of other people, and in spite of the rivalry between them".[98] In this analysis Merleau-Ponty is following the view expressed by Heidegger that "discourse in itself is temporal, since all talking about ——— , of ——— , or to ——— , is grounded in the ecstatical unity of temporality".[99] This is to say, "In order to become the unlimited milieus that human

[93] M. M-P., *Phenomenology*, p. 240.
[94] M. M-P., *Phenomenology*, pp. 425-426.
[95] M. M-P., *Phenomenology*, p. 422. See Edmund Husserl, *The Phenomenology of Internal Time-Consciousness*, ed. by Martin Heidegger, trans. J.S. Churchill (Bloomington: Indiana University Press, 1964). See M. M-P., *The Bergsonian Heritage*, ed. Thomas Hanna (New York: Columbia University Press, 1962), pp. 136-146.
[96] M. M-P., *Phenomenology*, p. 333.
[97] M. M-P., *Phenomenology*, p. 452.
[98] M. M-P., *Sense*, p. 40.
[99] Heidegger, *Being and Time*, p. 400.

experience finds in them, space and time demand symbolic activity".[100]

The two concepts of spatiality and temporality as they exist in Merleau-Ponty are a complex synoptic fabric that is in part a theory of sensation and intellection that allows the unitary existence of man as a body. This body is in turn the union of a "psyche" and its visual body, which is a lived-body of virtual space creating time. The transition of the body-subject from a world of private perception to a world of shared experience occurs through the agency of the Other as lived encounter with myself. All of these elements in the various agencies of essential becoming and existential being are in fact "perception" in the lived-body experience. There is a primacy to this perception that is synoptic of these elements, yet it could not be known as synoptic unless the parts were present first as individual, reciprocal entities.

In a sense, the highest point of philosophy is perhaps no more than rediscovering these truisms: thought thinks, speech speaks, the glance glances. But each time between the two identical words there is the whole spread one straddles in order to think, speak, and see.[101]

The "whole" that one straddles is the ambiguity of human existence that perception in its primacy of synergism clarifies and gives meaning to by moving from thought to speech to the understanding that is *seeing*.

1.5.3. *Perception as Synopsis*

The return to the existential moment in which the lived-body experience is in essence the primacy of perception *is* the "return to the things themselves". "Perception grounds everything because it shows us, so to speak, an obsessional relation with being; it is there before us, and yet it touches us from within".[102] For the philosopher perception becomes the absolute knowledge, it is the source and confirmation of all knowledge. It is in this sense that Merleau-Ponty speaks of a finality in which we are present to the world — "we are condemned to meaning".[103]

---

[100]   M. M-P., *Structure*, p. 104.
[101]   M. M-P , *Signs*, p. 21. See John O'Neill, "Situation and Temporality", *Philosophy and Phenomenological Research* XXVIII (March, 1968), pp. 413-422.
[102]   M. M-P., *Praise*, p. 16.
[103]   M. M-P., *Phenomenology*, p. xix. See *Humanism*, p. 58.

By these words, the "primacy of perception", we mean that the experience of perception is our presence at the moment when things, truths, values are constituted for us; that perception is a nascent *logos*; that it teaches us, outside all dogmatism, the true conditions of objectivity itself; that it summons us to the tasks of knowledge and action. It is not a question of reducing human knowledge to sensation, but of assisting at the birth of this knowledge, to make it as sensible as the sensible, to recover the consciousness of rationality. This experience of rationality is lost when we take it for granted as self-evident, but is, on the contrary, rediscovered when it is made to appear against the background of non-human nature.[104]

In this definition Merleau-Ponty has confirmed an earlier formula that the primacy of perception is constitutive of three synoptic elements : (1) non-positing experience; (2) pre-objective experience; and (3) pre-conscious experience.[105] This schema for primary perception is the formulation for phenomenological description that is characteristic of the three levels of Merleau-Ponty's existential phenomenological method. This is to say, phenomenological description as the first reflection is the determination of non-positing experience. In turn, phenomenological reduction is the specification of pre-objective experience and the radical *cogito* (as intentionality) is the manifestation of preconscious experience.

For the moment, the consideration of the primacy of perception will deal only with the modality of description, that is, with non-positing experience. "To perceive is to render oneself present to something through the body". In turn this means that "all the while the thing keeps its place within the horizon of the world, and the structurization consists in putting each detail in the perceptual horizons which belong to it".[106] Perception is therefore the act of placing oneself in relation to the things as a figure to a background in which the figure is presupposed by the background. In this way perception does not focus upon the consciousness one has of the object, but rather on the object itself as I confront it. In such a relation to the object, one does not posit the act of perception as part of a personal, subjective experience. Rather, the perception is a transcendent reflection on the immanence of self and object which is the stable structure that allows for the "experience of objectivity".[107]

---

104   M. M-P., *Primacy*, p. 25.
105   M. M-P., *Phenomenology*, p. 242. Even this formulation is preceded in looser form in *Structure*, p. 190.
106   M. M-P., *Primacy*, p. 42; see also, *Phenomenology*, pp. x-xi.
107   M. M-P., *Phenomenology*, p. 239.

Every primary act of perception presupposes and precedes an explicit act which may be either sensation or intellection as synthetic correlates of the other, that is —— if you will, stimulus and response. Perceptions that do emerge as explicit acts are the result of the attitude one assumes or are an answer to a presupposed question. There is a simple cause to effect or stimulus-response schema that is merely completed through the agency of perception. In this sense, perceptions as explicit actions always remain ambiguous to us. Yet, every perception presupposes in the body-subject a certain past and the abstract function of perception as the synoptic emergence of objects known by us that are an elaboration of our environment.[108] This is to say, in every creative act of perception there is the recognition of the present as it fades or gives way to a new present. The experience of the past (fading presence) shows the abstract function of perception that is the emerging structure that is *presence*. The presence is the perception made primary by my encounter in time with structure (as self, Other, or thing).

The present analysis may be clarified by pausing for a moment to designate the structure of the body-subject or person who is simultaneously transmitter and receiver for perception as a primary description of lived-experience. For example, Laing offers a brief definition.

I wish to define a person in a twofold way: in terms of experience, as a center of orientation of the objective universe; and in terms of behavior, as the origin of actions. Personal experience transforms a given field onto a field of intention and action: only through action can our experience be transformed.[109]

Some of Merleau-Ponty's previous postulations may now take on a new dimension as the body-subject is seen as the synoptic agency of perception. In point of fact, the act of knowing existence is perception whether that perception be the consciousness of experience or behavior as cited in the quotation above.[110] "Perception is a moment of the living dialectic of a concrete subject; it participates in its total structure and, correlatively, it has as its original object, not the 'unorganized mass', but the action of other human subjects".[111]

We observe at once that it is impossible, as has often been said, to decompose a perception, to make it into a collection of sensations, because in it the whole

---

[108]   M. M-P., *Phenomenology*, p. 281.
[109]   Laing, *The Politics of Experience*, p. 23.
[110]   M. M-P., *Structure*, p. 224.
[111]   M. M-P., *Structure*, p. 166.

is prior to the parts — and the whole is not an ideal whole. It is necessary that meaning and signs, the form and matter of perception, be related from the beginning and that, as we say, the matter of perception be "pregnant with its form".[112]

There can be little doubt that Merleau-Ponty intends that perception be the synoptic and synergic functioning of a semiology in which signs are the signifieds of sensation and the signifiers of reflection. Later, the process of speaking as the same semiology will form an expression, whereas the semiology is here a perception. The semiology that is the agency or dialectic of expression and perception is "the movement of Thought and Speech, and, in short, of the perceptible world's explosion within us".[113] Such a semiology as method allows the movements, the reversibly, between "verbal perception" (expression) and "lived perception" (primary perception).[114]

Perception is a synoptic agency for the body-subject in that what is perceived is not posited by an other's experience, but is rather the immanence and transcendence that is lived by me in the encounter with the object of perception.

The perception of the world by the others cannot enter into competition with my own perception of it, for my position is not comparable to theirs; I live my perception from within, and, from within, it has an incomparable power of ontogenesis.[115]

There is a danger that one might reduce perception to the thought of perceiving in which case one is dealing only on the level of immanence in which existential certitude is impossible, even obliterated by singular essential certitude.[116] In this matter, perception and the percept necessarily have the same existential modality because perception is inseparable from the consciousness which has it. However, to suppose that the percept is thus true, while the perception is always error ridden, is a mistake. The essential modality of both perception and the percept leaves them both open to error with any edge going to perception which has the primacy of being the synoptic agency of the percept *and* its signification.[117]

Merleau-Ponty specifically points out that thought as an intellectual

---

[112]   M. M-P., *Primacy,* p. 15.
[113]   M. M-P., *Signs,* p. 20.
[114]   M. M-P., *Structure,* p. 185ff.
[115]   M. M-P., *Visible,* p. 58.
[116]   M. M-P., *Visible,* p. 36.
[117]   M. M-P., *Phenomenology,* p. 374.

synthesis does not occur in perception, hence confirming the primacy
of perception in the description of non-posited phenomena.

Being supported by the prelogical unity of the body image, the perceptual
synthesis no more holds the secret of the object than it does that of one's own
body, and this is why the perceived object always presents itself as transcendent,
and why the synthesis seems to be effected on the object itself, in the world,
and not at that metaphysical point occupied by the thinking subject. Herein
lies the distinction between the perceptual synthesis and the intellectual.[118]

In the dialectic of perception there is a presence that is an immanence
and a transcendence, or "presence" and absence. This can be illustrated
indirectly by citing two illnesses in which there is a lack of synoptic
perception. In the person who has a phantom limb there is only a felt
presence when in fact there is no limb. Or, in anosognosia where a
felt absence occurs when in fact there is an actual presence. "In both
cases we are imprisoned in the categories of the objective world, in
which there is no middle term between presence and absence".[119] In
the lived-world there is the middle term of the lived-body where the
immanent and the transcendent form a synoptic unity in which what
is essential can be known as existential. "The presence and absence of
external objects are only variations within a field of primordial
presence, a perceptual domain over which my body exercises
power".[120]

The commonality that perception and speaking have in the semiology
of immanence and transcendence is explicitly summarized by Dufrenne.

What separates is always in the first instance the same as what unites: Everywhere man is a creature who speaks; hence whatever the diversity of languages
may be, they at least have in common that they are spoken; and this, in turn,
implies that everywhere man has the same basic relation to the world. Indeed,
it is the exigencies of this very relation to the world that are responsible for
man's being man everywhere and for such a thing as humanity to be possible.
Similarly, one must needs [sic] come back again from the study of language
to the study of speech, because language is nothing more than a mediation
between man and the world.[121]

The transition from the phenomenology of perception to a phenomenology of speaking described by Dufrenne is a recognition that the

---

[118]   M. M-P., *Phenomenology*, p. 233.
[119]   M. M-P., *Phenomenology*, p. 80.
[120]   M. M-P., *Phenomenology*, p. 92.
[121]   Dufrenne, *Language and Philosophy*, p. 40.

method of phenomenology as a semiology is applicable to perception
and expression alike. That Merleau-Ponty follows Husserl in his view
is apparent.

Thus it was that, having started with a "static phenomenology", he [Husserl]
ended with a "genetic phenomenology" and a theory of "intentional History" —
in other words, a logic of history. In this way he, more than anyone else, con-
tributed to describing consciousness incarnate in an environment of human
objects and in a linguistic tradition.[122]

It becomes strikingly obvious therefore that "perceptual behavior
emerges from these relations to a situation and to an environment which
are not the workings of a pure, knowing subject".[123] This is to suggest
that the perspectival appearance that is "perception" is not a sequence
of conscious states nor is it the logical organization of thoughts which
accounts for perception. Perception is an external relation which is
not a quantification of perspectival appearances because such appearances are representations of each other — at best an artificial synthesis.
There is also the presupposition of a "mind" in possession of its object
while "my will is without direct action on the unfolding of the perceived perspectives and because their concordant multiplicity is organized of itself".[124]

In the affinity of perception and expression, the philosopher finds
the semiology in the things themselves that will "make them speak".[125]

The root of the matter is that the sensible indeed offers nothing one could not
state if one is not a philosopher or a writer, but that this is not because it would
be an ineffable in Itself, but because of the fact that one does not know how
to speak. Problems of the "retrospective reality" of the true — It results from
the fact that the world, Being, are polymorphism, mystery and nowise a layer
of flat entities of the in itself.[126]

Merleau-Ponty's intent with this analysis is to indicate that there is
first a circular process of perception and expression which utilizes the
same semiology, and second, that both modalities of method are
centered in the lived-body-subject.

To this extent, every perception is a communication or a communion, the taking
up or completion by us of some extraneous intention or, on the other hand,

122   M. M-P., *Sense,* p. 135.
123   M. M-P., *Primacy,* p. 4.
124   M. M-P., *Structure,* p. 187.
125   M. M-P., *Visible,* p. 4.
126   M. M-P., *Visible,* p. 252.

the complete expression outside ourselves of our perceptual powers and a coition, so to speak, of our body with things.[127]

The force of the semiology is a dialectic perception and expression creating a meaning in the lived-experience. The perception of the phenomena brings forth the meaning that they have and expression causes them to have meaning. Such a synoptic perception is perception *as* expression — this is the lesson of the semiotic phenomenology.[128]

As Merleau-Ponty graphically suggests, "my perception accedes to the things themselves, for these perspectives are articulated in a way which makes access to interindividual significations possible; they 'present' a world".[129] Within this context there is a specific truism, namely, that the primacy of perception or expression displays the lived-experience regardless of its "truth" or "falsity" in comparison to a physical or intellectual schema of probability.

Each perception [or expression] is mutable and only probable — it is, if one likes, only an *opinion*; but what is not opinion, what each perception, even if false, verifies, is the belongingness of each experience to the same world, their equal power to manifest it, as *possibilities of the same world*.[130]

It is in this sense that Merleau-Ponty says that "the theory of body image [schema] is, implicitly, a theory of perception".[131] This correlation unites the felt experience of the body and the resulting structure of perception with the possibility of expression in which "what" one experiences is probablity like "what" the Other experiences. There is a unity of process in perception and expression that is the sign as signification and the agency of that process is the body experience as lived.

1.6. *Body*

Body is the synoptic perception of the "things themselves" which exercises a freedom that allows the lived-body to emerge in experience. Sartre views this process as a primary function of freedom and appropriately suggests it as the finality that is the human experience in the world, or in his own phrase : we are condemned to freedom. In contrast to the Sartrian view which suggests the negative meaningless-

---

[127] M. M-P., *Phenomenology*, p. 320.
[128] M. M-P., *Phenomenology*, p. 36.
[129] M. M-P., *Structure*, p. 218.
[130] M. M-P., *Visible*, p. 41.
[131] M. M-P., *Phenomenology*, p. 206.

ness of the constant human choice, Merleau-Ponty suggests the positive interpretation. That is, in his view we are "condemned to meaning" which is to say the freedom that is the human choice is a designation and fulfillment of the lived-experience. Thus, I *am* what I perceive and express.

In the earlier part of this chapter, the concept of Other was discussed. In particular, an examination of the four relationships by which one knows himself as psyche and body, and the Other as body and psyche. The purpose of this present section is to examine closely the *body* as that agency which allows for the operation of the phenomenological dialectic on several levels. The body is the vehicle for perception and expression and it is the agency that allows one to engage in the reversible process of being in public and private existence. The body allows sensation and intellection to emerge as perception, and later on, the body will be seen as the medium in which language becomes speaking.

Merleau-Ponty advances the idea that the body is a unitary existence which is neither subject or object, the body is a "perceiving thing", a "subject-object". The "relationship between my body and things is that of the absolute here and there, of the source of distances to distance. My body is the field within which my perspective powers are localized".[132] In this sense the body is a "vital structure"[133] in which the systemic effect works beyond its own limits and thereby constitutes a milieu for itself. "For us the body is much more than an instrument or a means; it is our expression in the world, the visible form of our intentions".[134] Thus it is in the body existence that one comes to know the essential manifestation that is self and knowledge of the Other. "It is in this becoming conscious of myself as I am that I am able to see essences, and in this context the real and the possible are not distinct".[135] Which is to say, the operation of the body is both subjective and objective in function without being defined as either *per se*. In a strict sense, the artificial bifurcation of subject and object in the body existence is to fabricate essence in two modalities. Nor, is it any more valid to suggest that body is mere object or simple subject in deference to its counterpart.

---

[132] M. M-P., *Signs*, p. 166.
[133] M. M-P., *Structure*, pp. 145-146.
[134] M. M-P., *Primacy*, p. 5. See *Themes*, pp. 80-82.
[135] M. M-P., *Primacy*, p. 73.

The appropriate view of the body, in terms of the above discussion, is that it "inhabits" space and time, but it is not *in* either one.[136] If it were in space or time it would be a mere object to be acted upon and not an acting agent itself. "The body is the vehicle of being in the world, and having a body is, for a living creature, to be intervolved in a definite environment, to identify oneself with certain projects and be continually commited to them".[137] This is to say, the body itself is an on-going synthesis of time and space.[138]

When I find again the actual world such as it is, under my hands, under my eyes, up against my body, I find much more than an object: a Being of which my vision is a part, a visibility older than my operations or my acts. But this does not mean that there was a fusion or coinciding of me with it: on the contrary, this occurs because between my body looked at and my body looking, my body touched and my body touching, there is overlapping or encroachment, so that we must say that the things pass into us as well as we into the things.[139]

It is in this sense, then, that Merleau-Ponty says that "the body is our general medium for having a world".[140]

"Is my body a thing, is it an idea ? It is neither, being the measurant of the things".[141] The body in its modality as being existent and a becoming essence is what Merleau-Ponty calls *flesh* to indicate the synthetic presence of the object and subject in one element.[142] One gets a sense of this notion in the idea that a body — as yours — has neither a here or now (space or time) except indirectly as not being there or then. By this "sort of reflection" one comes to know his body as an "enclosure" which is visible and which one leaves because it is visible.[143] The flesh is thus the *one (on)* which is a *presence* (a synergic, co-present immanence and transcendence).

The body's modality of being is a pre-knowing or "pre-meaning" which is to say it is a "silent knowing".[144] What Merleau-Ponty wishes to convey by this presentation is that the meaning of the body (not the lived-body) is a perception, not yet an expression.

---

136   M. M-P., *Phenomenology*, p. 139.
137   M. M-P., *Phenomenology*, p. 82.
138   M. M-P., *Phenomenology*, pp. 140-141.
139   M. M-P., *Visible*, p. 123.
140   M. M-P., *Phenomenology*, p. 146.
141   M. M-P., *Visible*, p. 152.
142   M. M-P., *Phenomenology*, p. 198.
143   M. M-P., *Visible*, p. 263.
144   M. M-P., *Visible*, p. 178.

My body *in* the visible. This does not simply mean: it is a particle of the visible, there, there is the visible and here (as variant of the there) is my body. No. It is *surrounded* by the visible. This does not take place on a plane of which it would be an inlay, it is really surrounded, circumvented. This means: it sees itself, it is a visible — but it sees itself seeing, my look which finds it *there* knows that it is here, at its own side —— Thus the body *stands* before the world and the world upright before it, and between them there is a relation that is one of embrace. And between these two vertical beings, there is not a frontier, but a contact surface ——
The flesh = this fact that my body is passive-active (visible-seeing), mass in itself *and* gesture —— [145]

It is the awareness of this "body" that allows the individual to come to know or be aware of his psyche or consciousness *as his body*. "For a being who has acquired the consciousness of self and his body, who has reached the dialectic of subject and object, the body is no longer the cause of the structure of consciousness; it has become the object of consciousness".[146]

Merleau-Ponty draws a distinction between the "natural body" which is always present to the world and the "cultural body" which is the sedimentation of the spontaneous acts of the natural body. In this sense the perception of the body is a process of sensation and thought that once spontaneous can be recalled or reconstituted from past perceptions.[147] The function of spontaneous and sedimented perception via the body is revealed in the following comment.

If perhaps there is for me no sense in saying that my perception and the thing it aims at are "in my head" (it is certain only that they are "*not elsewhere*"), I cannot help putting the other, and the perception he has, *behind his body*. More exactly, the thing perceived by the other is doubled: there is *the one he perceives*, God knows where, and there is the one I see, outside of his body, and which I call the true thing — as he calls the true thing the table *he sees* and consigns to the category of appearances the one I see.[148]

In this example both the other and I have a spontaneous perception that is real for us, yet we know each others perceptions are like our own from the commonalities that persist in our future perceptions. These recalled commonalities that mark out perception for us are sedimented phenomena and indicate our participation in the world as

[145]   M. M-P., *Visible*, pp. 270-271.
[146]   M. M-P., *Structure*, p. 204. See *Visible*, pp. 136-138.
[147]   M. M-P., *Structure*, pp. 210 and 249, n. 50.
[148]   M. M-P., *Visible*, pp. 9-10.

a cultural body for others, while in fact we remain by our spontaneous act our own natural body.

What, then, is the body as body ?

To say that I have a body is simply another way of saying that my knowledge is an individual dialectic in which intersubjective objects appear, that these objects, when they are given to knowledge in the mode of actual existence, present themselves to it by successive aspects which cannot coexist; finally, it is a way of saying that one of them offers itself obstinately "from the same side" without my being able to go around it.[149]

The two elements that distinguish the body in Merleau-Ponty's philosophy are the aspect of freedom and the lived modality. This is to say, the freedom that is the body is the conscious phenomenon of the lived-body experience.

1.6.1. *Freedom*

"There is free choice only if freedom comes into play in its decision, and posits the situation chosen as a situation of freedom".[150] Within this definition of freedom Merleau-Ponty advances a structure similar to that of the body with its coterminous subject and object. Here freedom is the occurrence of choice which by its very nature suggests the limits or situation of consciousness in which the choice is made. In a phrase, the figure sets the background.

There is, then, ultimately nothing that can set the limits to freedom, except those limits that freedom itself has set in the form of its various initiatives, so that the subject has simply the external world that he gives himself. Since it is the latter who, on coming into being, brings to light significance and value in things, and since no thing can impinge upon it except through acquiring, thanks to it, meaning and value, there is no action of things on the subject, but merely a signification (in the active sense), a centrifugal *Sinngebung.*[151]

Freedom thus comes to function in the body phenomena as a meeting of the inner and outer, of the subject with object, of the body with other. In any event, there is always a "field of freedom" and a "conditioned freedom" (following Husserl's terminology) which are the poles of the synthetic "freedom" that the body creates in the act of choice.[152]

The freedom that one derives from others is the "conditioned free-

---

149 M. M-P., *Structure*, p. 213.
150 M. M-P., *Phenomenology*, p. 437. See *Humanism*, pp. xiv-xxiv.
151 M. M-P., *Phenomenology*, p. 436.
152 M. M-P., *Phenomenology*, p. 454.

dom" that "is generic at our most individual, since our freedom waits for the recognition of other people and needs them to be what it is".[153] In this modalilty of freedom the body is seen as Other and functions to be objective in the Other's presence. Hidden in this modality is the choice to act according to Others, to let Others constitute the "field of freedom".

The only authentic free choice, that which is self generated, is in the "field of freedom" as limited by the body itself, not as the body-object of others. "There is free choice only if freedom comes into play in its decision, and posits the situation chosen as a situation of free-dom".[154] This is to say that the body's modality in any sense becomes a free choice when the modality is spontaneous rather than sedimented. The body is like unto the world, "it is the *phenomenon, that which* appears and has no interior".[155]

The body in the act of freedom which is a "field" comes to create by its spontaneous modality of perception a *space.* The space may be social, cultural, or symbolic.[156] In any event, the particular space modality that is free choice can and does come into contrast with conditioned freedom. The result is *time.* As Merleau-Ponty phrases it, "It is unconditional freedom which makes us capable of absolute attachment".[157]

Our freedom does not destroy our situation, but gears itself to it: as long as we are alive, our situation is open, which implies both that it calls up specially favoured modes of resolution, and also that it is powerless to bring one into being by itself.[158]

Since it is the body which is the agency of essential limitation, there is in the existential modality of the body the dialectic of immanence and transcendence that establishes for the body its *presence.* This presence is the intentionality that *is* the lived-body.

1.6.2. *The Lived-Body*

In so far as the body comes into the reality of the world, the subjective venture is a situation defined by the objectivity of the body. The essen-

[153] M. M-P., *Sense,* p. 45. See *Humanism,* pp. 10-11.
[154] M. M-P., *Phenomenology,* p. 437. See *Humanism,* p. xxxix.
[155] M. M-P., *Praise,* p. 6.
[156] M. M-P., *Praise,* p. 56.
[157] M. M-P., *Signs,* p. 210.
[158] M. M-P., *Phenomenology,* p. 442.

tial presence of the *subject* in the world is "one" with his body as lived; and, the *object* which his body is in the world exists as that same *essential presence*.[159] In this sense, "philosophy is indeed, and always, a break with objectivism and a return from *constructa* to lived experience, from the world to ourselves".[160] This is to say, "the lived experience can no longer recognize itself in the idealizations we draw from it".[161] In short, the lived-body experience is the spontaneous and primordial presence at the world which is the *phenomenal body*.[162]

The first philosophical act would appear to be to return to the world of actual experience which is prior to the objective world, since it is in it that we shall be able to grasp the theoretical basis no less than the limits of that objective world, restore to things their concrete physiognomy, to organisms their individual ways of dealing with the world, and to subjectivity its inherence in history. Our task will be, moreover, to rediscover phenomena, the layer of living experience which other people and things are first given to us, the system 'Self-others-things' as it comes into being ....[163]

Merleau-Ponty's concept of the lived-body is the notion that existence is the perception of essences in their primordial or immanent structure. It is this immanence that is taken up in the act of transcendence to become the "presence" that is existence. In short, the essential spontaneity is the material of existential analysis through a phenomenological method. "To experience a structure is not to receive it into oneself passively: it is to live it, to take it up, assume it and discover its immanent meaning".[164]

The phenomenal body which is the lived-experience is primordial structure that is itself temporality.[165] This is to suggest that the existential presence of the body is the common structure that is manifest in the on-going immanence and transcendence that is spatiality *in genesis*. It is only through this structure that the lived experience is manifest. The *flesh* is the visible-seer, the audible-hearer, the tangible-touch — the sensitive-sensible. The lived-body experience can be illustrated in the grasp of your right hand with the left.[166] For each instant of time that this union of hands creates, one hand is object and one hand is subject. Yet, they are reversibly subject and object only with the

159   M. M-P., *Phenomenology*, p. 408.
160   M. M-P., *Signs*, p. 113.
161   M. M-P., *Visible*, p. 87.
162   M. M-P., *Structure*, p. 156.
163   M. M-P., *Phenomenology*, p. 57.
164   M. M-P., *Phenomenology*, p. 258.
165   M. M-P., *Phenomenology*, pp. 431-432.
166   M. M-P., *Phenomenology*, p. 315.

union to each other. This is the immanence and transcendence that is the phenomenal presence. Each such presence creates the limits of its own spatiality and the movements of the phenomenal presence within those limits is their *time*. It is obvious that the clasped hands do not remain static in their roles as subject and object; each hand is first subject, then object, then subject, and so on. In any event, the felt or lived phenomena is known and expressed through the agency of the body. In addition, the perception or expression that takes place is an intentional act. The elements of experience that become relational through a dialectic of immanence and transcendence constitute a presence (a temporality and spatiality) only when the intent of the body-subject (body-psyche) directs the composition of that structure. "In order to perceive things, we need to live them".[167]

To have a body is to possess a universal setting, a schema of all types of perceptual unfolding and of all those inter-sensory correspondences which lie beyond the segment of the world which we are actually perceiving. A thing is, therefore, not actually *given* in perception, it is internally taken up by us in so far as it is bound up with a world, the basic structures of which we carry with us, and of which it is merely one of many possible concrete forms. Although a part of our living experience, it is nevertheless transcendent to our life because the human body, with its habits which weave round it a human environment, has running through it a movement towards the world itself.[168]

There is no ideal or arbitrary limitation that exists to guide the dialectic of perception in the lived-body experience, it is present with the individual himself. At times the "lived distance" between the person and the world fluctuates so as to allow the body-subject to exist in a realm of absolute freedom (recall : the condemnation to freedom) which has the negative effect of a forced choice of continuing to be. On the other hand, the lived distance may become so great or so small that events cease to have significance with those closest to oneself, thus becoming obsessional. "They enshroud me like night and rob me of my individuality and freedom. I can literally no longer breathe; I am possessed".[169] It is in this structure of perception that the lived-body *becomes* totally subject, object, or Other.

The lived-body experience is fundamentally the recognition by the person that his body is the agency of his psyche so that one is a body-subject in the phenomena of living.

---

[167] M. M-P., *Phenomenology,* p. 325.
[168] M. M-P., *Phenomenology,* pp. 326-327.
[169] M. M-P., *Phenomenology,* p. 286.

Knowledge and communication sublimate rather than suppress our incarnation, and the characteristic operation of the mind is in the movement by which we recapture our corporeal existence and use it to symbolize instead of merely to co-exist. This metamorphosis lies in the double function of our body.[170]

This is to say that the lived-body is the unitary agent through which the reception of the world and Others, as well as oneself, is accomplished. And, through it one is known to Others as "at the world" and known to oneself in expression.

My body is the seat or rather the very actuality of the phenomenon of expression *(Ausdruck)*, and there the visual and auditory experiences, for example, are pregnant with one another, and their expressive value is the ground of the antepredicative unity of the perceived world, and, through it, of verbal expression *(Darstellung)* and intellectual significance *(Bedeutung)*.[171]

There is no doubt that the lived-body is the semiotic agency of perception and expression alike.

We are not, then reducing the significance of the word, or even of the percept, to a collection of 'bodily sensations' but we are saying that the body, in so far as it has 'behaviour patterns', is that strange object which uses its own parts as a general system of symbols for the world, and through which we can consequently 'be at home in' that world, 'understand' it and find significance in it.[172]

Thus, the body-subject in the lived-body experience *is* the semiotic of being — an existence — that is manifest, and thus known, through the essential agencies of perception and expression. In the First Reflection of Merleau-Ponty's phenomenological method (description) there is indeed a primacy of perception that is the lived-body experience.

2. RADICAL REFLECTION AS *GESTALT*

Merleau-Ponty's familiarity with Gestalt Psychology and the influences of Heideggerian ontology are manifest in what may be called the "radical gestalt" which is in fact the Second Reflection of method in Merleau-Ponty. In order to set the limits of the phenomenological reduction according to Merleau-Ponty, the Husserlian notion of *epoché*

---

[170] M. M-P., *Primacy*, p. 7.
[171] M. M-P., *Phenomenology*, p. 235.
[172] M. M-P., *Phenomenology*, p. 237. For an analogous theory resembling that of Merleau-Ponty, see Hans-Eduard Henstenberg, "Phenomenology and Metaphysics of the Human Body", *International Philosophical Quarterly* III, no. 2 (May, 1963), pp. 165-200.

or the "bracketing of experience" needs to be explained. And, Heidegger's notion of the "primordial" must be noted.

2.1. *Epoché*

Edmund Husserl suggests that "by epoché we effect a reduction to our pure meaning (*cogito*) and to the meant, purely as meant".[173] The epoché is a methodology within Husserl's phenomenology which consist in focusing on any part or all of one's intentional experience, and then observing, analyzing, abstracting, and describing that experience by removing oneself from the immediate and lived engagement in it. And yet, "the epoché can also be said to be the radical and universal method by which I apprehend myself purely : as Ego, and with my own pure conscious life, in and by which the entire Objective world exists for me and is precisely as it is for me".[174] In this statement of method, there is the key notion of reduction in which one leaves out of consideration those aspects of human existence, as an experience of the world, which are extraneous to the pure, presented phenomena proper.

Although Spiegelberg's rendering of phenomenological method as it has historically evolved through several philosophers was presented in chapter one of this study, it is relevant to briefly spell out Husserl's method in particular. Such a presentation will allow an explanation of the term "radical" in Merleau-Ponty's phenomenological method.

Husserl in the bulk of his writings and in particular in his *Ideas* introduced a five step method which he called "phenomenology". This method is a series of conceptual reductions. The first such reflection is termed the "philosophical reduction". At this initial level one must "bracket" or suspend any philosophical theories which may be implicitly supposed in one's apperception of the world. Second, one must assume in his perception a *Lebenswelt* or life-world by the reduction of scientific experiences and the quotidian experiences that lend them validity; this is the "scientific reduction". .

The third step in the reductive method is the "epoché" or "phenomenological reduction" in which one suspends belief in the very existence of the objective phenomenon under scrutiny. This step lays the ground for the next two reductions. The "eidetic reduction" focuses upon and abstracts the general properties, ideas, or forms of the phenomenon under investigation, rather than examining the differentiating and par-

---

173 Husserl, *Cartesian Meditations*, p. 56.
174 Husserl, *Cartesian Meditations*, p. 21.

ticularizing elements of the object in question. And finally, the "transcendental reduction" occurs when everything, literally, has been bracketed. This is to say, the transcendental reality is bracketed and all that remains is "pure" Ego.

At this juncture it may be apparent that Husserl's early theory represents in the main what has been denominated "phenomenalism" in the present study inasmuch as Husserl's approach works from the basis of an objective knowing to a purely subjective existence. The later, redirecting influence of the Cartesian outlook is apparent. What is termed *existential phenomenology* is precisely a concern with Husserl's third step, the epoché, in the sense of limiting one's investigation to the lived-experience or *Lebenswelt*. And, it is in this sense that Merleau-Ponty's "radical reflection" is a "radical" reduction — radical by its departure from the early Husserl. To understand the radical reflection as *gestalt*, a brief examination of Heidegger's primordial situation is required.

2.2. *Primordial Situation*

Heidegger suggests that every interpretation or hermeneutic is based upon certain presuppositions which are its "fore-having, its fore-sight, and its fore-conception".[175] The totality of these presuppositions constitutes a "hermeneutical Situation" that must be clarified in relation to the object to be disclosed in experience and in terms of the experience itself.

If, however, the ontological Interpretation is to be a *primordial* one, this not only demands that in general the hermeneutical Situation shall be one which has been made secure in conformity with the phenomena; it also requires explicit assurance that the *whole* of the entity which it has taken as its theme has been brought into forehaving. Similarly, it is not enough just to make a first sketch of Being of this entity, even if our sketch is grounded in the phenomena. If we are to have a fore-sight of Being, we must see it in such a way as not to miss the *unity* of those structural items which belong to it and are possible. Only then can the question of the meaning of the unity which belongs to the whole entity's totality of Being, be formulated and answered with any phenomenal assurance.[176]

Within Heidegger's approach is the notion of *gestalt* in which the operation of the foreground and the background in its unity posit the "situation" as a construction from the priomordiality of Being. This is

175 Heidegger, *Being and Time*, p. 275.
176 Heidegger, *Being and Time*, p. 275.

to say that a situation specified in its primordiality is "to be in a situation"[177] which can be known as existential or authentic in meaning. The *gestalt* is a unity of structure that both specifies itself and sets the limits of that definition. In consequence, the hermeneutic that leads to primordial interpretation is an existential phenomenology. And, it is in this sense that Merleau-Ponty takes up the Heideggerian direction within the Husserlian epoché to arrive at the radical reduction which is possible in the *gestalt* of perception or expression.

2.3. *Radical Gestalt*

Originally the German word "Gestalt" meant a shape of form, but in the psychology of Wolfgang Kohler *gestalt* came to mean the "meaning" of a concrete entity *per se* which has form or structure as one of its characteristics.[178] This specification of the term became well established in Kohler's use of it, particularly with the wide acceptance of Kurt Koffka's master work *Principles of Gestalt Psychology*.[179] Although Merleau-Ponty rejects much of what Gestalt Psychology has to offer, he does see in it the direction of theory that can enhance and promote phenomenology.

For Merleau-Ponty the *gestalt* is "a spontaneous organization beyond the distinction between activity and passivity, of which the visible patterns of experience are the symbol".[180]

Without doubt one of the most important acquisitions of this theory has been its overcoming of the classical alternatives between objective psychology and introspective psychology. Gestalt Psychology went beyond this alternative by showing that the object of psychology is the structure of behavior, accessible from within and from without.[181]

There is a coupling of the methodological insights of *gestalt* theory and phenomenological reduction in that "the perception of forms, understood very broadly as structure, grouping, or configuration should

---

[177]   *Ibid.*, p. 346.
[178]   Wolfgang Kohler, *Gestalt Psychology* (New York: The New American Library, 1947), pp. 104-105.
[179]   New York: Harcourt, Brace, and World, Inc., 1963, pp. 682-683. For a brief explanation of the Kohler-Koffka psychology see: T.R. Miles, "Gestalt Theory", in *Encyclopedia of Philosophy*, ed. Paul Edwards (New York: Macmillan Co. and The Free Press, 1967), III, pp. 318-323.
[180]   M. M.-P., *Primacy*, p. 77. See *Themes*, p. 5.
[181]   M. M.-P., *Primacy*, pp. 23-24.

be considered our spontaneous way of seeing".[182] The next step is almost obvious in light of the phenomenology of body that Merleau-Ponty develops. This is to say, "my body *is* a *Gestalt* and it is co-present in every *Gestalt*. It is a *Gestalt;* it also, and eminently, is a heavy signification, it is flesh; the system it constitutes is ordered about a central hinge or a pivot which is openness to ..., a bound and not a free possibility".[183]

Within the dialectic of immanence and transcendence which is like the "figure" and "ground" of the *gestalt,* "one's lived-body is the third term, always tacitly understood, in the figure-background structure, and every figure stands out against the double horizon of external and bodily space".[184] This concept is critical to both perception and expression sinse "it is *that separation* (écart) first of all that is the perceptual *meaning*".[185] In short, the *gestalt* is not a physical reality, but an object of perception — an intentional object.[186]

"We experience a perception and its horizon 'in action' [*pratique-ment*] rather than by 'posing' them or explicitly 'knowing' them. Finally the quasi-organic relation of the perceiving subject and the world involves, in principle, the contradiction of immanence and transcendence".[187] One should not be misled by the use of the word "contradiction" since Merleau-Ponty's intent is not a polarity but a paradox or ambiguity born of polymorphism where the given presence is at once immanence then transcendence.[188] This is to say,

If ... we want to give an unprejudiced definition of gestalt psychology's philosophical meaning, we would have to say that, by revealing "structure" or "form" as irreducible elements of being, it has again put into question the classical alternative between "existence as thing" and "existence as consciousness", has established a communication between and a mixture of, objective and subjective, and has conceived psychological knowledge in a new way, no longer as an attempt to break down these typical ensembles but rather an effort to embrace them and to understand them by reliving them.[189]

By seizing upon the paradigm of the *gestalt,* Merleau-Ponty opens

---

182   M. M-P., *Sense,* p. 49. See *Visible,* pp. 194-195.
183   M. M-P., *Visible,* p. 205.
184   M. M-P., *Phenomenology,* p. 101.
185   M. M-P., *Visible,* p. 197. See *Humanism,* p. 130.
186   M. M-P., *Structure,* p. 143.
187   M. M-P., *Primacy,* p. 13.
188   M. M-P., *Visible,* p. 208.
189   M. M-P., *Sense,* p. 86.

philosophy to "a way beyond the subject-object correlation which has dominated philosophy from Descartes to Hegel".[190]

The *gestalt* lends itself to the notion of a presence which is the perspective of perception in that the object-horizon structure is at once the perspective of immanence and transcendence.[191] This is to say, a semiology operates in which signs are the *gestalt* seen in comparison and contrast as the perceived perspective that is meaning. For example, the phenomena that one experiences as "depth" is a perceived presence that has the meaning of spatiality since height and width and depth suggest solidity. The "depth" is a lived presence that is known through the perception of immanent and transcendent signs (any structure of width and height) given in the *gestalt* as figure and ground which are such only by their comparison and contrast.[192]

Depth, thus understood is, rather, the experience of the reversibility of dimensions, of a global "locality" — everything in the same place at the same time, a locality from which height, width, and depth are abstracted, of a voluminosity we express in a word when we say that a thing is *there*.[193]

At this level of analysis it may be apparent why Merleau-Ponty refers to perception as "the archetype of the originating encounter".[194] The semiotic apparent in perception is the visual paradigm of meaning in any of its modalities. This judgment reflects the view that reality in its "world-structure" exists and is known in two stages : sedimentation or immanence and spontaneity or transcendence.[195] Thus, "all perception, all action which presupposes it, and in short every human use of the body is already *primordial expression*".[196] This is to say, "In actual perception taken at its origin, before any word is uttered, the sign offered to sense and the meaning are not even theoretically separable".[197]

The implications of the *gestalt* for expression are that perception and expression are themselves a larger *gestalt* in which there is the

190   M. M-P., *Signs*, p. 123.
191   M. M-P., *Phenomenology*, p. 68.
192   M. M-P., *Primacy*, pp. 172-173.
193   M. M-P., *Primacy*, p. 180.
194   M. M-P., *Visible*, p. 158.
195   M. M-P., *Phenomenology*, p. 130. See *Visible*, p. 231.
196   M. M-P., *Signs*, p. 67.
197   M. M-P., *Phenomenology*, p. 38.

"circular process" of knowing the situation and expressing the situation.[198]

Language must surround each speaking subject, like an instrument with its own inertia, it own demands, constraints, and internal logic, and must nevertheless remain open to the initiatives of the subject (as well as to the brute contributions of invasions, fashions, and historical events), always capable of the displacement of meanings, the ambiguities, and the functional substitutions which give this logic its lurching gait. Perhaps the notion of *gestalt*, of structure, would here perform the same service it did for psychology, since both cases involve ensembles which are not the pure manifestations of a directive consciousness, which are not explicitly aware of their own principles, and which nevertheless can and should be studied by proceeding from the whole to the parts.[199]

Merleau-Ponty does not mean that perception and expression are a theory of "sign-gestalt", which is in fact a theory of mere *signaling*.[200] This is to say, a sign *per se* does not give rise to a signification that has the force of a total meaning; this is phenomenalism. Rather, *signs* must be the *significations* that, as a presence, constitute the meaning of a *gestalt*. Such a *gestalt* is manifest in the lived experience of the body-subject as the perception or expression that genetically allows self knowledge or the knowing of the Other.

When Merleau-Ponty is using the concept of the radical *gestalt* in perception as the paradigm for expression he uses a new term to designate the linguistic *gestalt,* namely, *chiasm.* "It is the simultaneous experience of the holding and the held in all orders. *What* it says, its *significations,* are not absolutely invisible : it shows by words. Like all literature. It does not install itself in the reverse of the visible : it is on both sides".[201] The chiasm is that reversibility of perception and expression that allows the structure of "I — the world" and "I — the other".[202] This reversibility is a teleology that is the dialectic of semiotic that grounds both perception and expression.

The chiasm, reversibility, is the idea that every perception is doubled with a counter-perception (Kant's real opposition), is an act with two faces, one no longer knows who speaks and who listens. Speaking-listening, seeing-being seen, perceiving-being perceived circularity (it is because of it that it seems to

[198]   M. M-P., *Structure,* p. 130.
[199]   M. M-P., *Sense,* pp. 87-88.
[200]   M. M-P., *Visible,* p. 266.
[201]   M. M-P., *Visible,* p. 266.
[202]   M. M-P., *Visible,* p. 264.

us that perception forms itself *in the things themselves*) — — Activity = passivity.[203]

In this sense, all reflection as the second step in Merleau-Ponty's phenomenological method should establish the *gestalt* of perception or expression that derives directly from the description of lived-experience. "Our research must be concentric rather than hierarchized".[204]

2.3.1. *Film : A Temporal Paradigm*

Merleau-Ponty's only specific discussion of film occurs in a address given on March 13, 1945 to L'Institut des Hautes Etudes Cinématographiques.[205] This lecture on "The Film and the New Psychology" draws an amazingly accurate parallel between the notion of *gestalt* in perception and expression, and cinemotagraphy.

The present concern with film reflects an inquiry into perception and not expression. And, in terms of the preceding discussions of Merleau-Ponty's notion of *gestalt* it must be noted that film is *not* a spatial *gestalt*. The film captures only time. "Let us say right off that a film is not a sum total of images but a temporal *gestalt*".[206] And, "what we have just said about visual films also applies to sound movies, which are not a sum total of words or noises but are likewise a *gestalt*".[207] Yet, the analysis of sound films must wait until we have examined Merleau-Ponty's concept of expression.

As to silent films, they are captured segments of time that are their own *gestalt* and become our *gestalt* when our relation to the film is my relation to the Other. Why is the *gestalt* of space absent in the film ?

When, in a film, the camera is trained on an object and moves nearer to it to give a close-up view, we can *remember* that we are being shown the ash tray or an actor's hand, we do not actually identify it. This is because the screen has no horizons. In normal vision, on the other hand, I direct my gaze upon a sector of the landscape, which comes to life and is disclosed, while the other objects recede into the periphery and become dormant, while, however, not

---

[203] M. M-P., *Visible*, pp. 264-265.
[204] M. M-P., *Primacy*, p. 36. See John F. Bannan, "Philosophical Reflection and the Phenomenology of Merleau-Ponty", *Review of Metaphysics* VIII, no. 3 (March, 1955), pp. 418-442.
[205] M. M-P., "Le Cinéma et la nouvelle psychologie", *Les Temps Modernes* III, no. 26 (November, 1947), pp. 930-943. Trans., in M. M-P., *Sense*, pp. 48-59.
[206] M. M-P., *Sense*, p. 54.
[207] M. M-P., *Sense*, p. 55.

ceasing to be there. Now with them I have at my disposal their horizons, in which there is implied, as a marginal view, the object on which my eyes at present fall. The horizon, then, is what guarantees the identity of the object throughout the exploration; it is the correlative of the impending power which my gaze retains over the objects which it has just surveyed, and which it already has over the fresh details which it is about to discover. No distinct memory and no explicit conjecture could fill this role: they would give only a probable synthesis, whereas my perception presents it as actual.[208]

This is to say that in the spatial configuration present on the screen one sees an on-going immanence of objects and acts. The pseudo-transcendence which appears to make the immanent stand out against the background is the shift of camera focus from stationary to "close-up". Or, another ready example of the *gestalt* that creates time by eliminating spatial considerations in the film is *montage*.

The consequence of antithesis is that the effect of any one shot differs sharply from that of its precursor and successor, resulting in an impasse of the sensations and concepts derived from contiguous shots; and from this impasse ma arise a third concept different from that of either of the components which produced it. This we shall call montage.[209]

This is to say, the movement of perspectives (shots) form a linearity of time either explicit (stationary to close-up) or implicit (montage) by the synthesis of immanent elements. Although the montage is a synthesis it is not a transcendence. In montage immanent shots are counterposed to allow synthetic views of another perspective which is itself linear and possible because the synthesis is a natural progression from the recalled shots preceding and/or following it. In each case, the immanent "figure" is always present without the "ground" which would allow transcendence. The film viewer uses his own visual ground to pose the immanent figures, hence time becomes a product of the dialectic of "figures" of immanent objects in the film seen. The viewer's subjective concept of time is the synoptic result of his space in terms of the film's time; all movement is against the viewer's stability.

To summarize this analysis, time is created for the viewer by the film in the on-going, linear progression of perspectives. The film itself has no spatiality. Spatiality is a product of the viewer and the film where the viewer places himself as the ground with respect to the film as a figure. Hence, the viewer *and* the film create a spatial gestalt.[210]

[208]   M. M-P., *Phenomenology,* p. 68.
[209]   Raymond Spottiswoode, *A Grammar of the Film: An Analysis of Film Technique* (Berkeley: University of California Press, 1967), p. 202.
[210]   See Ralph Stephenson and J.R. Debrix, "Space-Time in the Cinema" Chapter V

If time is a factor of duration in space, how does the film create time without its own spatial *gestalt* ? "Cinema portrays movement, but *how* ? Is it, as we are inclined to believe, by copying more closely the changes of place ? We may presume not, since slow-motion shows a body floating among objects like algae but not moving *itself*".[211]

Indeed, if we project the consecutive image of a movement on to a homogeneous field containing no object and having no outline, the movement takes possession of the whole space, and what is shifting is the whole visual field, as in the Haunted House at the fair. If we project on to the screen the post-image of a spiral revolving round its centre, in the absence of any fixed framework, space itself vibrates and dilates from the centre to the periphery.[212]

Thus, for example, "that is why the train coming toward us, at the cinema, increases in size much more than it would in reality".[213] In this manner, space becomes a creation of viewer in terms of the time present in the film. The train as an immanent figure is rapidly approaching the viewer *as the ground* — synoptic presence occurs, the viewer closes his eyes, turns away, etc. to avoid the train. The train is an "expanding figure" that is static while its context (ground) is actually the immanent "shrinking figure" of which one's body is the actual ground. The entire film screen and the images upon it are figures put into the lived-space (virtual space) of the viewer.

A good sence of the spatiality that is created by the viewer's perception of the screen images as immanent figures or *objects* in relation to him as transcendent ground is found in filmed reflections and lighting.

Reflections and lighting in photography are often badly reproduced because they are transformed into things, and if, in a film for example, a person goes into a cellar holding a lamp, we do not see the beam of light as an immaterial entity exploring the darkness and picking out objects, because it becomes solidified and can no longer display to us the object at its far end.[214]

This is to say that the light as the present image on the screen is immanent and therefore an object to the viewer, whereas in the lived-experience the light is the background or transcendence against which is placed the immanent object or that which the light forces into the

in *The Cinema as Art* (Baltimore: Penguin Books, Inc., 1965), pp. 123-138, esp. 133-134.
[211]   M. M-P., *Primacy*, p. 185.
[212]   M. M-P., *Phenomenology*, p. 270.
[213]   M. M-P., *Phenomenology*, p. 260.
[214]   M . M-P., *Phenomenology*, p. 309.

foreground. In the film the light is the next object in the linear presentation of objects which creates time, but destroys space in a virtual
sense. In short, spatial synopsis is not possible in film, although the
synthesis of immanent objects in montage can "spatialize" time (pseu-
dotranscendence) by substituting a succession of temporal *gestalt* to
infer a spatial *gestalt*. Often the inference does not succeed and one
loses interest in the film, yet when the inference is successful one is
enveloped in the temporal *gestalt* to the extent that objective time (in
contrast to the film time) stops, causing degrees of spatial disorientation
(one avoids the on-coming train by turning away).[215]

By using the film as a paradigm of the temporal *gestalt* which
preceeds the spatial *gestalt,* Merleau-Ponty comes very close to illustra-
ting his concept of the *pre-objective.* This is to say, "just as I grasp
time through my present and by being present, I perceive others through
my individual life, in the tension of an experience which transcends itself".[216] The experience of the dialectic presence which comes from the
perception of the immanent and its transcendent is the "miraculous
multiplication of perceptible being" in which the "other side" of the
perceptible is known through the actual perceptible.[217]

It has been possible to show that we do not recognize our own hand in a photograph, and that many subjects are even uncertain about identifying their own
handwriting among others, and yet that everyone recognizes his own silhouette
or his own walk when it is filmed. Thus we do not recognize the appearance of
what we have often seen, and on the other hand we immediately recognize
the visual representation of what is invisible to us in our own body.[218]

Merleau-Ponty suggests in this line of analysis that perception is a
dialectic of presence and absence in the lived experience of a time-
space *gestalt.* Yet, when that life world is made static in the photo-

---

[215] M. M-P., *Sense,* p. 14. "The discontinuous images of the cinema prove nothing
with regard to the phenomenal truth of the movement that connects them before the
eyes of the spectator — moreover, they do not even prove that the life world involves
movements without a mobile: the mobile could well be projected by him who perceives." M. M-P., *Visible,* p. 157. An excellent examination of this point appears in
Andre Bazin, "The Ontology of the Photographic Image" in *What is Cinema?*, trans. H.
Gray (Berkeley: University of California Press, 1967). This edition contains selections
from *Qu'est-ce que le cinéma?*, 4 vols., (Paris: Editions de Cerf, 1958-1965).
[216] M. M-P., *Primacy,* p. 27.
[217] M. M-P., *Signs,* pp. 16-17.
[218] M. M-P., *Phenomenology,* p. 149. See Joseph A. Kockelmans, "Merleau-Ponty's
View on Space-Perception and Space", *Review of Existential Psychology and Psychiatry* IV, no. 1 (Winter, 1964), pp. 69-105. Cf., William S. Haymond, "Merleau-Ponty
on Sensory Perception", *Modern Schoolman* XLIV, no. 2 (January, 1967), pp. 93-111.

graph perception is no longer a dialectic process. The still photograph solidifies time and space and constitutes an object. The motion picture is similar in freezing space into an object, yet time remains as the virtual possibility of one's relation to the object. And it is this constant possibility that is the "other side" of any given perception that a viewer sees in a motion picture. This other side is the pre-objective that preceeds the objective reality of the world which is accessible only through radical reflection as a *gestalt* to be discovered.

2.3.2. *Radical Reflection as Method*

For the sake of clarity it should be noted again that Merleau-Ponty uses the terms "radical reflection" and "radical reduction" in synonymous ways and that both designate the reduction of the phenomenological description to its *gestalt* or primordial structure. This is in distinction to the "new cogito" or "radical cogito" as a Third Reflection in which the intentionality of reflection is sought in the preconscious. In this Second Reflection the purpose of the method (radical reflection) is to determine the form or *gestalt* derived from the pre-objective phenomena.

2.3.2.1. *Pre-Objective Phenomena*

The pre-objective phenomena are those "of which we have experience, on the hither side of any formation of ideas...".[219] This is to say, those phenomena that exist in perception for us prior to any conceptualization about their form or presence to us as a unified structure and content.

The world is there before any possible analysis of mine, and it would be artificial to make it the outcome of a series of syntheses which link, in the first place sensations, then aspects of the object corresponding to different perspectives, when both are nothing but products of analysis, with no sort of prior reality.

When I begin to reflect my reflection bears upon an unreflective experience; moreover my reflection cannot be unaware of itself as an event, and so it appears to itself in the light of a truly creative act, of a changed structure of consciousness, and yet it has to recognize, as having priority over its own operations, the world which is given to the subject, because the subject is given to himself. The real has to be described, not constructed or formed.[220]

---

[219] M. M-P., *Phenomenology*, p. 220.
[220] M. M-P., *Phenomenology*, p. x.

The pre-objective phenomena are those perceptions of reality which are the "unreflective experience of the world" of which reflection on them is a mode of being.[221] Our perception as body-subjects teaches us that there is a "first truth" which "prejudges nothing and cannot be contested" that "there is presence, that 'something' is there, and that 'someone' is there".[222]

There is a pre-existence of the world with regard to our perception, of the aspects of the world which the other perceives to the perception I will have of them later, of my world to that of men yet to be born, and all these "words" make one unique world, but do so only in that the things and the world are objects of thought with their intrinsic properties, are of the order of the true, of the valid, of the signification, and are not of the order of events.[223]

In short, the pre-objective phenomena are those things and persons who are to be known prior to any conceptions about them or their structural and substantial presence. They must be encountered as existences in their essential presence prior to reflection on the relationship between existence and essence.

2.3.2.2. *Reflective Reduction*

By engaging in the process of reflection one reduces his perception to a structure in which the phenomenal essence points to an existential structure or manner of being. This is the return to the phenomena. "In the realm of 'reduction' there is no longer anything but consciousness, its acts, and their intentional object".[224] This is to suggest that "reflection is truly reflection only if it is not carried outside itself, only if it knows itself as reflection-on-an-unreflective-experience, and consequently as a change in structure of our existence".[225]

Merleau-Ponty presents several formulations of the reflective act of radical reduction. The following is one of the briefer, yet more explicit accounts.

---

[221] M. M-P., *Phenomenology*, p. 241.
[222] M. M-P., *Visible*, p. 160. See Michael Kullman and Charles Taylor, "The Pre-Objective World", *Review of Metaphysics* XII, no. 1, issue 45 (September, 1958), pp. 108-132. Cf., H.L. Dreyfus and S.J. Todes, "The Three Worlds of Merleau-Ponty", *Philosophy and Phenomenological Research* XXII, no. 4 (June, 1962), pp. 559-565. [Dreyfus and Todes *incorrectly* cite the Kullman and Taylor article as "The Pre-objective World of Maurice Merleau-Ponty", *The Philosophical Review*, October, 1958, p. 108; there is no such article.]
[223] M. M-P., *Visible*, pp. 47-48.
[224] M. M-P., *Signs*, p. 162.
[225] M. M-P., *Phenomenology*, p. 62.

The philosophical *I* is going to withdraw from every condition of fact, as well as from every way of perceiving and understanding them, in order to leave nothing unnoticed. And the task of philosophy will then be to explain, with complete lucidity, how both the manifestations of the external world and the realizations of the incarnate self are possible. Every intentional object refers to consciousness but to a consciousness which is not the incarnate individual that I am as a man, living at a certain moment of time and in a certain position in space. When I carry out the phenomenological reduction, I do not bring back information concerning an external world to a self that is regarded as a part of being, nor do I substitute an internal for an external perception. I attempt rather to reveal and to make explicit in me that pure source of all the meanings which constitute the world around me and my empirical self.[226]

Of course, "the most important lesson which the reduction teaches us is the impossibility of a complete reduction".[227] Thus, the reductive reflection is an on-going process that approaches the existential presence of reality through the essences of things and others without ever arriving at a definitive knowledge beyond self awareness that is the lived-body experience of the body-subject which only he possesses in the joint modalities of existence and essence.

The valid operation of the radical reduction must begin within the form or *gestalt* of perceived phenomena. "It is essential to the reflective analysis that it start from a *de facto* situation".[228] If the reflection does not start from the perceived situation there results an intellectualism that arbitrarily thematizes the objects and consciousness and the object becomes "what is" and consciousness of it becomes a mere concept.[229] Such a reflection ignores the pre-objective phenomena in favor of constructed phenomena which are a hypostatization.

In the last analysis the phenomenological reduction operates on the basic formula : "What do I know ?"[230] This is to say that the reduction belongs to existentialism as a methodology of "being-in-the-world" as a perceiving body-subject capable of knowing the lived-body-experience.[231] Being-in-the-world is a modality of the pre-objective phenomena that one comes to know in the reduction of experience to objects of intentionality. In short, "my personal existence must be

---

[226]   M. M-P., *Primacy*, p. 56. The same analysis with an example appears in *Phenomenology*, pp. 324-325. See *Signs*, pp. 160-161; *Visible*, pp. 203-204.
[227]   M. M-P., *Phenomenology*, p. xiv.
[228]   M. M-P., *Visible*, pp. 43-44.
[229]   M. M-P., *Phenomenology*, pp. 218-219.
[230]   M. M-P., *Phenomenology*, p. 399.
[231]   M. M-P., *Phenomenology*, p. xiv.

the resumption of a prepersonal tradition".[232] And, that prepersonal tradition in experience is the lived-body. As the lived-body addressing itself in the radical reflection one becomes aware of living, seeing, doing and becoming thing, world, and history.[233] This is to say the lived-body-subject is enveloped by corporeal life and is "one" with all of human life.

3. RADICAL *COGITO*

The phenomenological reduction or radical reflection in Merleau-Ponty's methodology is the second step after phenomenological description (primacy of perception) and the forerunner of the Third Reflection or *radical cogito*. From the non-posited elements discovered in the phenomenological description one moves to the radical *gestalt* in which the elements are connected in the perceptible essences that in their relationships constitute the structure of perception and expression. Yet, inherent within such essences are the pre-objective phenomena whose structure allows the *gestalt* to be radically known to reductive description. The return to the phenomena, as "the return to the things themselves", is not an attempt to specify entities in their objective appearance. Rather, the specification of pre-objective phenomena allows the *pre-conscious, intentional meaning* that is the *a priori* structure of the phenomena of the lived-body experience — if you will — the radical *cogito*.

A complete analysis of the radical cogito requires a progressive movement from the idea of the pre-objective to the *cogito* (and the radical *cogito*) and then to intentionality. Although the radical *cogito* is the designation of intentional objects of the pre-objective, analysis is facilitated by moving from the pre-objective to intentionality.

The vision that Merleau-Ponty has given to philosophy by opening new dimensions of perception and of human consciousness, and by pointing at the obscurity of the region of the pre-conscious, has no parallel in the history of philosophy. This vision assumes nothing; nor does it claim to have explored the exact nature of anything. Merleau-Ponty's quest is the perpetual quest of a consciousness for the knowledge of its own beginning.[234]

---

[232] M. M-P., *Phenomenology*, p. 254. See Edward G. Ballard, "On Cognition of the Pre-Cognitive", *Philosophical Quarterly* XI (July, 1961), pp. 238-244, esp. 240.
[233] M. M-P., *Visible*, pp. 83-84.
[234] Ramakant Sinari, "The Phenomenology of Maurice Merleau-Ponty", *Philosophical Quarterly of India* XXXIX, no. 2 (July, 1966), p. 140.

Sinari's remark indicates the composition of the radical *cogito* inasmuch as Merleau-Ponty moves from a strict concern with the pre-objective to the more existential level of the pre-conscious. This is to say, at the higher level of the Third Reflection one attempts to specify the intentionality of the body-subject. While the pre-objective is a concern with the intentional-object as a *gestalt,* the pre-cognitive is concerned with the origin of that intentionality.

3.1. *Pre-Conscious*

The very heart of phenomenology is a concern with the pre-conscious in Merleau-Ponty's philosophy because phenomenology is "... a study of the *advent* of being into consciousness, instead of presuming its possibility as given in advance".[235] A typical example of this "advent of being into consciousness" occurs prior to a communication between two people in which one begins to sense a sharp distinction between the one who communicates and the one with whom he communicates. "But there is initially a state of pre-communication (Max Scheler), wherein the other's intentions somehow play *across* my body while my intentions play across his".[236] This pre-conscious awareness under reflection emerges as one becomes aware of his body and of what radically distinguishes it from the other person's body. At the same time one begins to live his intentions in the facial expressions of the other person just as the other's volitions begin to live in one's own gestures and bodily position. "It is in becoming conscious of myself as I am that I am able to see essences, and in this context the real and the possible are not distinct".[237]

To return to the things themselves is to return to that world which precedes knowledge, of which knowledge always *speaks*, and in relation to which every scientific schematization is abstract and derivative "sign-language" [signification], as is geography in relation to the countryside in which we have learnt beforehand what a forest, a prairie or a river is.[238]

The reduction to the pre-conscious is "the description of the lived world (*Lebenswelt*), where Cartesian distinctions have not yet been made".[239] It is an attempt to describe consciousness incarnate in the

235   M. M-P., *Phenomenology,* p. 61.
236   M. M-P., *Primacy,* p. 119.
237   M. M-P., *Sense,* p. 72.
238   M. M-P., *Phenomenology,* p. ix.
239   M. M-P., *Sense,* p. 135.

environment of human objects and in a linguistic tradition in which the Other is encountered.

The pre-conscious is the "tacit *cogito*" that precedes the "verbal *cogito*" in the encounter of the Other and the world.

Behind the spoken *cogito*, the one which is converted into discourse and into essential truth, there lies a tacit *cogito*, myself experienced by myself. But this subjectivity, albeit imperious, has upon itself and upon the world only a precarious hold.

The tacit *cogito*, the presence of oneself to oneself, being no less than existence, is anterior to any philosophy, and knows itself only in those extreme situations in which it is under threat: for example, in the dread of death or of another's gaze upon me. What is believed to be thought about thought, as pure feeling of the self, cannot yet be thought and needs to be revealed.[240]

This is to say, the pre-conscious which is the lived-body experience emerges under reflection as a spoken *cogito* which seeks to make the existential phenomena knowable as essences of the self in its relation to Others and the *gestalt* of the perceived reality. The pre-conscious is in fact the *pre-reflexive cogito* that is prior to the tacit cogito (itself prior to the verbal cogito). The pre-reflexive *cogito* is the awareness that is destroyed in the knowledge of "myself" that then leads to the knowing of "myself as psyche". It is the existence prior to the primordiality of corporeal awareness.[241]

3.2. *Cogito*

In Merleau-Ponty's writings there is an on-going development of the "new" of "radical" or "true" *cogito* which is always counterposed to the "old" or Cartesian *cogito*.

In consciousness, appearance is not being, but the phenomenon. This new *cogito*, because it is anterior to revealed truth and error, makes both possible. The lived is certainly lived by me, nor am I ignorant of the feelings which I repress, and in this sense there is no unconscious.[242]

Merleau-Ponty in this remark clearly marks out the Cartesian *cogito* as a verbal *cogito* in which language is the medium of knowing existence rather than the lived-experience. Merleau-Ponty formulates the argument this way.

---

[240]   M. M-P., *Phenomenology*, pp. 403-404.
[241]   M. M-P., *Signs*, pp. 152-153; *Visible*, p. 69.
[242]   M. M-P., *Phenomenology*, pp. 296-297.

By following the meaning of the words and the argument [of Descartes], I reach the conclusion that indeed because I think, I am; but this is merely a verbal *cogito*, for I have grasped my thought and my existence only through the medium of language, and the true formula of this *cogito* should be: 'One thinks, therefore one is.' The wonderful thing about language is that it promotes its own oblivion: my eyes follow the lines on the paper, and from the moment I am caught up in their meaning, I lose sight of them.[243]

The point of view that Merleau-Ponty expresses is that the *cogito* should, indeed must, be known in an impersonal and indirect way through the lived-experience rather than as the personal experience of a cognitive idealism. The two propositions, "I think" and "I am" (taken in that order), are indeed necessary to the *cogito* but not in the relationship which Descartes suggests.

Nevertheless we must be clear about the meaning of this equivalence: it is not the 'I am' which is pre-eminently contained in the 'I think', not my existence which is brought down to the consciousness which I have of it, but conversely the 'I think', which is re-integrated into the transcending process of the 'I am', and consciousness into existence.[244]

This is not Merleau-Ponty's means of proclaiming the faith of existentialism in the Sartreian dictum "that existence precedes essence, or, if you prefer, that subjectivity must be the starting point".[245] "On the contrary it recognizes my thought itself as an inalienable fact, and does away with any kind of idealism in revealing me as 'being-in-the-world' ".[246] This is to say, Merleau-Ponty rejects the position of Sartre that the *cogito* can lead to a synthesis of the For-itself (Consciousness) and the In-itself (Being) by saying that both elements are already present (synoptically) in the lived-experience — the presence-at-the world (être-au-monde). In short, Merleau-Ponty argues that existence and essence are primordially present to a radical *cogito* which "teaches us that the existence of consciousness is indistinguishable from the consciousness of existing, and that therefore there can be nothing in it of which it is unaware, and that conversely, everything that it knows with certainty it finds in itself..."[247]

---

[243] M. M-P., *Phenomenology*, pp. 400-401.
[244] M. M-P., *Phenomenology*, p. 383.
[245] Jean-Paul Sartre, *Existentialism and Human Emotions* (New York: Philosophical Library, 1957), p. 13.
[246] M. M-P., *Phenomenology*, p. xiii.
[247] M. M-P., *Phenomenology*, pp. 335-336. Cf., M. M-P., *Primacy*, pp. 21-22.

With the radical *cogito* firmly defined, Merleau-Ponty's use of it as a reflection in phenomenological method can be indicated.

The *cogito* not only discloses to me the certitude of my existence, but more generally it provides me with access to a whole field of knowledges by giving me a general method: the method of searching, by reflection, for the pure thought in each domain which defines it; with regard to perception, for example, of analyzing the thought of perceiving and the meaning of the perceived which are immanent in the sight of a piece of wax, which animate it and sustain it internally.[248]

For example, the method of the radical *cogito* allows one to know the presence (être-au-monde) which is the semiotic — that which is prior to perception or expression. This semiotic is *intentionality* that is both perception and expression or, if you will, intentionality that is a "physiognomic perception".[249] Such a reflection reveals the *gesture* as the lived-semiotic that is synoptically expression and perception. It is "myself-my psyche", and "introceptive image-visual body".[250]

Metaphysics begins from the moment when, ceasing to live in the evidence of the object — whether it is the sensory object or the object of science — we apperceive the radical subjectivity of all our experience as inseparable from its truth value. It means two things to say that our experience is our own: both that it is not the measure of all imaginable being in itself and that it is nonetheless co-extensive with all being of which we can form a notion. This double sense of the *cogito* is the basic fact of metaphysics: I am sure that there is being — on the condition that I do not seek another sort of being than being-for-me.[251]

In short, the radical *cogito* is the method of reflection which allows the body-subject to know the pre-conscious existence which is the presence-at-the-world. The use of this method is, however, a function of intentionality.

3.3. *Intentionality*

Edmund Husserl describes the term intentionality as "an inclusive title for a number of pervasive phenomenological structures".[252] Specifically, phenomenological intentionality is "the unique peculiarity of experiences 'to be the consciousness *of* something'".[253] In his later

---

248   M. M-P., *Structure,* p. 196.
249   M. M-P., *Phenomenology,* p. 132.
250   *Supra,* p. 108.
251   M. M-P., *Sense,* p. 93.
252   Husserl, *Ideas,* p. 222.
253   Husserl, *Ideas,* p. 223.

writings, hence in closer relation to Merleau-Ponty's view of the radical *cogito*, Husserl says *"this essence of consciousness, in which I live as my own self, is the so-called intentionality"*.[254] Husserl elaborates these definitions by suggesting that intentionality methodologically functions as an actuality and potentiality within a lived-"horizon" (figure and ground).[255]

The intentionality that ties together the stages of my exploration, the aspects of the thing, and the two series to each other is neither the mental subject's connecting activity nor the ideal connections of the object. It is the transition that as carnal subject I effect from one phase of movement to another, a transition which as a matter of principle is always possible for me because I am that animal of perception and movements called a body.[256]

The *gestalt* of intentionality is the body-subject in the lived-experience. The paradigm here is sexuality.

Security "is one more form of original intentionality" that "has internal links with the whole active and cognitive being" in which perception, motility, and representation are "three sectors of behavior displaying one typical structure, and standing in a relationship to each other of reciprocal expression".[257]

Thus sight, hearing, sexuality, the body are not only the routes, instruments or manifestations of personal existence: the latter takes up and into itself their existence as it is anonymously given. When we say that the life of the body, or the flesh, and the life of the psyche are involved in a relation of reciprocal *expression*, or that the bodily event always has a psychic *meaning*, these formulations need to be explained.[258]

That is, there is no mind/body dualism but the recognition that there is a "deeper intentionality" below the intentionality displayed in the "myself-my psyche" relationship that is the lived-body-experience.[259] Thus, the intentionality of related acts is a *thetic intentionality* the preconditions for which are found in an *operative intentionality*.[260] The operative intentionality is the radical *cogito* of the pre-conscious or

[254] Husserl, *The Paris Lectures*, pp. 12-13.
[255] Husserl, *The Paris Lectures*, p. 19; Husserl, *Cartesian Meditations*, p. 44. See Paul Ricoeur, *Fallible Man*, pp. 41-42.
[256] M. M-P., *Signs*, p. 167.
[257] M. M-P., *Phenomenology*, p. 157.
[258] M. M-P., *Phenomenology*, p. 160.
[259] M. M-P., *Phenomenology*, p. 121, n. 5.
[260] M. M-P., *Phenomenology*, pp. 428-429.

what Heidegger calls "transcendence".[261] This is to say, the operative intentionality is like "arranging that a detour to an object *be made* [which] is to trace by our every gesture the symbol of the movement which we would have to make if we were in its place; it is to establish a relation between relations; it is a structure or an intention of the second power".[262]

The distinction between the intentionalities might be fairly described in saying that thetic intentionality is the genetic essence of lived-experience while the operative intentionality is a singular and lived-experience constituted from the thetic. "... It is to make an intention explode in the phenomenal field in a cycle of significative gestures, or to join to the things in which he lives the actions which they solicit by an attraction comparable to that of the first unmoved mover".[263] Yet, Merleau-Ponty explains that "the more energetic our intention to see the things themselves, the more the appearances by which they are expressed and the words by which we express them will be interposed between these things and us".[264]

In arriving at the distinction between the preconscious and the consciousness of the lived-body, Merleau-Ponty points to the *intentional object* which is the thetic intentionality or essence of lived existence. The intentional object is the realization *of* lived existence (operative intentionality). "Consciousness is in the first place not a matter of 'I think that' but of 'I can' ".[265] The radical *cogito* is the awareness of the intentional object by the lived-body-subject.

As soon as there is consciousness, and in order that there may be consciousness, there must be something to be conscious of, an intentional object, and consciousness can move towards this object only to the extent that it 'derealizes' itself and throws itself into it, only if it is wholly in this reference ... something, only if it is a pure meaning-giving act. If a being is conscious, he must be nothing but a network of intentions. If he ceases to be definable in terms of the act of sense-giving, he replaces into the condition of a thing, the thing being precisely what does not know, what slumbers in absolute ignorance of itself and the world, what consequently is not a true 'self', i.e., a 'for-itself', and has only a spatio-temporal form of individuation, existence in itself. Consciousness, therefore, does not admit of degree.[266]

In short, the movement of intentionality must be a "phenomenon of

---

261   M. M-P., *Phenomenology*, p. 418.
262   M. M-P., *Structure*, p. 118.
263   M. M-P., *Structure*, p. 188. See also p. 211.
264   M. M-P., *Praise*, p. 20.
265   M. M-P., *Phenomenology*, p. 137.
266   M. M-P., *Phenomenology*, pp. 120-121.

synergy" in which the radical *cogito* posits an intentional object in the *gestalt* of presence-at-the-world.[267] "The recognition of phenomena, then, implies a theory of reflection and a new *cogito*".[268] This is Merleau-Ponty's existential phenomenological method in one sentence, for the method is precisely the synergism of three reflections : description, reduction, and intentionality.

---

[267]   M. M-P., *Phenomenology,* pp. 232-233.
[268]   M. M-P., *Phenomenology,* p. 50.

IV

EXPRESSION : EXISTENTIAL PHENOMENOLOGY AS SPEAKING

In the working notes that form part of *The Visible and the Invisible,* Merleau-Ponty indicates his fear that the development of a philosophy of speech would lead to a corruption of method if "speaking" were allowed to form part of the notion of "writing". "There is a danger that a philosophy of speech would justify the indefinite proliferation of writing — and even pre-writings".[1] This is to suggest that a philosophy of speech must not be considered a subdivision, along with writing, of *expression*. Rather, speaking is to stand independently of writing as the authentic or existential modality of man as the counterpart of perception. Expression in its existential form is *speaking*.

"Expression is like a step taken in the fog — no one can say where, if anywhere, it will lead".[2] Yet, Merleau-Ponty is rather explicit in laying down the conditions for expression in its verbal modality. "Expression presupposes someone who expresses, a truth which he expresses, and the others before whom he expresses himself. *The postulate of expression and of philosophy is that it can simultaneously satisfy these three conditions*".[3] (My Italics.) It is important to show that the conditions for expression are analogous to those for perception, since this study postulates that both expression and perception derive from a common semiology. The three preconditions simultaneously necessary for expression are also present in primordial perception.

... An existence as consciousness (i.e., as pure *appearing to self*), it comes from the fact that I am he who: 1) has a visible world, i.e., a dimensional body, and open to participation; 2) a body visible for itself; 3) and therefore, finally, a self-presence that is an absence from self ——

[1] M. M-P., *Visible,* p. 239.
[2] M. M-P., *Sense,* pp. 3-4.
[3] M. M-P., *Praise,* p. 30. See Alphonse DeWaelhens, "The Philosophical Position of Merleau-Ponty", trans. R. Lauer, *Philosophy Today* VII, no. 2 (Summer, 1963), pp. 134-149, esp. 141. First published as "Situation de Merleau-Ponty", *Les Temps Modernes,* Année 17, nos. 184-185 (October, 1961), pp. 377-398.

The flesh of the world is not explained by the flesh of the body, nor the flesh of the body by the negativity or self that inhabits it — the 3 phenomena are *simultaneous* —— [4]

Merleau-Ponty's semiology consists, then, in a dialectic of signs and significations that constitute a presence. This presence in "perception" is the synoptic union of sensation and intellection, the immanence and transcendence of encountered experience. Similarly, "expression" is a dialectic of signs and significations that constitutes a presence. Here, the presence is the synoptic union of language and tongue, the immanence and transcendence of encountered speaking. In both modalities of this semiology (perception and expression) there is the paradigm of the *gestalt* with its figure and ground pointing to the three reflections of method : description and reduction in the synopsis of intentionality. Hence, "a philosophical life always bases itself on these three cardinal points. The enigma of philosophy (and of expression) is that sometimes life is the same to oneself, to others, and to the true".[5]

1.   EXPRESSION AS PHENOMENA

When one thinks of the phenomena that might constitute expression the fine arts are a probable selection. This is also typical of Merleau-Ponty who frequently uses painting to illustrate his thoughts, in particular the work of Cézanne.[6] The great importance of painting to Merleau-Ponty is the fact that it demonstrates itself as a singular mode of speech, which is to argue that expression is part of speaking and not contrarily. Painting as expression is a gesture for others to copy in coming to know the painter's intent or to know one's own intentions.

But we would see a relation if we understood that to paint, to sketch, is not to produce something from nothing, that the drawing, the touch of the brush, and the visible work are but the trace of a total movement of Speech, which goes unto Being as a whole, and that this movement contains the expression

---

[4]   M. M-P., *Visible*, p. 250. See Heidegger, *Being and Time*, p. 317.
[5]   M. M-P., *Praise*, p. 32.
[6]   M. M-P., "Le Doute de Cézanne", *Fontaine* VIII, no. 47 (December, 1945), pp. 80-100. Trans. in *Sense*, pp. 9-25; Abridged trans. Juliet Bigney, *Partisan Review*, XIII, no. 4 (September-October, 1946), pp. 464-478. [The Bigney translation omits approximately one hundred lines of text dealing with a discussion of Freud's analysis of Léonard de Vinci's psychological state as an artist, in particular his alleged homosexuality.]

with lines as well as the expression with colors, my expression as well as that of the other painters.[7]

In this sense, "Bergson was wrong in believing that the picture is 'a simple act projected on the canvas', since it is rather the sedimented result of a series of expressive efforts".[8] This is to say that the painting exists as the final product of a series of expressions that culminate in one intentional expression of the human condition. "The new sense-giving intention knows itself only by donning already available meanings, the outcome of previous acts of expression".[9]

In speaking of Cézanne, Merleau-Ponty points out that "he gradually learned that expression is the language of the thing itself and springs from its configuration".[10] The art of painting merely demonstrates that "when one goes from the order of events to the order of expression, one does not change the world; the same circumstances which were previously submitted to now become a signifying system".[11] This process holds true for other forms of expression also. For example, the speaker's communication with his listener is not a mere exchange of information through vocalization. Rather, the speaking is total signifying system. "In ordinary experience we find a fittingness and a meaningful relationship between the gesture, the smile and the tone of a speaker".[12]

As the sensible structure can be understood only through its relation to the body, to the flesh — the invisible structure can be understood only through its relation to logos, to speech — — The invisible meaning is the inner framework of speech — — The world of perception encroaches upon that of movement (which also is *seen*) and inversely movement has [eyes?] Likewise the world of ideas encroaches upon language (one thinks it) which inversely encroaches upon the ideas (one thinks because one speaks, because one writes) — —
The other's words make me speak and think because they create within me an other than myself, a divergence *(écart)* by relation to ... what I see, and thus designate it to me myself. The other's words form a grillwork through which I see my thought.[13]

Merleau-Ponty's theory suggests that both expression and perception operate from a common *gestalt* of signs and significations that account

[7]   M. M-P., *Visible,* p. 211.
[8]   M. M-P., *Praise,* p. 67, Note III.
[9]   M. M-P., *Phenomenology,* p. 183.
[10] M. M-P., *Phenomenology,* p. 322.
[11] M. M-P., *Signs,* p. 64.
[12] M. M-P., *Phenomenology,* p. 55.
[13] M. M-P., *Visible,* p. 224.

for meaning. It is the common structure of elements that allows the
reversibility of perception and expression. Such a common structure
and its respective entities are a simiology of phenomena that is existential. As existential phenomena, the semiotic elements exist only in
varying modalities as perceptions or expressions. One is never separate
from the other, which is to say, perception and expression operate in
the phenomenological dialectic of immanence and transcendence wherein the *presence* is the existent. Where perception is immanent, expression becomes its transcendent modality; and, where expression is
immanent, perception rises as its modal transcendent.

There is a circle of the touched and the touching, the touched takes hold
of the touching; there is a circle of the visible and the seeing, the seeing is not
without the visible existence; [what are these adhesions compared with those
of the voice and hearing?] there is even an inscription of the touching in the
visible, of the seeing in the tangible — and the converse; there is finally a
propagation of those exchanges to all the bodies of the same type and of the
same style which I see and touch — and this by virtue of the fundamental
fission or segregation of the sentient and the sensible which, laterally, makes
the organs of my body communicate and founds transitivity from one body to
another.[14]

More specifically, there is the synoptic union of the semiotic in every
perception and expression.

Already when I name the perceived or when I recognize it *as* a chair or tree,
I substitute the subsumption under a concept of experience of a fleeting reality;
even when I pronounce the word "this", I already relate a singular and lived
existence to the essence of lived existence. But these acts of expression or
reflection intend an original text which cannot be deprived of meaning.[15]

The fundamental notion that is embodied in the idea of expression as
phenomena is that "transcendence is identity within difference".[16] "It
is thus that one speaks *to the other* although one has only to do with
oneself".[17] The transcendence operates in opposition to immanence yet
requires that immanence to form the existential presence.

That general spirit which we all constitute by living our life in common, that
intention already deposited in the given system of the language, preconscious
because the speaking subject espouses it before he becomes aware of it and ele-
vates it to the level of knowledge, and yet which only subsists on the condition

[14]   M. M-P., *Visible,* p. 143 and 143n.
[15]   M. M-P., *Structure,* p. 211.
[16]   M. M-P., *Visible,* p. 225.
[17]   M. M-P., *Visible,* p. 225.

of being taken up or assumed by speaking subjects and lives on their desire for communication — this, in the field of linguistics, is indeed the equivalent of the psychologists' "form", equally alien to the objective existence of the natural process as to the mental existence of an idea. Being neither thing or idea, language, like individual consciousness, can be approached only by a method of "comprehension" which finds amid the multiplicity of facts a few intentions or decisive aims, the "profound and in a way secret facts upon which rest the construction of the language".[18]

Speech in this context becomes the "taking possession of an indefinite time and space".[19] Speech is the "advent of human action and of human perception" that is "irreducible to the vital dialectic of the organism and its milieu".[20] Rather, speech is the phenomena of expression that is the figure and ground of the *gestalt*.

But from the beginning the sonorous phenomena — whether I speak or another speaks — will be integrated into the structure: expression-expressed; the face — whether I touch my own or I see that of another — will be integrated into the structure: alter-ego.
In other words, as soon as nascent consciousness is taken as the object of analysis one realizes that it is impossible to apply to it the celebrated distinction between *a priori* form and empirical content.[21]

In short, perception is its own expression and expression contains within it the limits of its own perception. "Distinctions of figure and ground, sound and meaning, conception and execution are now blurred, as the limits of body and mind were previously".[22]

With this brief introduction to expression as a phenomena to be examined, the nature of *speaking* in its existential, phenomenological character may be explored. Necessarily, speaking must be examined in a progression from its dialectic parts to its unitary presence. This is to say, language is an existential modality in "speaking" that is primordial language which comes to be sedimented into essential language or a tongue. Language is a *gestalt* of existential speaking and sedimented speaking.

---

[18]   M. M-P., *Sense,* p. 88.
[19]   M. M-P., *Structure,* p. 176.
[20]   M. M-P., *Structure,* p. 176.
[21]   M. M-P., *Structure,* p. 171.
[22]   M. M-P., *Signs,* p. 233. "The language is an immediate object between sound and thought: it consists in *uniting both while simultaneously decomposing them.*" Roland Barthes, *Elements of Semiology,* p. 56.

2. LANGUAGE

"It is by considering language that we would best see how we are to and how we are not to return to the things themselves".[23] Through the vehicle of language, Merleau-Ponty explores the structure of a semiotic that casts perception as related to expression (or contrarily) as "the speech before speech".[24] This is to say with de Saussure, "language is speech less speaking".[25] At the risk of an extended quotation, the problem of language in its evolution from a systemic entity to a lived-experience as explained by Merleau-Ponty serves as an excellent introduction to his phenomenology of speaking.

Hence the problem of language is, if one likes, only a regional problem — that is, if we consider the ready-made language, the secondary and empirical operation of translation, of coding and decoding, the artificial languages, the technical relation between a sound and a meaning which are joined only by express convention and are therefore ideally isolable. But if, on the contrary, we consider the speaking word, the assuming of the conventions of his native language as something natural by him who lives within that language, the folding over within him of the visible and the lived experience upon language, and of language upon the visible and the lived experience, the exchanges between the articulations of his mute language and those of his speech, finally that operative language which has no need to be translated into significations and thoughts, that language-thing which counts as an arm, as action, as offense and as seduction because it brings to the surface all the deep-rooted relations of the lived experience wherein, it takes form, and which is the language of life and of action but also that of literature and of poetry — then this logos is an absolutely universal theme, it is the theme of philosophy. Philosophy itself is language, rests on language; but this does not disqualify it from speaking of language, nor from speaking of the pre-language and of the mute world which doubles them: on the contrary, philosophy is an operative language, that language that can be known only from within, through its exercise, is open upon the things, called forth by the voices of silence, and continues an effort of articulation which is the Being of every being.[26]

The direction of the above quotation should not be misleading; there is no attempt to arrive at a "verbalism" in the Scholastic tradition. The use of verbal language is an agency for knowing existence through essences (of which language is one), not an attempted phenomenalism

---

23 M. M-P., *Visible,* p. 125.
24 M. M-P., *Visible,* p. 201.
25 Ferdinand de Saussure, *Course in General Linguistics,* p. 77.
26 M. M-P., *Visible,* p. 126.

that views the word as a delimitation of essence. Language should indicate the nature of the essence as an existential modality, not the only
possible existence of an essential modality.[27] The same comment has
been made ratherly cynically by Cioran.

If I were asked what man I most envied, I should answer without hesitation:
the one who, taking his ease among words, lives there naively, by reflex, neither
questioning nor identifying them with signs, as if they correspond to reality
itself or as if they were an absolute strewn in the everyday.[28]

One must recognize that language is both the instrument and the
product of speaking. Language in speaking can be existential by
constituting meaning, or language can settle into a sediment after being
spoken which is an essential meaning. There is a dialectic of language
which "constitutes an organic whole developing through history as a
living being".[29] There is a clear project in Merleau-Ponty's scheme of
analysis as a result of this approach to language.

To reflect on language is, rather, to recover an experience which is anterior to
the objectivizing of language and certainly anterior to the scientific observation
of it. In this experience the subject, who speaks and writes, passes beyond language only by exercising it and taking it over.[30]

This return to the speaking subject is what Husserl referred to as "the
phenomenology of language".[31] But Merleau-Ponty goes beyond this
level to the primordial phenomenology of speaking that precedes that
of language. "We must study the subject who is actually speaking. To
the linguistic of language we must add the linguistic of the word".[32]
The phenomenology of speaking must unite language to the lived-
experience of the body-subject. Yet, this union must reflect the view
of language in the presence of the speaking subject that creates primordial meaning and also extends sedimented meaning. This is to say,
the "word" should be understood as that expressed meaning of the
lived-experience that progresses out of and goes beyond "language"
as past experience.

The difference between a "Word" and "Language" as they are used
above can be seen in two illnesses. For example, the amnesic aphasiac

---

27   M. M-P., *Primacy*, p. 74.
28   E.M. Cioran, *The Temptation to Exist*, p. 187.
29   George Gusdorf, *Speaking (La Parole)*, p. 31.
30   M. M-P., *Primacy*, pp. 81-82.
31   M. M-P., *Primacy*, p. 84.
32   M. M-P., *Primacy*, p. 84. See Martin Heidegger, *Being and Time*, p. 211.

does not lose his "words" but remains capable of employing them in automatic language. Yet, he does lose the power of *naming* since the person reduced to concrete, immediate experience becomes incapable of category selection. Also, in alexia a person may be able to read his name as a word, but not the letters that compose it taken separately.[33] In the aphasiac the lived-experience is not possible except as a recurring use of language, the "word" cannot be specified. Similarly, in alexia the word as a structure or "language" is usable, but its parts are not known. This is to say, structure is the sole determinant of content. Merleau-Ponty's point is that structure must come from a content that, in circular process, is contained by the structure. Content and structure must be co-present, which is to say the word must be the language and language should give rise to the word. In other words, transcendent meaning must be part of the immanent meaning and vice versa.

Merleau-Ponty suggests that the living body-subject is a mediation in language between the word as expressed and the word as perceived. This is to say, a mediation occurs in speaking that takes up language as perceived and uses it to create meaning. This created meaning may have the power of primordial signification or may merely repeat an already familiar meaning. The difference is between existential communication and essential communication. The body-subject is the agency of converting language as private use into public meaning or inversely. In any event, the speaking subject is the agency and language the instrument or code. And, the word in each instance is *not* a symbol standing in place of an object or a symbol indicating a given object. "Thus we refute both intellectualism and empiricism by simply saying that *the word has a meaning*".[34]

Far from harboring the secret of the being of the world, language is itself a world, itself a being — a world and a being to the second power, since it does not speak in a vacuum, since it speaks *of* being and *of* the world and therefore redoubles their enigma instead of dissipating it. The philosophical interrogation concerning the world therefore does not consist in referring from the world itself to what we say of the world, since it is reiterated within language.[35]

By defining the word as its own meaning, Merleau-Ponty is advancing an ontology of the word itself insofar as it is the union of the sign and signification. "Words have a physiognomy because we adopt towards

[33] M. M-P., *Structure*, p. 64.
[34] M. M-P., *Phenomenology*, p. 177.
[35] M. M-P., *Visible*, pp. 96-97.

them, as towards each person, a certain form of behavior which makes its complete appearance the moment each word is given".[36] This ability to know what a word means in a given usage makes the word transcend; its mere presence as a specific meaning is what is often referred to as a "semantic thickness".[37] This is to say, the word as an essential item by its use in speaking becomes an existential phenomena : it is its meaning. Speech and thought become a synoptic meaning since they "are intervolved, the sense being held within the word, and the word being the external existence of the sense".[38]

For Merleau-Ponty language is a depository of fixed significations because of its cumulative power which results from a "power of anticipation and of prepossession, because one speaks not only of what one does not know, in order to know it", but also of "an ontogenesis of which it is a part".[39] Language is a "repeated index" that functions to "name a circumscribed signification".[40] This is to say language functions in both a private and public role. The private use of language is a naming or specification by the speaking individual that sets the limit for meaning when encountered by the other.

There is a "languagely" ["*langagière*"] meaning of language which effects the mediation between my as yet unspeaking intention and words, and in such a way that my spoken words surprise me myself and teach me my thought. Organized signs have their immanent meaning, which does not arise from the "I think" but from the "I am able to".[41]

This is to say, language in speech constitutes the lived-reality that is created in the relation of man to man. It is in this sense that Merleau-Ponty says that the spoken word "reassumes the tragic resonance it has in ordinary language when a man speaks of what he has lived through".[42] The strange power of *speaking* is manifest when one recalls that "there

---

[36] M. M-P., *Phenomenology*, pp. 235-236. See James H. Charlesworth, "Reflections on Merleau-Ponty's Phenomenological Description of 'Word'", *Philosophy and Phenomenological Research* XXX, no. 4 (June, 1970), pp. 609-613.

[37] M. M-P., *Signs*, p. 75.

[38] M. M-P., *Phenomenology*, p. 182. See Joseph A. Kockelmans, "Merleau-Ponty's Phenomenology of Language", *Review of Existential Psychology and Psychiatry* III, no. 1 (Winter, 1963), pp. 39-82. Cf., Philip E. Lewis, "Merleau-Ponty and the Phenomenology of Language", *Yale French Studies*, nos. 36 and 37 (October, 1966), pp. 19-40.

[39] M. M-P., *Visible*, pp. 102-103.

[40] M. M-P., *Visible*, p. 130.

[41] M. M-P., *Signs*, p. 88.

[42] M. M-P., *Signs*, p. 65. See Mikel Dufrenne, *Philosophy and Language*, p. 81.

are situations which cannot be communicated and which can only be understood by living them".[43]

Speech in the guise of language is the lived-experience of perception which is only the " 'pilings' of our spoken words".[44] Yet, one must not take language as the residue of past acts of signification and a record of acquired meaning. From the phenomenological point of view, the speaking person, who makes use of his language as a means of communicating with a living community, makes the language regain its unity as primordial meaning. "From now on there is no other way to comprehend language than to dwell in it and use it".[45]

Consciousness of language is no longer the separated foundation of a language, which is secondary to it and derived. To know what language is, it is necessary first of all to speak. It no longer suffices to reflect on the language lying before us in historical documents of the past. It is necessary to take them over, to live with them, to speak them. It is only by making contact with this speaking subject that I can get a sense of what other languages are and can move around in them.[46]

Thus, language makes one enter into the realm of the *Lebenswelt* or life-world. The creation and sedimentation of lived values comes to be transmitted and stabilized in speaking. It is the creation of values by speaking that leads Merleau-Ponty to focus his attention on language and speaking as a means to existential phenomenology.[47]

In order to fully realize what Merleau-Ponty intends by language, its counterpart in the dialectic of speaking should be examined. This is to say that "silence" is the paired concept with language in the dialectic of immanence and transcendence which is articulated meaning.

2.1. *Silence*

Just as absolute emptiness is perceived only at the moment when it is filled with experience, language as expression allows the awareness of

---

[43] M. M-P., *Sense*, p. 33.
[44] M. M-P., *Signs*, p. 20.
[45] M. M-P., *Signs*, p. 232.
[46] M. M-P., *Primacy*, p. 83. See Richard B. Gregg, "A Phenomenologically Oriented Approach to Rhetorical Criticism", *Central States Speech Journal* XVII (May, 1966), pp. 83-90. With specific reference to Merleau-Ponty see my own analysis in "Rhetorical Criticism: An Interpretation of Maurice Merleau-Ponty", *Philosophy and Rhetoric* II, no. 2 (Spring, 1969), pp. 61-71.
[47] Brendan E. O'Mahony, "The Rediscovery of Language", *Studies* LIII (Spring, 1964), p. 77.

silence. Merleau-Ponty has defined silence as the absence of sounds which therefore "keeps us in contact with the being of sound".[48] This is to say that as "all absence is merely the obverse of a presence, all silence a modality of the being of sound".[49] Just as depth in perception is a dialectic presence, speaking is the dialectic result of language and silence.[50] And, it is in this context that "all language is indirect or allusive — that is, if you wish, silence".[51] Merleau-Ponty's intent is to indicate that speaking uses language to specify a human intentionality in a situation that is a "speechless want".[52] Silence is that private awareness of self that intends to be present-at-the-world by objectifying the lived-experience in speaking a language that at once is public and open to encounter.

For speech takes flight from where it rolls in the wave of speechless communication. It tears out or tears apart meanings in the undivided whole of the nameable, as our gestures do in that of the perceptible. To make language a means or a code for thought is to break it.[53]

Silence marks that period in the dialectic of perception and expression in which the semiotic of meaning transfers from reception to transmission in the lived-body-subject.

When the silent vision falls into speech, and when the speech in turn, opening up a field of the nameable and the sayable inscribes itself in that field, in its place, according to its truth — in short, when it metamorphoses the structures of the visible world and makes itself a gaze of the mind, *intuitus mentis* — this is always in virtue of the same fundamental phenomenon of reversibility which sustains both the mute perception and the speech and which manifests itself by an almost carnal existence of the idea, as well as by a sublimation of the flesh. In a sense, if we were to make completely explicit the architectonics of the human body, its ontological framework, and how it sees itself and hears itself, we would see that the structure of its mute world is such that all the possibilities of language are already given in it.[54]

The import of this argument is that speech as language in the process of becoming is an immanence that must always be contrasted against

[48]   M. M-P., *Phenomenology*, p. 328. "Silence = absence of the word due." *Visible*, p. 263.
[49]   M. M-P., *Phenomenology*, p. 364.
[50]   M. M-P., *Visible*, 236.
[51]   M. M-P., *Signs*, p. 43.
[52]   M. M-P., *Signs*, p. 90.
[53]   M. M-P., *Signs*, p. 17.
[54]   M. M-P., *Visible*, pp. 154-155. See Martin Heidegger, *Being and Time*, pp. 204 and 208.

the silence that is transcendent around it, i.e. as the range of possibility
that speech can always invoke. Language as a semiotic in this context
is a presence of signs that depend on those signs or absences which
are silence — the contrast that allows for meaning by composing a
gestalt. The world of silence is the perceived world that is the non-
language significations surrounding speech and thus allowing the
emergence of meaning. It is in this sense that Merleau-Ponty speaks
of the "silence of perception" which is "silent speech, without signification and yet rich in meaning".[55] Thus, "in the silence of primary
consciousness can be seen appearing not only what words mean, but
also what things mean : the core of primary meaning in which the
acts of signification and expression take shape".[56] In one's involvement
with the world and others, we come to practice a *hyper-reflection* which
is precisely the lived-body experience. One must determine, therefore,
"what in its silence *it means to say...*".[57]

Silence is not simply the inability to speak. Rather, it is the determinate choice of commitment that becomes obvious when one has the
potential to speak, but does not : "one keeps silence only when one
can speak".[58] In this sense there is a primordial silence that is the
possibility of speech and which signifies meaning because of this
possibility. When one comes to speak about things or people it is because what one expresses is anticipated and prefigured, although not
entirely accomplished, in the silence we share. Thus, one is constantly
in a *gestalt* of potentiality that communicates itself and is on the verge
of self-confirmation where silence is transcendent with speech. This
concept is particulary important with respect to the difference between
existential speaking and sedimented speech. In both cases silence is the
ground and terminator of the expressive *gestalt*. Silence is thus the
immediate dialectic element that allows for the meaning in speech by
accomplishing the second task of indicating the limits of the articulation.
Hence, silence is the frontier that is transgressed by speaking, yet
silence is the perceived boundary established by the word said — the
limit where actuality meets potentiality.

It may be apparent that the silence that embodies speech is the
lived-body. The body in its perceptive power is a modality of the

---

[55]   M. M-P., *Visible*, p. 268. See *Phenomenology*, p. 48.
[56]   M. M-P., *Phenomenology*, p. xv. An interesting extrapolation of this point occurs
in Philip Wheelwright, "A Preface to Phenosemantics", *Philosophy and Phenomenological Research* II, no. 4 (June, 1942), pp. 511-519.
[57]   M. M-P., *Visible*, p. 39.
[58]   M. M-P., *Phenomenology*, pp. 161-162.

potential, a claim to immediacy that waits for its manifestation. The lived-body is a "pre-meaning, a silent knowing" that becomes manifest in spoken language.[59] The lived-body experience which is perception becomes the *matrix* from which existential speaking issues to create the *Lebenswelt* reflected in sedimented speech. In this sense, silence can become that true commitment which develops beyond all argument and motive as the expressed value contained in the privacy of the lived-body and which is not open to public perception through articulation.[60] Silence becomes the risked commitment and "to be silent is not the same as to say why one does not wish to choose".[61]

Merleau-Ponty's development of silence does not evolve a solipsistic point of view inasmuch as being silent always presumes a community of men endowed with speech and by choosing to be silent one addresses himself to that community. This is to say, "the refusal to communicate, however, is still a form of communication".[62] Solipsism is avoided because "solitude and communication cannot be the two horns of a dilemma, but two 'moments' of one phenomenon, since in fact other people do exist for me".[63]

2.2. *Chiasm*

In the last chapter, "chiasm" was mentioned as the verbal *gestalt*. This point needs clarification in terms of what has been said about language and silence in their dialectic of meaning. The chiasm as Merleau-Ponty defines it is both a separation (écart) and a reversibility (chiasme). It is a separation in the sense that "it is more exactly that between someone who goes unto the world and who, from the exterior, seems to remain his own 'dream' ".[64] Thus, the lived-body-subject perceives his own exterior simultaneously with his interior. The dialectic of separation is the ground of a reversibility that is at once perception and expression, an alternating presence of immanence and transcendence.[65] Silence and communication, speaking and listening become mere "moments" of each other as two signs in a semiotic that join to display meaning. In the *gestalt* that is the chiasm "there is no other meaning

---

[59] M. M-P., *Visible*, p. 179.
[60] M. M-P., *Sense*, p. 32.
[61] M. M-P., *Praise*, p. 62.
[62] M. M-P., *Phenomenology*, pp. 360-361.
[63] M. M-P., *Phenomenology*, p. 359.
[64] M. M-P., *Visible*, pp. 214-215.
[65] M. M-P., *Visible*, pp. 264-265.

than carnal, figure and ground —— Meaning = their dislocation, their gravitation".[66]

"Like the natural man, we situate ourselves in ourselves *and* in the things, in ourselves *and* in the other, at the point where, by a sort of *chiasm,* we become the others and we become the world".[67] The use of the semiotic in perception that allows one to derive meaning from his structure relation to others and to things can also operate in language and silence. Here, the chiasm is a structure or *gestalt* that utilizes the semiotic formulations of perception to express a lived-meaning. This is to say, "that the perception-message analogy (coding and decoding) is valid, but on condition that one discerns a) the *flesh* beneath the discriminating behaviors b) speech and its 'comprehensible' diacritical systems beneath the information".[68]

The *gestalt* of expression as a chiasm is well reflected in the semiology of language, particularly as Merleau-Ponty has taken up De Saussure's analysis.

Merleau-Ponty's attention to structure, which he more accurately calls infra-structure [Chiasm], (and which has since created a minor intellectual industry in France called *le structuralisme*), owes its existence to an imaginative combin-ing of Ferdinand Saussure's linguistics with Husserl's later philosophy. The study of language becomes a study in the semiology (as C.S. Peirce called it) of a given society.[69]

This is to say that the semiotic of expression must be a *gestalt* in which one examines the perspective of the "speaking subject who lives in his language (and who in some cases may change it)".[70] Expression in this view is a totality to be studied and specified. Speech as language is a concrete and incarnate system. Signs are diacritical by functioning only through their differences from other signs and by the separation between them (also signs). Thus there is a unity in the divergence of signs that imposes a positive signification on language which "lies

---

[66] M. M-P., *Visible,* p. 265.
[67] M. M-P., *Visible,* p. 160.
[68] M. M-P., *Visible,* p. 201. See Richard M. Zaner, "Piaget and Merleau-Ponty: A Study in Convergence", *Review of Existential Psychology and Psychiatry* VI, no. 1 (Winter, 1966), pp. 7-23.
[69] Edward W. Said, "Labyrinth of Incarnations: The Essays of Maurice Merleau-Ponty", *Kenyon Review* XXIX, no. 1 (January, 1967), p. 65. For a good survey of structuralism in various applications, including language analysis, see: "Structuralism", [Special Issue] *Yale French Studies,* nos. 36-37 (October, 1966); and, "Structuralismes: idéologie et méthode", [Special Issue] *Esprit* XXXV, no. 360 (1967), pp. 769-976.
[70] M. M-P., *Sense,* pp. 86-87.

beneath a language's explicit signification, a systematization which is achieved in language before its conceptual principle is known".[71]

We must recognize as anterior to 'sense-giving acts' *(Bedeutungsgebende Akten)* of theoretical and positing thought, 'expressive experiences' *(Ausdruck-serlebnisse)*; as anterior to the signified meaning *(Zeichen-Sinn)*, the expressive meaning *(Ausdrucks-Sinn)*, and finally as anterior to any subsuming of content under form, the symbolic 'pregnancy' of form in content.[72]

The nature of the semiotic chiasm is illustrated rather clearly in the concept of "style" in expression. A style is a certain manner of re-cognizing and dealing with situations which specify an identity or sense of understanding as one encounters them in, e.g. individuals or writers. There is felt-experience of "taking over that manner myself in a sort of imitative way, even though I may be quite unable to define it...".[73] Hence, "I experience the unity of the world as I recognize a style".[74] This is to say, the structure that is perception for me can be expressed by another in such a way that his perspective signifies my own. His expression captures what I live ! This semiotic presence occurs as one realizes that "I am a psychological and historical structure, and have received, with existence, a manner of existing, a style. All my actions and thoughts stand in relationship to this structure, and even a phi-losopher's thought is merely a way of making explicit his hold on the world, and what he is".[75] Style is that personal way of ordering words and actions to indicate a meaning born of "a new correspondence between signs" which posits a language system.[76] However, such a system reflects the lived-experience of the person over the years of his language usage which implicitly reflects his values. Style is, then, more than a system of thought or a mere symbol system, *style is a system of speaking.*

2.3. Film : A Semiotic Paradigm

Just as the silent film is a temporal *gestalt,* the "talking" motion picture is a *gestalt* of time that results from spatial configurations *and sound*

---

[71] M. M-P., *Signs,* p. 117. See B.A. Farrell, "Intentionality and the Theory of Signs", *Philosophy and Phenomenological Research* XV, no. 4 (June, 1955), pp. 500-511.
[72] M. M-P., *Phenomenology,* p. 291.
[73] M. M-P., *Phenomenology,* p. 327.
[74] M. M-P., *Phenomenology,* p. 327.
[75] M. M-P., *Phenomenology,* p. 455.
[76] M. M-P., *Signs,* pp. 234-235.

structures. "A rhythm exists for sounds just as for images".[77] The soundtrack represents an internal organization of the film that should be taken in conjunction with visual images. The sound film is a new whole, a synergism, that cannot be reduced to its component parts.

A sound movie is not a silent film embellished with words and sounds whose only function is to complete the cinematographic illusion. The bond between sound and image is much closer, and the image is transformed by the proximity of sound. This is readily apparent in the case of dubbed films, where thin people are made to speak with the voices of fat people, the young have the voices of tiny ones — all of which is absurd if what we have said is true — namely, that voice, profile, and character form an indivisible unit. And the union of sound and image occurs not only in each character but in the film as a whole.[78]

This is to say the sound which is music, words, and the like, combines with silence to create an image. This is a signification composed of the visual image which is a sign and the presence (or absence) of sound (or silence) which is also a sign. The synopsis of such signs is a semiotic *gestalt.*

Barthes denies such a *gestalt* and suggests that the dual presentation of the visual and sound images is a redundancy or at least the sound completes the visual image.[79] Kwant follows this notion by noting that the sound film is like "ordinary language" which comes incomplete and has meaning only in the situation of use.[80] This view seems extreme inasmuch as the film's visual image would appear to present a constancy of perception that is little affected by the introduction of sound (that minor effect being semiotic repetition). Merleau-Ponty asserts that this is not the case.

The introduction of sound into the perceptual *gestalt* allows a more precise meaning as the result of a semiotic completion. This is to say the sound film tells or narrates a story or history (chaque film raconte une histoire).[81] In this formulation of the film as a history the analogy of actual history should be a guide to interpretation. "History admits of adumbrative significations. It is not a coherent system".[82] Just as

[77]   M. M-P., *Sense,* p. 55.
[78]   M. M-P., *Sense,* p. 55.
[79]   Roland Barthes, *Elements of Semiology,* p. 10. See David Funt, "Roland Barthes and the *Nouvelle critique*", *Journal of Aesthetics and Art Criticism* XXVI, no. 3 (Spring, 1968), pp. 329-340.
[80]   Remy C. Kwant, *Phenomenology of Language* (Pittsburgh: Duquesne University Press, 1965), p. 215. See M. M-P., *Humanism,* p. 141.
[81]   M. M-P., *Sense,* p. 57.
[82]   M. M-P., *Primacy,* p. 206.

actual history is a temporal *gestalt* with space the creation of the perceiver, so the sound film is a temporal *gestalt* with the sense of time intensified by the rhythm of the sound in a dialectic with the visual rhythm. The standard combinations of sound and sight in cinematography are as follows.

Synchronism is the same combination of sound and images as we would experience in real life (we look at a person and hear him talking). *Asynchronism* is a combination of sound and image we would not experience in real life (we look at an empty nursery and hear the voices of the children who have just been playing there). *Parallelism* is a combination in which sound and image repeat one another and one of the two is redundant — parallelism implies audiovisual pleonasm. Parallelism can be either synchronous or asynchronous.[83]

In these dialectic combinations, sound and image form two latent semiotics into a synoptic presence. What is given in sound is supplemented by image or contrarily. In any event, the *gestalt* is always completed in a sensuous admixture of rhythm.

The meaning of a film is incorporated into its rhythm just as the meaning of a gesture may immediately be read in that gesture: the film does not mean anything but itself. The idea is presented in a nascent stage and emerges from the temporal structure of the film as it does from the coexistence of the parts of a painting. The joy of the art lies in its showing how something takes on meaning — not by referring to already established and acquired ideas but by the temporal or spatial arrangement of elements.[84]

Merleau-Ponty characterizes the film in its sound and image modality as "finer-grained" than real-life experiences because in the lived-experiences perceptions have "blurs, smudges, and superfluous matter" which cause us to see and lose sight of things and people.[85] The sound film presents the viewer with a world that is more exact, the tiniest aesthetic item is present as the obvious. Perception is the key to meaning in the film just as in lived experience however. "A movie is not thought; it is perceived".[86] The consequence is that the viewer is drawn into the image action and the sound dialogue (or musical rhythm) as the ground of the immanent expression : the film. The film is the pre-objective experience made manifest. The camera directs one's perception by

[83] Stephenson and Debrix, *The Cinema as Art*, p. 192.
[84] M. M-P., *Sense*, pp. 57-58.
[85] M. M-P., *Sense*, p. 58.
[86] M. M-P., *Sense*, p. 58.

chosing the figure in the *gestalt* that must constantly contrast with the ground that is my lived-experience. What one sees and hears in the sound film is a "primacy of perception" which the film director has chosen for us. The sound film gives us the actor's *thoughts* in an audio-visual structure of time that has only one meaning : what I perceive, what I live when the expression (sound film) *is* my perceived reality.

When there is a disparity of semiology in the sound film the viewer is immediately aware of it since the perception is in discordance with the way he would express the same situation. In the "dubbed" film one immediately recognizes the discrepancy between what is heard and the speaking of the actors, that is, the divergence between the word and image. The viewer searches for those words that are really being spoken — the ones he perceives in the semiotic comparison of image and "dubbed" word which place the meaning *in the silence* of the image. This phenomenon is immediately apparent in a sound film that suddenly loses its sound or with a silent film and the disharmony of the drunk piano player with the film's action. The result is a complete change in the spectacle on the screen.

The face which was so recently alive thickens and freezes, and looks non-plussed, while the interruption of the sound invades the screen as a quasistupor. For the spectator, the gestures and words are not subsumed under some ideal signification, the speaking takes up the gesture and the gesture the speaking, and they inter-communicate through the medium of the body. Like the sensory aspects of my body they are immediately and mutually symbolical, precisely because my body is a ready-made system of equivalents and transpositions from one sense to another. The senses translate each other without any need of an interpreter, and are mutually comprehensible without the intervention of any idea.[87]

In this analysis Merleau-Ponty has described the breakdown of the sound film *gestalt* that is immediately replaced by the lived-experience of the viewer — just as the viewer would have perceived the film if it were silent in the first place.

A positive disposition of Merleau-Ponty's analysis may clarify the nature of the sound film as a paradigm of the semiotic of the lived-body-experience that is a dialectic of expression and perception. First, the visual image and the sound image operate as a sign in De Saussure's sense of the term. Both images are counterposed to their absence, which is to say sound is reflected against silence and the visual perspective

[87]   M. M-P., *Phenomenology*, pp. 234-235.

is countered by the perspective not shown (or the simultaneous and multiple perspectives in montage). Then there is the dialectic of sound images as opposed to visual images (both combinations of signs). At all these levels of sign combination there is a given perspective that is the limitation one experiences as time. The possibilities of the dialectic pull the viewer into its movement or rhythm and a sense of space is established. Hence, the semiotic that is the sound image and the semiotic of the visual image are joined in an expression which enters as a whole into a semiotic relationship with the viewer's perception, a perception defined by its own semiotic structures of the *lived-experience* of sound and sight images. Thus, when any part of the semiotic of the film breaks down or is absent (a silence) in the film expression, the viewer finds meaning by substituting in his lived-experience.

However, the viewer accomplishes the same completion in a normal viewing of a sound film by constantly filling in the possibilities not specified in the sight-sound semiotic. The perception of the film is undertaken as any normal perception, except that the film automatically chooses the foreground of perception leaving the background as the semiotic to be completed by the viewer. This is true of any given movement whether visual, audible, or both. Thus, the viewer is the creator of space by his perception which links foregrounds to backgrounds. Time is measured in the movement of the foreground (a virtual time) which is the "film time" that predominates over "actual time" in the film experience. This is to say, the sound film creates a total *gestalt* save only a sense of space. And, in this structure the sound film is singularly an expression to be perceived.

The parallels between the role of expression and perception in the sound film are a strong analogy to Merleau-Ponty's method of description of the lived-experience. This is to suggest that the visual image of a film is like the "visual image" that one sees in the lived-experience of others and things. In kind, the awareness of one's psyche by the body in constituting the body-subject is strikingly close to the film semiotic of sound image and visual image as a synoptic presence on the screen. The most important aspect of the sound film, however, is one's ability to perceive the screen action and sound as a foreground *like* the foreground I could see or have already seen in actual life. This phenomenon is like one's ability to know or perceive some of the other person's perspectives because they are like one's own. In these complex relationships, the sound film stands as an audio-visual paradigm of the lived exchange of persons and things that is expression and perception.

The sound film captures part of the semiotic that is the dialectic of immanence and transcendence of the body-subject.

The general direction of the present analysis of the sound film semiotic has been suggested by Peter Wollen in his application of Peirce's semiology to film analysis.[88] Although he asserts that "Peirce's categories [icon, index, symbol] are the foundation for any advance in semiology",[89] he follows the direction of de Saussure in saying that the categories must be seen as "co-present".[90] His conclusion as to the semiology of cinema is forthright : "For the cinematic sign, the language or semiotic of cinema, like the verbal language, comprises not only the indexical and the iconic, but also the symbolic".[91] Yet, "it is the symbolic which is the submerged dimension".[92] Wollen's use of the Peirceian semiotic is obviously a phenomenalism using the subject/object dualism as the basis for its demensions : (1) the icon being the signifier-signified relation by analogy; (2) the index being the existential bond of signifier and signified; and (3) the symbol being the signifier or signified substitute for its opposite number.[93]

The point to be made is that Wollen's semiotic cannot describe the film paradigm accurately unless the three types of signs are used interchangeably and simultaneously. This of course escapes the pitfalls of phenomenalism, yet destroys the very semiotic of Peirce in the process ! Although this objection is left unresolved by Wollen, the possible solution is that of Merleau-Ponty which is the application to film of the semiotic common to perception and expression.[94] This is to suggest that any element of perception or expression can be taken as a sign that relates to other signs in a signification that is the presence or meaning of an immanence and transcendence of the signs *per se*. Recall that the semiotic of Merleau-Ponty is a dialectic within a *gestalt*. Film should be taken as that *gestalt* which captures a segment of lived-experience, a virtual potential in the act of becoming real.

---

[88]   Peter Wollen, *Signs and Meaning in the Cinema*, p. 116ff.
[89]   Wollen, *Signs and Meaning ...*, p. 123.
[90]   Wollen, *Signs and Meaning ...*, p. 141.
[91]   Wollen, *Signs and Meaning ...*, p. 153.
[92]   Wollen, *Signs and Meaning ...*, p. 143.
[93]   Wollen, *Signs and Meaning ...*, pp. 122-123.
[94]   A semiotic phenomenology without any existential implications is presented in Chapter VII, "Naissance d'une raison, Épanouissement d'un Langage", of Edgar Morin's *Le Cinéma ou L'Homme Imaginaire: Essai d'Anthropologie Sociologique* (Paris: Les Éditions de Minuit, 1956), pp. 175-204. Cf., William Earle, "Revolt Against Realism in the Films", *Journal of Aesthetics and Art Criticism* XXVII, no. 2 (Winter, 1968), pp. 146-151.

3. TONGUE

Heidegger has commented that "what is expressed becomes, as it were, something ready-to-hand within-the-world which can be taken up and spoken again".[95] The circularity of expression and perception is assumed as a reversible semiotic of lived-experience. With respect to language (langage), one is aware of this fact in the experience of speaking. This is to say, language is a symbolic code (langage) which is used by man to express his perceptions — this is the act of speaking (parole) which reflects his value orientation toward a situation. This value orientation can become a structure of social direction which is contained, then, in the possible meaning of language (langue).

Speech as a primary form of expression bears a semiotic structure like that of perception and is composed of an analogus form of presence-at-the-world. The previous examination of perception as the lived-body experience suggests its counterpart in expression can be understood in a like manner. This is to suggest that the structure of speaking (parole) is obscured by the sediments of language or a "tongue" (langue), just as "the structure of the perceived world is buried under the sedimentations of later knowledge".[96] The dialectic function of language as an authentic expression and a sedimented record of common values (Weltanschauung) is reflected rather precisely by Heidegger.

Language has the task of making manifest in its work the existent, and of preserving it as such. In it, what is purest and what is most concealed, and likewise what is complex and ordinary, can be expressed in words. Even the essential word, if it is to be understood and so become a possession in common, must make itself ordinary.[97]

The process that Heidegger illustrates is a movement from authentic speaking (signs which mark the lived-value of personal encounter : Lebenswelt) to sedimented speaking or a tongue (signs which specify the social value of interpersonal encounter : Weltanschauung). In both cases the medium or agency of movement is the codified language. Thus Heidegger demonstrates the appropriateness of de Saussure's remark that language is speech less speaking.

de Saussure, whom Merleau-Ponty adds to, maintains that in separating language from speaking there is respectivily a division of the

---

[95] Martin Heidegger, *Being and Time*, p. 266.
[96] M. M-P., *Primacy*, p. 5.
[97] Martin Heidegger, *Existence and Being*, p. 275. See Edmund Husserl, *Ideas*, p. 175.

social from the individual, the essential from the accessory. Here, language is not a function of the speaker, but a product assimilated by the individual with reflection entering only for clarification.[98] The result of this postulation is a further division in speech. First, there is the speech that is purely social and independent of the individual; it is primarily psychological and constitutes a "tongue" (langue). Second, there is speech that is exclusively individual as the act of speaking; it is primarily psychophysical and constitutes "speaking" (parole).[99] This twofold division of the *mention* and *use* functions of language that linguistics makes in the study of language (langage) as an *object* is not the final explanation for Merleau-Ponty.[100]

We speak and we understand speech long before learning from Descartes (or rediscovering for ourselves) that thought is our reality. We learn to meaningfully handle language *(langage)*, in which we install ourselves, long before learning from linguistics the intelligible principles upon which our tongue *(langue)* and every tongue are "based" (supposing that it does teach them).[101]

Merleau-Ponty views the process of speaking as a dialetic of *thought* and *language* not as separate modalities, but as interlocking branches of each other. Thus, there is one modality called "thought" which is in fact "sensible speech". Secondly, there is the modality called "language" which is properly "abortive speech".[102] Expression therefore occurs between "thinking language" and "speaking thought". The difference may be illustrated in this way. Inarticulate thought appears in language that one does not understand — to say that "those are words there" instead of "I see". On the other hand there is accomplished thought in which our own discourse is pure thought for us. The difference is a concern "with an expressive value rather than with logical signification".[103] In short, the semiotic of perception and expression is the same in emphasizing the primacy of meaning in the signs as opposed to the interpretation of convention of sign-signification vectors.

We need therefore to understand how temporal thought links up with itself and brings about its own synthesis [synopsis]. The fact that the normal subject

98   Ferdinand de Saussure, *Course in General Linguistics,* p. 14.
99   De Saussure, *Course,* p. 18.
100   This analysis is carried into great detail by Richard Schmitt, "Maurice Merleau-Ponty", *Review of Metaphysics* XIX, no. 3 (March, 1966), pp. 493-516; XIX, no. 4 (June, 1966), pp. 728-741.
101   M. M-P., *Visible,* p. 12. Cf., p. 153.
102   M. M-P., *Signs,* p. 18.
103   M. M-P., *Phenomenology,* p. 6.

immediately grasps that the eye is to sight as the ear is to hearing shows that the eye and ear are immediately given to him as means of access to one and the same world, and furthermore that one *world* is for him antepredicatively self-evident, so that the equivalence of the 'sense-organs' and their analogy is to be read off from things and *can be lived before being conceived.*[104] (My italics.)

In short, "neither the word nor the meaning of the word is, in fact *constituted* by consciousness".[105] That meaning which is revealed in semiotic formulations "will be *that without which* there would be neither world nor language nor anything at all — it will be the essence".[106]

The unique characteristic of the tongue is that it is a speech "able to settle into a sediment and constitute an intersubjective acquisition"[107] In this operation speech becomes formulated into institutions of grammar and vocabulary that summarize and yet establish value norms. "We live in a world where speech is an *institution.* For all these many commonplace utterances, we possess within ourselves ready-made meanings".[108] This is to say, "we may speak several tongues [langue], but one of them always remains the one in which we live".[109] Merleau-Ponty expresses in these formulations the dialectic of language which is a codification of learned values specified in one set of values by one's action and intention in speaking. The reversible effect is that one's speaking contributes to the linguistic institution by either preserving it or modifying it. The power of speaking is a power of the individual which is manifest in the semiotic structures that make perception and expression necessary to one another's meaning. "Take any word, repeat it a number of times, examine it : it will vanish, and in consequence something will vanish in you. Take more, and continue the operation. By degrees you will reach the culminating point of your sterility, the antipodes of verbal demiurgy".[110]

Cioran is correct in saying that the act of speaking can cause something to disappear in the speaker, yet the act is an intentional movement of subjectivity that is intersubjectivity.[111] What disappears *in me* also appears *for me* (en soi et pour soi).

---

104   M. M-P., *Phenomenology,* p. 129.
105   M. M-P., *Phenomenology,* p. 402.
106   M. M-P., *Visible,* p. 107.
107   M. M-P., *Phenomenology,* p. 190.
108   M. M-P., *Phenomenology,* p. 184.
109   M. M-P., *Phenomenology,* p. 187.
110   E.M. Cioran, *The Temptation to Exist,* p. 190.
111   M. M-P., *Phenomenology,* p. xx.

... just as a man once launched the first word, not knowing whether it will be anything more than a shout, whether it can detach itself from the flow of individual life in which it originates and give the independent existence of an identifiable *meaning* either to the future of that same individual life or to the monads coexisting with it or to the open community of future monads.[112]

Merleau-Ponty's view is that language is first acquired as a tool which is the result of habitual usage. For example, the child in learning to speak comes to learn the system that is speech not by an intellectual operation, but by a "kind of *habituation*".[113] The child comes to know through experience the principles that govern speech, its morphology and its syntax. The result is the "child's assimilation of the linguistic system of his environment in a way that is comparable to the acquisition of any habit whatever : the learning of a structure of conduct".[114] The child comes to learn what is taken for granted in the adult's world of expression, namely, that "in ordinary experience we find a fittingness and a meaningful relationship between the gesture, the smile and the tone of a speaker".[115] In this reciprocal relationship which presents the human body as the outward manifestation of a "style" of being-at-the-world there is authentic or existential communication that adheres to the tongue. The primordial structure inhabits the sedimented structure and thus affirms it or changes it. The sedimented structure is the synopsis of existential structures.

Merleau-Ponty views sedimented speech as a conceptual or verbal "fixation" which is only a first "moment of analysis" but which is indispensable to a reflection of primordial speech.[116] "The procedure of reflection, as an appeal to 'the interior', retreats from the world, consigns the faith in the world to the rank of things said or *statements*".[117] Merleau-Ponty specifies this analysis in an analogy with painting, although the implications for spoken language are markedly clear.

Both Valéry and the surrealist have in view what Francis Ponge was to call the "semantic thickness" and Sartre the "signifying humus" of language, that is the characteristic power that language as gesture, accent, voice, and modulation of existence has to signify in excess of what it signifies part by part according to existing conventions. It is not very far from what Claudel calls the word's

112   M. M-P., *Sense*, p. 19.
113   M. M-P., *Primacy*, p. 99.
114   M. M-P., *Primacy*, p. 99.
115   M. M-P., *Phenomenology*, p. 55.
116   M. M-P., *Visible*, p. 67.
117   M. M-P., *Visible*, p. 50.

"intelligible mouthful". And the same feeling for language is found even in contemporary definitions of prose.[118]

The direction of this analysis from language as spoken to its sedimentation in literature borders on the edge of opening Pandora's box, nonetheless prose offers an excellent illustration of Merleau-Ponty's concept of a tongue.

3.1. *Literature*

In the act of reading one must discover that common intention that binds the words together in a meaning that is recognizable to us. "We are capable of this kind of reading because we carry in our incarnate being the alphabet and the grammar of life, but this does not presuppose an achieved meaning either in us or in it".[119] Rather reading is "the art of grasping a meaning in a style before it has been put into concepts. And finally *the thing itself* is the virtual focal point of these convergent formulations".[120] The critically important notion of "reading" in this sense is that prose is a tongue of actual usage made *virtual*. This is to say, prose adopts actual language as used in ordinary life and presents it (via writing) *as* an actual usage, although it is imaginary (the character in the novel does not actually *speak* as I speak). In short, prose displays an imaginary actuality of language that is a potential meaning for the reader.[121] However, this potential is twofold. If the reader "sees" the prose as simply the general meaning of language as it is sedimented, the literary piece merely presents a tongue (langue) — an imaginary actuality — that in fact corresponds to a tongue as one experiences it in the lived, or actual, experience of language (langue). On the other hand, the prose tongue as an imaginary actuality may correspond to one's personal lived-experience that one recognizes *as* sedimented in the prose expression. This is to suggest the prose tongue can be a *virtual usage* of the primordial or existential language (parole) experience. Such an achievement by a writer is what Barthes calls "writing degree zero".[122] The distinction being drawn by Merleau-

---

[118]   M. M-P., *Signs,* p. 234.

[119]   M. M-P., *Praise,* p. 23. See Hiram Caton, "Speech and Writing as Artifacts", *Philosophy and Rhetoric* II, no. 1 (Winter, 1969), pp. 19-36.

[120]   M. M-P., *Praise,* p. 19.

[121]   This distinction is what Aristotle referred to as poetic style. For a detailed analysis, see my "Two Species of Style in Aristotle", *Dialogue* (Journal of Phi Sigma Tau) X, no. 1 (May, 1968), pp. 1-5.

[122]   Roland Barthes, *Writing Degree Zero,* trans. A. Lavers and C. Smith (London:

Ponty between a tongue (as written) which remains sedimented as opposed to a tongue that reflects the existential is illustrated in the difference between a "news item" and a "novel". The news item being a virtual, existential expression and the novel being an "actualized" sediment of language.

Yet there is more and less in the novel than there is in true little incidents [of news items]. It foreshadows momentary speech and gesture, and comments on them. The author lends himself to the character, makes us enter his inner monologue. The novel gives the context. The news item on the contrary strikes us because it is a life's invasion of those who were unaware of it. The news item call things by their name; the novel names them only through what the characters perceive.[123]

This is to say, the news item is a gesture while the novel is a message, the one is respectively transcendent and the other immanent.[124]

All great prose is also a re-creation of the signifying instrument, henceforth manipulated according to a new syntax. Prosaic writing, on the other hand, limits itself to using, through accepted signs, the meanings already accepted in a given culture. Great prose is the art of capturing a meaning which until then had never been objectified and of rendering it accessible to everyone who speaks the same language. When a writer is no longer capable of thus founding a new universality and of taking the risk of communicating, he has outlived his time.[125]

Thus, Merleau-Ponty sees in prose an objectified account of the spoken language as sedimented — a tongue. A tongue is the use of an instrument (langage) to specify those cultural values that individuals share in their common, lived-experiences. This is the world of ordinary language, the sediments of multifarious verbal encounters that the individual finds are a convergence of his experience and the perception of others. This is the phenomenon of the news item — another human being has lived what "I" avoid living (e.g., death). The tongue which appears in the prose of the novel differs from this world of ordinary language only in that it is a virtual manifestation. It is a sediment that "I" live or do not live only if the character's perception is *my* perception, his expression my expression. The prose tongue is an object that one *can* live.

Jonathan Cape, Ltd., 1967), pp. 82-83, 93.
[123] M. M-P., *Signs,* p. 313. See *Themes,* pp. 12-18.
[124] M. M-P., *Signs,* p. 63.
[125] M. M-P., *Primacy,* p. 9.

3.2. *Myth*

The myth represents another modality of the "tongue" just as literature is an instrument for expressing cultural values. Following the direction of Merleau-Ponty's distinction between the tongue as lived-experience and as virtual experience, Ihde has suggested the myth has two levels : the rational and the myth *per se*. This is to say, the myth has a "literal significance" or rational structure that tends to deal with objective phenomena and it has an "imaginative significance" which is the symbolic (mythos) level.[126] The consequence of this bifurcation is to assign to myth a *"gestalt-function"* for the imagination in which the symbolic function is primary.[127]

Merleau-Ponty suggests that the myth functions as does a tongue in that "the myth holds the essence *within* the appearance; the mythical phenomenon is not a representation, but a genuine presence".[128]

Since mythical consciousness has not yet arrived at the notion of a thing or of objective truth, how can it undertake a critical examination of that which it thinks it experiences; where can it find a fixed point at which to stop and become aware of itself as pure consciousness, and perceive, beyond its phantasms, the real world?[129]

This is to say that a myth like the phantasms of dreaming, one's idle thoughts, or even poetic imagery does not fix its meaning as a sign to a signification. Such phenomena "really contain their meaning, which is not a notional meaning, but a direction of our existence".[130] For example, primitive peoples whose world is myth bound do not separate out the virtual space from the lived space, the essential from the existential. Thus, dreams come to count for as much as actual perception.[131] The function of myth as a tongue (langue) is clarified by Merleau-Ponty in the following manner.

Primitive man lives his myths against a sufficiently articulate perceptual background for the activities of daily life, fishing, hunting and dealings with civilized people, to be possible. The myth itself, however diffuse, has an identifiable significance for primitive man, simply because it does form a world, that is, a whole in which each element has meaningful relations with the rest. It is

---

[126]   Don Ihde, "Rationality and Myth", *Journal of Thought* II, no. 1 (January, 1967), p. 12.
[127]   *Ibid.,* pp. 14-15.
[128]   M. M-P., *Phenomenology*, p. 290.
[129]   M. M-P., *Phenomenology*, p. 290.
[130]   M. M-P., *Phenomenology*, p. 285.
[131]   M. M-P., *Phenomenology*, p. 285.

true that mythical consciousness is not a consciousness of any thing. This is to say that subjectively it is a flux, that it does not become static and thus does not know itself. Objectively, it does not posit before itself terms definable as a certain number of properties, which can be isolated from one another and which are in fact interlinked.[132]

Merleau-Ponty's view is fairly well illustrated in Claude Lévi-Strauss's analysis of myth in relation to language, or more specifically speech.[133] This is to say, the tongue (langue) is a structural entity of reversible time. The tongue is speech sedimented into a form capable of reference to the past, present, or future. In short, the structure allows for a sign-signification relationship. Now, the tongue is distinguished from speaking (parole) in that speaking is not structural, but statistical, indicating its presence in non-reversible time. Speaking specifies phenomena in a given time as given occurrences. As Merleau-Ponty specifies, speaking is its own sign, the sign is its own signification.

A specific determination of the myth suggests, in consequence, that speaking is sedimented into a tongue which is to say individual phenomena in certain times and places signify a common structure. The common structure is viewed as part of the past, applicable to events of the present, and likely to occur in the future. Over a period of time the structure (tongue) comes to be *timeless*. The signification of the sign is dropped. The meaning of the myth becomes a continuous process of occurrence *as probability,* while the structure of the myth is discontinuous. The myth becomes a *symbolic* construction.[134]

As the faithful, in the Dionysian mysteries, invoke the god by miming scenes from his life, I call up the visitation of sleep by imitating the breathing and posture of the sleeper. The god is actually there when the faithful can no longer distinguish themselves from the part they are playing, when their body and their consciousness cease to bring in, as an obstacle, their particular opacity, and when they are totally fused in the myth.[135]

Merleau-Ponty is suggesting that the myth is a "shrinking in the space directly experienced, a rooting of things in our body, the overwhelming proximity of the object, the oneness of man and the world...".[136] Such experience is repressed in one's everyday experiences or artificially eliminated by objective thought. By reflection one comes to know that

---

[132]   M. M-P., *Phenomenology,* p. 292.
[133]   Claude Lévi-Strauss, *Structural Anthropology,* pp. 205-206, 226.
[134]   M. M-P., *Visible,* pp. 187-188. Cf., p. 182.
[135]   M. M-P., *Phenomenology,* p. 163.
[136]   M. M-P., *Phenomenology,* p. 291.

the virtual meaning of the myth, its structure, is a possible actuality. Yet, the actuality is never achieved because the very structure of the myth remains symbolic, detached from the rationality that links sign to signification. Myth is the use of a tongue (langue) sedimented from a forgotten "speaking". The use of the myth in literature is a confirmation that given perspectives can suggest a meaning for the myth, although such a meaning neither explains the myth (by making it objective) nor totally obscures the myth's intent (by making it subjective).

There is little doubt that an understanding of myth requires a phenomenology of language and speaking that can specify the polarity and condensation of speaking and the spoken.[137]

To want to understand myth as a proposition, in terms of what it says, is to apply our own grammar and vocabulary to a foreign language. Then the whole myth has to be decoded without our even being able to postulate, as cryptographers do, that the code we are looking for has the same structure as ours. Leaving aside what myth tells us at first sight, which would tend to divert us from its true meaning, let us study its inner articulation, taking episodes only insofar as they have what Saussure calls a diacritical value and produce such and such a recurrent relation or contrast.[138]

Merleau-Ponty points to the necessity of a base semiology or structure of meaning that allows one to see the divergence and convergence of perception and expression in language. This concern with meaning, particularly with the semiotic of myth, is generally denominated *hermeneutic* or a theory of interpretation. Because of the connotation applied to myth and theological exegesis, hermeneutic is rarely conceived in terms of semiology. However, hermeneutic is precisely what is meant by our own term (in Chapter II) a "semiotic semiology" or a theory of signs which will allow an interpretation of all modalities of being and becoming. In short, the myth points out Merleau-Ponty's continuing interest in the application of his hermeneutic which is an existential, phenomenological semiology. The myth embodies the idea of tongue (langue) in its symbolic modality, a modality that displays the immediate link between language (langage) and tongue as the structure of lived-experience — sedimented values.[139]

---

[137] Richard E. Palmer, *Hermeneutics: Interpretation Theory in Schleiermacher, Dilthey, Heidegger, and Gadamer* (Evanston, Ill.: Northwestern University Press, 1969), p. 70. Cf., Don Ihde, "From Phenomenology to Hermeneutic", *Journal of Existentialism* VIII (Winter, 1967-68), pp. 111-132, esp. 129.
[138] M. M-P., *Signs*, p. 120-121.
[139] M. M-P., *Sense*, p. 25.

Hermeneutic properly attempts to find the meaning of the tongue in its various forms. This concern is manifest in Merleau-Ponty's work in his study of "speaking" as the existential source of the lived-body-presence. Speaking represents the act of expression that is the joint summation and propagation of perception. The act of speech in its lived modality of "speaking" is a semiotic of intentionality that is fundamental to existential phenomenology. Such a semiotic is the source of knowing the structures of the body-subject in its dialectical encounters with itself, others, and things.

4. SPEAKING

Merleau-Ponty's semiology is a system of signs in which expression and perception are linked by the agency of speaking. This is to say, "there is no experience without speaking, as the purely lived-through has no part in the speaking life of man. The fact remains, however, that "the primary meaning of speaking is to be found in that text of experience which is trying to communicate".[140] The nature of the speaking subject within the dialectic of perception and expression who experiences language (langage) in its existential mode as speaking (parole) and its essential becoming as tongue (langue) is roughly phrased by Merleau-Ponty this way :

We know simply that, if it is to remain dialectical, speech can no longer be statement, *Satz*, it must be thinking speech, without reference to a *Sachverhalt*, speaking *(parole)* and not language *(langage)* (and in fact it is indeed the speaking, not the language [*la langue*] that aims at the other as a behavior, not as a "psychism", that responds to the other before he would have been understood as "psychism", in a confrontation that repels or accepts his utterances as utterances, as events —— It is indeed speaking that constitutes, *in front of* myself as a signification and a subject of signification, a milieu of communication, an intersubjective diacritical system which is the spoken tongue [*la langue*] in the present, not a "human universe", an objective spirit) —— The problem is to restore this, in the present and in the past, the *Lebenswelt* history, to restore the very presence of a culture. The failure of the dialectic as thesis or "dialectical philosophy" is the discovery of this intersubjectivity which is not perspectival but vertical, which is, extended into the past, existential eternity, savage mind *(esprit sauvage)*.[141]

---

140   M. M-P., *Phenomenology*, p. 337. See *Themes*, pp. 117-121.
141   M. M-P., *Visible*, p. 175. Cf., Claude Lévi-Strauss, *The Savage Mind*, anon. trans. (Chicago: University of Chicago Press, 1966). First published in 1962 as *La*

Although the form of these comments betray their status as working notes, they are a concise statement of Merleau-Ponty's phenomenology of speaking. Speaking emerges as a "verbal gesticulation" which suggests a consciousness of ... which is not present to everyone and thus must be communicated. From the cultural background captured in the tongue available meanings of former expressions are called forth in speaking to create a common world. It is the lived-experience "to which the words being actually uttered in their novelty refer as does the gesture to the perceptible world".[142]

Since the body-subject cannot have direct access to the psyche of another, it must be realized indirectly in its bodily experience. In the physical encounter, one also realizes the psychic meeting of self and Other. "I see you in flesh and bone; you are there".[143] Nonetheless what the Other is thinking is not laid bare to objectivity, "I can suppose it, guess at it from your facial expression, your gestures, and your words — in short from a series of bodily appearances of which I am only the witness".[144] The lesson of this experience in which one encounters the speaking of the Other as a tongue is that the relation of self to speech must be as self to body. The semiotic of speaking is the semiotic of perceiving. The reflexivity that is the body-subject of speaking-listening is the "I" as lived. In the knowledge of the self (as lived-body) one comes to realize that subjectivity *that is* intersubjectivity.[145] This existential knowledge is the product of a distinction that Merleau-Ponty makes in his semiology of speech. This is to say, speech has two modalities which have previously been cited in this study as tongue and speaking (la langue et la parole). The tongue is *empirical speech* and speaking is *existential* or *authentic speech*. The semiotic is

... a distinction between empirical speaking — the word as a phenomenon of sound, the fact that a certain word is uttered at a certain moment by a certain

---

Pensée sauvage. See also, C. Lévi-Strauss, *The Scope of Anthropology,* trans. Sherry O. and Robert A. Paul (London: Jonathan Cape, 1967), pp. 28-30, 43-44. First published in 1960 as *Leçon inaugurale.* And Georges Charbonnier, *Conversations with Claude Lévi-Strauss,* trans. John and Doreen Weightman (London: Jonathan Cape, 1969), pp. 101-132, 146-155. First published in 1961 as *Entretiens avec Claude Lévi-Strauss.*

[142]   M. M-P., *Phenomenology,* p. 186.
[143]   M. M-P., *Primacy,* p. 114.
[144]   M. M-P., *Primacy,* p. 114.
[145]   M. M-P., *Visible,* p. 246. "The phenomenology of speech is among all others best suited to reveal this order to us." *Signs,* p. 97.

person, which may happen independently of thought — and transcendental or authentic speaking, that by which an idea begins to exist.[146]

The difference between "secondary speech" (tongue) and "originating speech" (speaking) reflects the dialectic in which all words which have become mere signs for a univocal thought are derived from originating words. The speaker recalls the "richness" that empirical speech draws from its relation to the originating speech which once fulfilled the primordial function of expression.[147] In semiotic terms, existential speaking is the use of authentic language — those signs whose signification is self-possessed. The sign is its own signification, its own meaning. The signs of existential speaking are primordial ideas, which is to say the *presence* of speaking-thought or thinking-speech. On the other hand, empirical speaking is the "opportune recollection of a pre-established sign".[148]

Critical to the understanding of the subtle distinction between existential and empirical speaking is the notion of *gestalt* as applied to the dialectic of semiotic elements. This is to say, immanence and transcendence account for the meaning of signs in any given usage. Within existential speaking there is the articulation of primordial signs whose meaning is dialectic presence of those signs expressing a lived-intentionality as the breaking of silence (also a sign). The existential speaking is the intentional transcendence of an immanent silence which has meaning as the intentional object chosen in the spontaneity of the lived-experience. The alternative intentional object is the silence which is itself an intentional transcendence (silent speaking) of an immanently possible speech which has the meaning of an intentional object. The reversibility of the semiotic of existential speaking is the *gestalt* of signs which dialectically presume each other in their own presence. Just as the body is experienced as the lived-body of the subject and the subject is experienced as the lived-subject of the body, silence and existential speaking are reversibly lived as a *synoptic presence*.

The semiotic status of empirical speaking can be explained in a fashion similar to existential speaking. Since empirical speech is a pre-established sign recalled, the pre-established sign in conjunction with silence (also a sign) forms a dialectic *gestalt*. Either sign can be the transcendent element in contradistinction to the immanent element and

---

[146]   M. M-P., *Phenomenology*, p. 390.
[147]   M. M-P., *Phenomenology*, p. 389.
[148]   M. M-P., *Signs*, p. 44.

vice versa. However, the fact that some of the signs are already known and are thus pre-established informs one that empirical speaking is not primordial. Empirical speech does not present an intentionality which specifies an existential object, rather empirical speech is geared to essences. Empirical speech is of the descriptive or instrumental domain of communication, while existential speech is an originating or intentional creation of meaning.[149] In short, empirical speech is a tongue (langue).

4.1. *The Speaking Subject*

"The phenomenologist tries to recover an awareness of what a speaking subject really is. He is certainly not in the attitude of a learned observer who is confronting something external to him".[150] Merleau-Ponty speculates that the study of the speaking subject requires a determination of existential speaking before any empirical study can begin.

The eidetic of language should therefore be established at the very beginning. The empirical study of language should come afterward, directing itself to the relevant facts, clarifying them, and then reconstructing them in the light of the essences already determined.[151]

To reflect on language as speaking is to recover the language experience that is anterior to the objectivizing of language and certainly anterior to the scientific observation of it. The lived-experience of the speaking subject who gestures, writes, speaks, and who is bodily a presence-at-the-world, passes beyond language (langue) only by exercising it and taking it over by inhabiting it (parole).

It might be said, restating a celebrated distinction, that *languages* [langages] or constituted systems of vocabulary and syntax, empirically existing 'means of expression', are both the repository and sedimentation of acts of *speaking*, in which unformulated meaning not only finds the means of being conveyed outwardly, but moreover acquires existence for itself, and is genuinely created as meaning. Or again one might draw a distinction between the *speaking word* [parole parlante] and the *spoken word* [parole parlée]. The former is the one

---

[149]   The pragmatic application of this speech duality with an emphasis on the existential aspects is generally presented in Charles T. Brown and Charles Van Riper, *Speech and Man* (Englewood Cliff, New Jersey: Prentice-Hall, Inc., 1966), Chapter III, pp. 35-48; and in Gordon Wiseman and Larry Barker, *Speech — Interpersonal Communication* (San Francisco: Chandler Publishing Co. ,1967), Chapter III, pp. 38-62.

[150]   M. M-P., *Primacy*, p. 80. See *Themes*, pp. 19-26.

[151]   M. M-P., *Themes*, p. 79.

in which the significant intention is at the stage of coming into being. Here existence is polarized into a certain 'meaning' which cannot be defined in terms of any natural object. It is somewhere at a point beyond being that it aims to catch up with itself again, and that is why it creates speech as an empirical support for its own not-being. Speaking is the surplus of our existence over natural being.[152]

The speaking subject is the exercise of existential speaking (parole parlante) gives rise to new forms of grammar and syntax which emerge on the foundation of old linguistic structure (parole parlée) or in opposition to those foundations. In any case, the speaking is organized according to an expressive intention which constitutes a new system or allows the positing of a new *gestalt*. "As the discriminant in a new type of thought and a new symbolism, it sets up for itself a field of application which is incommensurable with its origins and can be understood only from within".[153] Merleau-Ponty contends that the speaking subject at the level of existential speaking is that subjectivity (lived-body) which is *primordial communication* or intersubjectivity in the intentional, lived presence-at-the-world (the inseparable synopsis of expression-perception).

It is thus necessary that, in the perception of another, I find myself in relation with another 'myself', who is, in principle, open to the same truths as I am, in relation to the same being that I am. And this perception is realized. From the depths of my subjectivity I see another subjectivity invested with equal rights appear, because the behavior of the other takes place within my perceptual field. *I understand this behavior, the words of another.* I espouse his thought because this other, born in the midst of my phenomena, appropriates them and treats them in accord with typical behaviors which I myself have experienced. Just as my body, as the system of all my holds on the world, founds the unity of the objects which I perceive, in the same way the body of the other — as bearer of symbolic behaviors and of the behavior of true reality — tears itself away from being one of my phenomena, offers me the task of a *true communication*, and confers on my objects the new dimension of *intersubjective being* or, in other words, of objectivity.[154] (My italics.)

In this description of the perception-expression synopsis which is existential speaking, Merleau-Ponty illustrates the power of speaking as the application of his phenomenological method to reduce essences to existence. The movement from empirical speaking back to exis-

---

[152] M. M-P., *Phenomenology*, pp. 196-197. This critically important and definitive passage occurs in the French edition at page 229.
[153] M. M-P., *Signs*, p. 130.
[154] M. M-P., *Primacy*, pp. 17-18.

tential speaking is first a description of speech as reduced to its essential presence in the *gestalt,* i.e. a tongue or empirical speech. By reflection one can determine the intentionality present in the speaking which is speaking at the existential level, that speech that sedimented into the tongue. The existential speech is determined to be that modality of expression that constitutes its own *gestalt,* the chiasm that is known to perception only in its mirror presence as expression.[155] In the presence of lived perception and expression the body-subject becomes an inherence in the world, in history, and in language. "Philosophy turns towards the anonymous symbolic activity from which we emerge, and towards the personal discourse which develops in us, and which, indeed, we are".[156]

As the world is behind my body, the operative essence is behind the operative speech also, the speech that possesses the signification less than it is possessed by it, that does not speak *of it,* but speaks *it,* or speaks *according to it,* or lets it speak and be spoken within me, breaks through my present.[157]

Merleau-Ponty explains the dialectic of perception and expression in the lived-body experience in the parallel notion that the body expresses existence at every moment just as a word expresses thought. In specific terms of the speaking subject's language, primordial communication is a process of signification in which the sign does not exist apart from the expression. The signification is an incarnate sign in the same manner that the body is an incarnate existence. For example, a specification of speech in which the signification is made to exist apart from the sign results in an impression of indigence which is empirical speech sedimented from the existential expression. This phenomena occurs in an audio-recording of a conversation.

The presence of those who were speaking, the gestures, the physiognomies, and the feeling of an event which is coming up and of a continuous improvisation, all are lacking in the recording. Henceforth the conversation no longer exists; it *is,* flattened out in the unique dimension of sound and all the more deceptive because this wholly auditory medium is that of a text read.[158]

In point of fact, Merleau-Ponty is suggesting that the separation of a *gestalt* into analytic elements destroys the expression present leaving

---

155   M. M-P., *Phenomenology,* p. 194.
156   M. M-P., *Praise,* pp. 57-58.
157   M. M-P., *Visible,* p. 118. Cf., Helmuth Plessner, "On Human Communications", in *Phenomenology: Pure and Applied,* ed. Erwin W. Strauss, (Pittsburgh: Duquesne University Press, 1964), pp. 63-74, esp. 67-68.
158   M. M-P., *Signs,* p. 57.

only an object to be perceived. The existential speaking present becomes a sediment. It is in this sense that Merleau-Ponty speaks of the "world of silence, the perceived word" which is "an order where there are non-language significations".[159]

The task of the philosopher, Merleau-Ponty suggests, is to realize that man is situated in language that "he *is* speaking" and that phenomenological reduction cannot be limited to the conditions without which there would be no language.[160] In the speaking subject phenomenology must concern itself with the subject whose existential speaking is a comprehension of the on-coming future or "field of presence" of the lived-experience. Speaking should be the realization by the speaking subject of his lived-world (Lebenswelt) as a *gestalt* in transcendent relation to a value-world (Weltanschauung) that is immanent, and which together are an ever intentional presence-at-the-world (être-au-monde).

4.2. *Speech : A Definition*

The lived-body experience allows one to perceive the *gestalt* of phenomena which is a structure with the semiotic force of an "existential signification".[161] This "immanent meaning" is the product of a "lived through logic" of signs present to the perceiving body-subject.[162] For example, in the phenomena of love one is involved in an authentic or inauthentic expression and perception. The determination of authenticity or total commitment of the whole person in this situation requires a separation between experience and lived-experience. The person who can designate and circumscribe the limits of his love is dealing on the level of empirical experience. In contrast, one who perceives an authentic and lived-experience finds it nameless; it is a way in which he establishes his relations with the world; "it is an existential signification".[163] In the lived act of a man who gives his lover a bouquet of flowers, the "love *is* in the flowers" just as it is in the caress.[164] There is no signification in the sign as an effect generated by a cause; the sign *is* its own signification *per se*. In short, "there is, of course, every reason to distinguish between an authentic speech which formulates for the

159 M. M-P., *Visible*, p. 171.
160 M. M-P., *Signs*, pp. 104-105.
161 M. M-P., *Phenomenology*, p. xix.
162 M. M-P., *Phenomenology*, p. 49.
163 M. M-P., *Phenomenology*, p. 381.
164 M. M-P., *Phenomenology*, p. 321.

first time, and secondary expression, a speaking about speech, which constitutes the empirical language of ordinary usage. Only the first is identical with thought".[165]

The power of the speaking subject in the medium of oral communication is not representation in which words disclose thoughts. "The orator does not think before speaking, nor even while speaking; his speaking is his thought. In the same way the listener does not form concepts on the basis of signs"[166] This is to say, the speaker's thought is empty while he is speaking and the listener is not conscious of thought marginal to the oral communication. The articulated words fully occupy the mind of speaker and listener and "we feel the necessity of speech. Although we are unable to predict its course, we are possessed by it". Therefore, "the end of the speech or text will be the lifting of a spell. It is at this stage that thoughts on the speech or text will be able to arise".[167]

In the context of all that has been said thus far, Merleau-Ponty offers the following definition of speech.

Speech, as distinguished from language, is that moment when the significative intention (still silent and wholly act) proves itself capable of incorporating itself into my culture and the culture of others — of shaping me and others by transforming the meaning of cultural instruments. It becomes "available" in turn because in retrospect it gives us the illusion that it was contained in the already available significations, whereas by a sort of *ruse* it espoused them only in order to infuse them with a new life.[168]

This definition of speech assumes implicitly a theory of semiotic in which the speaking subject is capable of two modalities of communication. First, the speaker uses language as an immanent meaning within transcendent silence which is existential speaking. It is the direct presentation of signs — which can be perceived as such. Or secondly, the speaker uses language as a transcendent meaning within immanent language which is empirical speaking. It is the direct presentation of significations which reflect signs — pre-established in existential speech. In other words, existential speaking is primordial communication (parole parlante) which uses language (langage) as unqualified signs. Empirical speaking is secondary communication (parole parlée) which

[165] M. M-P., *Phenomenology*, p. 178n. See *Signs*, p. 80.
[166] M. M-P., *Phenomenology*, p. 180.
[167] M. M-P., *Phenomenology*, p. 180.
[168] M. M-P., *Signs*, p. 92.

uses language (langage) as a qualified sign (pre-established) which is signification or tongue (langue).

Within this semiotic it is quite possible that empirical speech *appears to hide* the existential speaking so that when the intentionality of the existential speech is manifest, it seems to be like a "ruse" of language. This is frequently the case when silence (as a sign) is an act in a *gestalt* (the other signs) that signifies meaning in opposition to speaking that is secondary or empirical. However, it is more often the situation in which speech appears to be secondary because the signs are familiar, but the combination of these signs in the present *gestalt* is actually a unique, primordial structure that in fact signifies *per se*. What appears to be signification is sign.

I understand or think I understand the words and forms of French; I have a certain experience of the literary and philosophical modes of expression offered me by the given culture. I express when, utilizing all these already speaking instruments, I make them say something they have never said. We begin reading a philosopher giving the words he makes use of their "common" meaning; and little by little, through what is at first an imperceptible reversal, his speech comes to dominate his language, and it is his use of words which ends up assigning them a new and characteristic signification. At this moment he has made himself understood and his signification has come to dwell in me. We say that a thought is expressed when the converging words intending it are numerous and eloquent enough to designate it unequivocally for me, its author, or for others, and in such a manner that we all have the experience of its presence in the flesh in speech.[169]

In short, Merleau-Ponty maintains that in thought made manifest as speech, both empirical and existential, "I am installed on a pyramid of time which has been me. I take up a field and invent myself (but not without my temporal equipment), just as I move about in the world (but not without the unknown mass of my body)".[170]

It is the very process of putting thoughts into spoken words and spoken words into thought that constitute "transformations of private into public" by making events into meditations that are an "echo coming from everywhere [which] makes it such that in speaking to others we also speak to ourselves, and speak of what exists".[171] At the existential level, speaking becomes synonymous with thought as is illustrated in the experience of poetic language. The very words of poetry are their meaning as signs which serve to communicate a lived-

---

169   M. M-P., *Signs*, p. 91. See *Visible*, p. 129.
170   M. M-P., *Signs*, pp. 14-15. See *Visible*, p. 101; *Structure*, p. 210.
171   M. M-P., *Signs*, p. 20.

experience. One cannot sum up the poems he reads, rather to regain the meaning the poems must be re-read. For, in poetic language the idea is not produced by the words as a result of empirical language (lexical significations) which reflect ordinary usage, but as a result of more "carnal relations of meaning, the halos of signification words owe to their history and uses — as a result, in short, of the life that words lead within us, a life which from time to time ends up in those meaning-laden accidents, the great books".[172]

In the last analysis, the definition of speech must be understood as that reversible semiology of perception and expression that is ever present in the lived-body experience of existential communication which sediments into the values which mean respectively, life and history.

The theory of signs, as developed in linguistics, perhaps implies a conception of historical meaning which gets beyond the opposition of *things* versus *consciousness*. Living language is precisely that togetherness of thinking and thing which causes difficulty. In the act of speaking, the subject, in his tone and in his style, bears witness to his autonomy, since nothing is more proper to him, and yet as the same moment, and without contradiction, he is turned towards the linguistic community and is dependent on his language. The will to speak is one and the same as the will to be understood.

The constant need for communication leads us to invent and to accept a new usage which is not deliberate and yet which is systematic. The contingent fact, taken over by the will to expression, becomes a new means of expression which takes its place, and has a lasting sense in the history of this language. In such cases, there is a rationality in the contingent, a lived logic, a self-constitution of which we have definite need in trying to understand the union of contingency and meaning in history, and Saussure, the modern linguist, could have sketched a new philosophy of history.[173]

These remarks presented to the Collège de France on January 15, 1953 were intended as a prognosis of problems to be solved in the years to come. Merleau-Ponty achieved that end in determining the very definition of speech that united his own theories of perception and expression into a semiotic of being and knowing. Although Merleau-Ponty relies on the basic structuralist schema of the De Saussure semiology, his theory of existential speaking is a major progression beyond De Saussure by an incorporation of Husserl[174] and an interpretation of the Heideggerian metaphysics.[175] Yet, Merleau-Ponty's postulation of

172   M. M-P., *Signs*, p. 234.
173   M. M-P., *Praise*, pp. 54-55. See *Signs*, pp. 87-88.
174   Edmund Husserl, *Ideas*, pp. 308-308ff., 324ff.
175   Martin Heidegger, *Being and Time*, pp. 196-197, 199, 211-212.

parole parlante and *parole parlée* as an *être-au-monde* is an original contribution beyond the phenomenology of speaking. The force of this philosophy is made explicit in the theme that Merleau-Ponty found most influential in the later Husserl, that is, that subjectivity is inter-subjectivity.[176] Or, Merleau-Ponty conceives it as the existential speaking that is dialogue as a maieutic conversation [entretien].

4.3. *Dialogue As Maieutic*

By dialogue Merleau-Ponty does not mean an empirical speech that reflects the common values of men; the dialogue is not a synonym for a tongue. Dialogue, then, is not that common experience called a *"collective consciousness* but intersubjectivity, a living relationship and tension among individuals".[177] This is to say, a person's view of social or intersubjective relations is meaningful only by analogy or contrast with those that he has lived. There is the necessity of submitting those lived-experiences of the individual to an "imaginary variation".[178] Yet, the effect is that the lived-experience takes on a new meaning as a result of this reflection. The semiotic principle of synopsis emerges to make meaning the product of the signs in conjunction, rather than in isolation.

What "precedes" intersubjective life cannot be numerically distinguished from it, precisely because at this level there is neither individuation nor numerical distinction. The constitution of the others does not come after that of the body; others and my body are born together from the original ecstasy. The corpo-reality to which the primordial thing belongs is more corporeality in general; as the child's egocentricity, the "solipsist layer" is both transitivity and con-fusion of the self and other.[179]

Merleau-Ponty is here describing the dialectic movement of semiology whether it be manifest in perception or in expression. In fact, the semiotic dialectic is a maieutic because perception is never complete without expression and expression always relies on perception. What is perceived becomes the object of expression and the very act of expressing becomes an object of perception. This phenomenon is dem-onstrated each time one speaks or listens — to oneself or to others — inasmuch as one's perception is a constant monitoring of his expression.

---

176   Edmund Husserl, *The Paris Lectures*, p. 35.
177   M. M-P., *Sense*, p. 90.
178   M. M-P., *Signs*, p. 100.
179   M. M-P., *Signs*, p. 174.

In turn, one's expression is a recurring scrutiny of perception. Merleau-Ponty observes that the principle involved in this phenomenon of reversibility that is manifest in one semiotic is a discovery of Hegel.[180]

The dialectic is, Hegel said approximately, *a movement which itself creates its course and returns to itself* — and thus a movement which has no other guide but its own initiative and which nevertheless does not escape outside itself but cuts across itself again and confirms itself at long intervals.

So the Hegelian dialectic is what we call by another name the phenomenon of expression, which gathers itself up and launches itself again through the mystery of rationality.[181]

Expression thus defined is a specification that the individual in the act of speaking brings about the junction of the personal and the universal. This is to say, one does not choose between the *pour soi* and the *pour autri* or between thought according to myself and thought by others, but that at "the moment of expression the other to whom I address myself and I who express myself are incontestably linked together".[182] In this context, the perceiving individual no longer thinks his ideas when he speaks them. "A discussion is not an exchange or a confrontation of ideas...".[183] Rather, one speaks and the others who hear him are immediately marked out by their divergencies in the relation they have to his words and it is the speaker who determines the nature of this divergence. The lived-experience and ideas become reversible in the commitment of the speaker within the lived *gestalt*. The speaking person is guided by his own speaking and the responses he receives from others led by his initial thought which is no longer the sole possession of his subjectivity — it is intersubjective.

Merleau-Ponty specifies the spoken dialogue as a maieutic by indicating that the basic model of subjectivity as an intersubjectivity must be a system of "self-others-world" in which self and other together constitute a world, yet where the world is more than the sum of self and other.[184] At the level of maieutic the transcendental subject emerges precisely because of the body-subjectivity that is a lived-experience in which intentionality marks out its object in the other, as in itself. "Historical meaning is immanent in the inter-human event, and is as

---

[180] Merleau-Ponty is thinking of the discussion that occurs in G.W.F. Hegel, *The Phenomenology of Mind*, p. 122.

[181] M. M-P., *Signs*, p. 73. Cf. G.W.F. Hegel, *The Phenomenology of Mind*, pp. 142, 183, 338-340.

[182] M. M-P., *Signs*, p. 73.

[183] M. M-P., *Visible*, p. 119.

[184] M. M-P., *Phenomenology*, p. 60.

fragile as this event. But precisely because of this, the event takes on the value of a genesis of reason".[185] This is to say, the intersubjective dialectic "accedes to things themselves, for these perspectives articulated in a way which makes access to inter-individual significations possible; they 'present' a world".[186] Merleau-Ponty illustrates this point in the use of the semiotic paradigm, the gesture.

The sense of the gestures is not given, but understood, that is, seized upon by an act on the spectator's part. The whole difficulty is to conceive this art clearly without confusing it with a cognitive operation. The communication or comprehension of gestures comes about through the reciprocity of my intentions and the gestures of others, of my gestures and intentions discernible in the conduct of other people. It is as if the other person's intention inhabited my body and mine his. The gesture which I witness outlines an intentional object. This object is genuinely present and fully comprehended when the powers of my body adjust themselves to it and overlap it. The gesture presents itself to me as a question, bringing certain perceptible bits of the world to my notice, and inviting my concurrence in them. Communication is achieved when my conduct identifies this path with its own. There is mutual confirmation between myself and others.[187]

In the maieutic every thought and event in the lived-experience is communicated and shared, every intention is immediately interpreted and made into the felt "we-ness" of intercorporeality.[188] Indeed, the very essence of a society is to be found in its interpersonal relations. Just as the person in the lived-body experience is an expression of mental and moral structures displayed at the beckoning of the slightest reflex, the social dialogue that is maieutic expresses "the total subject's fundamental way of being in the world".[189] The existential force of subjectivity as the lived-body is the creation of the *body-subject* which is intersubjectivity in all its intentional elements.

4.4. *Film : Maieutic Icon*

Merleau-Ponty singles out dialogue in film as an icon or faithful model which copies lived-maieutic. The film offers the union or bond of image

---

[185]   M. M-P., *Primacy*, p. 51.
[186]   M. M-P., *Structure*, p. 219. See *Visible*, p. 13.
[187]   M. M-P., *Phenomenology*, p. 185. See James L. Bemis and Gerald M. Phillips, "A Phenomenological Approach to Communication Theory", *Speech Teacher* XIII (November, 1964), pp. 262-269. Cf., George A. Schrader, "Inter-Personal Communication", *Review of Existential Psychology and Psychiatry* II, no. 1 (February, 1962), pp. 65-74.
[188]   M. M-P., *Sense*, p. 30. See *Signs*, p. 225; Martin Heidegger, *Existence and Being*, pp. 277-278.
[189]   M. M-P., *Sense*, p. 108.

and sound in a *gestalt* that illustrates the reversibility of perception and expression. For Merleau-Ponty three formulations of dialogue are possible in the cinema : expository, tonal, and dramatic. Expository dialogue serves "to make the circumstances of the dramatic action known. The novel and the film both avoid this sort of dialogue...".[190] This type of dialogue is shunned in film because it cannot duplicate the multifarious nature of a shifting *gestalt* which a dialogue constitutes in its modality of pointing to limits and perspectives between perception and expression.

The thresholds of perception in an organism, as we were saying, are among the individual constants which express its essence. This signifies that the organism itself measures the action of things upon it and itself delimits its milieu by a circular process which is without analogy in the physical world.[191]

This is to say, the visual and sonorous dialectic of one's lived-experience is already a milieu against which the film is contrasted. When the film itself attempts to suggest what this lived milieu *is* — in deference to the viewer's own experience — the cinematic *gestalt* is negated. This point is illustrated in a comment by Godard in which he *by-passes* the very problem of an expository dialogue.

One of the texts in the presentation is a speech of Bukharin's. Right after it's read there comes a title: "Bukharin made this speech". Next, you see a photo of Bukharin's accuser. Of course, I could have used a photo of Bukharin himself. *But I didn't need to: you'd just "seen" him in the person who reads the speech.* So, I had to show his adversary: Vichynski — and, eventually, Stalin. Okay: photo of Stalin. And because it's a young man who speaks in of Bukharin, the Stalin in the photo is young.[192] (My italics).

The second type of dialogue that can occur in the film is "tonal dialogue". It "gives us each character's particular accent and which dominates, for example, in Proust where the characters are very hard to visualize but are admirably recognizable as soon as they start to talk".[193] Thus, this form of dialogue is also avoided in film to a great extent because the visual presence of the actor with his own peculiar manner of behaving rarely lends itself to it. On the contrary, tonal effect is achieved through "decomposition" of the visual element to

---

[190]   M. M-P., *Sense,* p. 56.
[191]   M. M-P., *Structure,* p. 148.
[192]   Jean-Luc Godard, "Struggle on Two Fronts: A Conversation with Jean-Luc Godard", *Film Quarterly* XXI, no. 2 (Winter, 1968-69), p. 25.
[193]   M. M-P., *Sense,* p. 56.

specify the audio element in the *gestalt*. For example, a tonal dialogue is achieved indirectly in filming a courtroom speech by a lawyer. The film does not fix on the lawyer throughout his speech, rather the following *gestalt* is developed.

Shot 1. The lawyer addresses the courtroom.
        (Long shot)
Shot 2. The lawyer addresses the jury.
        (Medium shot)
Shot 3. The jury listens intently.
        (Medium shot)
Shot 4. The lawyer speaking.
        (Close-up)
Shot 5. The prisoner at the bar listening intently to the speech.
Shot 6. The prisoner's wife in the audience listening intently.
Shot 7. The prosecutor grimly taking notes upon the speech.
Shot 8. The Judge pondering as he weighs the lawyer's words.
Shot 9. The entire courtroom tense ....[194]

This visual decomposition coupled with the on-going speech creates a dialectic of image and sound that is "tonal dialogue" with respect to the "speaking" only. The visual patterns allow for the "particular accent" which allows one to immediately identify a speech in defense of the accused person — the defense lawyer speaking — but one does not immediately recognize the lawyer as a personality. This is to say, in film the visual presentation can achieve what Merleau-Ponty calls tonal dialogue, but the addition of sound makes it an indirect technique which is precisely the third type of dialogue.

"Finally, we have dramatic dialogue which presents the discussion and confrontation of the characters and which is the movies' principal form of dialogue".[195] In this variety of dialogue one moves beyond the "metrics of vision and sound" to the dialectics of "words and silence" which in their advanced complexity superimpose their metric on that of vision and sound.[196] This is to say, the "unity of sound and image is realized by an interplay of meanings which results ... in a more exact rendering of nature than its superficial copying".[197] This icon of maieutic dialogue can be seen in a filmed conversation involving three or more persons.

[194] Joseph and Harry Feldman, *Dynamics of the Film* (New York: Hermitage House, Inc., 1952), p. 238.
[195] M. M-P., *Sense*, p. 56. See *Themes*, pp. 10-11.
[196] M. M-P., *Sense*, p. 56.
[197] V.I. Pudovkin, *Film Technique and Film Acting*, trans. Ivor Montagu (New York: Lear Publishers, 1949), p. 156.

For example, the spectator's interest may be held by the speech of the first, and — with the spectator's attention — we hold the close-up of the first person lingering with him when his speech is finished and *hearing* the voice of the commenced answer of the next speaker before passing on to the latter's image. We see the image of the second speaker only *after* becoming acquainted with his voice. Here sound has preceded image.[198]

However, in the final analysis the sound film is not the lived maieutic of speaking body-subjects for the film remains visual with sound added. Audio expression is always dependent on visual perception before the *gestalt* explains the audio perception. In the lived-experience expression and perception are not separated elements, they are synoptic. The film in the director's cutting room is always a chosen perspective which can be no more than an icon of any given life. In the end, "le cinéma, s'adjoignant la parole, reste visuel".[199]

4.5. *Speaking As Maieutic*

"In a dialogue, the participants occupy both poles at once, and it is this that explains why the phenomenon of 'speaking' can pass into that of 'hearing' ".[200] In the experience of dialogue the persons conversing constitute between themselves a common ground of perception and expression in which meaning is a joint venture. Words are inserted into the *gestalt* in a dialectic exchange in which neither person is the sole creator, rather the genesis of meaning is truly maieutic. "Our perspectives merge into each other, and we co-exist through a common world".[201] It is in this context that Merleau-Ponty suggests that speaking is a reflection of the things themselves, because "expression is the language of the thing itself and springs from its configuration".[202]

The character of speaking in its maieutic stance is exemplified at the intrapersonal level in the child who comes to understand that in dialogues he is referred to as a subject although the verbalization is objective. "The *I* arises when the child understand that every *you* that is addressed to him is for him an *I*; that is, that there must be a consciousness of the reciprocity of points of view in order that the word *I*

[198] Pudovkin, *Film Technique* ..., p. 159.
[199] Edgar Morin, *Le Cinema*, p. 146. See Allen Leepa, "A Painter Looks At Film", *Journal of University Film Associations* XX, no. 2 (1968), pp. 34-38.
[200] M. M-P., *Primacy*, p. 134.
[201] M. M-P., *Phenomenology*, pp. 355-356.
[202] M. M-P., *Phenomenology*, p. 322. See *Themes*, p. 4.

may be used".[203] However, maturity does not dissolve the subjectivity/ objectivity split, for the other person who addresses *me* is never the *I* which I am. Rather, the other person is as expressive of himself as he is expressive of me. He remains his own *I* even if one conceives him totaly as one's alter-ego.[204] "I borrow myself from others; I create others from my own thoughts. This is no failure to perceive others; it is the perception of others".[205]

The maieutic power that exists in the person himself which is re-doubled in interpersonal relations is precisely that lived realization that one's perceptions are one's expressions. In this analysis Merleau-Ponty affirms Husserl. "It seemed to him that to reflect on language is to clarify the activity of the speaking subject, to find a reason already incorporated in these means of expression, this language which I know because I am it".[206] Because "man is a mirror for man"[207] what is perceived becomes the power to express and expression becomes the power to perceive. The dialectic or "ambiguity" that is the lived maieutic becomes the *gestalt* in which experience is renewed and continues on in the process of private into public world. One comes to know the "projection-injection" that denies the dualism of the For Itself and the For the Other by establishing the maieutic system : "I-Other Other-I".[208] This existential system is described explicitly as a phenomenology by Heidegger.

Communication is never anything like a converging of experiences, such as opinions or wishes, from the interior of one subject into the interior of another. Dasein-with is already essentially manifest in a co-state-of-mind and a co-understanding. In discourse Being-with becomes 'explicitly' *shared*; that is to say, it *is* already, but it is unshared as something that has not been taken hold of and appropriated.[209]

The *gestalt* that perception and expression form in the maieutic of speaking is an ambiguity that Merleau-Ponty formulates as a metaphysics and ethics. Speaking as a phenomenology is an existentialism of the lived-experience of a presence-at-the-world. The philosophic import of the proposition "I am speaking" is an ontological semiotic.

203   M. M-P., *Primacy*, p. 150.
204   M. M-P., *Structures*, p. 126.
205   M. M-P., *Signs*, p. 159.
206   M. M-P., *Primacy*, p. 82.
207   M. M-P., *Primacy*, p. 168.
208   M. M-P., *Visible*, pp. 263-264.
209   Martin Heidegger, *Being and Time*, p. 105.

The study of perception could only teach us a "bad ambiguity", a mixture of finitude and universality, of interiority and exteriority. But there is a "good ambiguity" in the phenomenon of expression, a spontaneity which accomplishes what appeared to be impossible when we observed only the separate elements, a spontaneity which gathers together the plurality of monads, the past and the present, nature and culture into a single whole. To establish this wonder would be metaphysics itself and would at the same time give us the principle of an ethics.[210]

---

[210] M. M-P., *Primacy*, p. 11. See *Humanism*, pp. 187-189.

INTRODUCTION TO THE PROSE OF THE WORLD

"The existential-ontological foundation of language is speaking [Rede]".[1] This proposition announced by Martin Heidegger summarizes the theme of Merleau-Ponty's philosophy of existential, phenomenological communication as it has been presented in this study. Although the ontological nature of Merleau-Ponty's phenomenology of perception and expression appears strikingly clear at times, he himself was in the process of specifying that direction when he died. The scattered indications of an ontological *logos* that appear in his published works are embellished to some extent by the working notes published as part of *The Visible and The Invisible*. Yet, his precise thoughts about the hermeneutic inherent in the dialectic of perception and expression remain obscure. Thus, in the pages that follow an attempt is made to piece together the possibilities of a phenomenology of speaking that is, indeed, metaphysics.

Jean-Paul Sartre, the intimate companion of Merleau-Ponty, suggests in his reflections after Merleau-Ponty's death that "through phenomenology, and without ever departing from it, Merleau-Ponty hoped to rejoin the imperatives of ontology".[2] The validity of this comment was foreshadowed at least twice in the work of Merleau-Ponty. In a prospectus of his work sent to Martial Gueroult at the time of his candidacy to the Collège de France, Merleau-Ponty indicated an initial interest in the ontological significance of the perception-expression synergism.[3] His intention was to write a specific analysis which was to be called *The Origin of Truth (L'Origine de la vérité)*. However, this work never appeared. Nonetheless, this first speculation surfaced a second time in a

---

[1] Martin Heidegger, *Being and Time*, p. 203. [The precise translation of "Rede" is something between the formality of "discourse" and the colloquiality of "talk". In this instance the context appears to justify using the translation "speaking".]
[2] Jean-Paul Sartre, *Situations*, p. 217.
[3] M. M-P., *Primacy*, p. 8.

fragment posthumously published in 1967 with the title "La Prose du Monde" in which some tenets of an ontology were suggested.[4]

It is now clear with the posthumous publication of Merleau-Ponty's working notes that he intended to devote the final section of his book *The Visible and The Invisible* to an analysis and reflection on the ontology of speaking.

My plan: I The visible
II Nature
III Logos [5]

To this schema Merleau-Ponty adds the following specifications of his intent: "The Part III is neither logic, nor teleology of consciousness, but a study of the language that has man", and "Logos also as what is realized in man, but nowise as his *property*".[6] There is little doubt that the *logos* which Merleau-Ponty is describing is a semiotic in which perception and expression are incarnate. "Metaphysics is the deliberate intention to describe this paradox of consciousness and truth, exchange and communication, in which science lives and which it encounters in the guise of vanquished difficulties or failures to be made good but which it does not thematize".[7]

Denying the dualism of Sartre, Merleau-Ponty argues that "an ontology from within" which does not have to be constructed like being and negentity is a transcendence of Being.[8] The transcendence or structure is a realization that "*reversibility* is not an actual *identity* of the touching and the touched".[9] This is to say, the cardinal principle of ontological reversibility is that a dialectic can be substituted for all modalities of being and nothingness. *Within* the systems touching-touched and speaking-speech there is reversibility and *between* the

---

[4] M. M-P., "Pages d'Introduction à la Prose de Monde", *Revue de Métaphysique et de Morale* LXXII, no. 2 (Avril-Juin, 1967), pp. 139-153. A complete set of notes and writings have appeared posthumously as *La Prose du monde*, ed. Claude Lefort (Paris: Éditions Gallimard, 1969); a translation by John O'Neill, *The Prose of the World*, is forthcoming from Northwestern University Press, Evanston, Ill. The importance of these notes, probably written in the early 1950's, must be largely discounted as it is clear from the work on *The Visible and the Invisible* that "La Prose du monde" was abandoned as an approach by M. M-P. However, it is only fair to note that some of the material would undoubtedly have been reformulated and redirected by M. M-P. as part of his development of the "logos" section of *The Visible and the Invisible*.
[5] M. M-P., *Visible*, p. 274.
[6] M. M-P., *Visible*, p. 274.
[7] M. M-P., *Sense*, pp. 94-95. See pp. 97-98.
[8] M. M-P., *Visible*, p. 237.
[9] M. M-P., *Visible*, p. 272.

systems there is reversibility. The *logos* is a semiotic in which "an interconnection among all these phenomena is possible, since they are all symbolisms, and perhaps even the translation of one symbolism into another is possible".[10] Thus for Merleau-Ponty "each philosophy is also an architecture of signs".[11]

The precise statement of an ontology of speaking is made by Merleau-Ponty in an explanation of the *logos* as the reversibility that is the structure of the presence-at-the-world : the intentional lived-body.

Among my movements, there are some that go nowhere — that do not even go find in the other body their resemblance or their archetype: these are the facial movements, many gestures, and especially those strange movements of the throat and mouth that form the cry and the voice. Those movements end in sounds and I hear them. Like crystal, like metal and many other substances, I am a sonorous being, but I hear my own vibration from within; as Malraux said, I hear myself with my throat. In this, as he also has said, I am incomparable; my voice is bound to the mass of my own life as is the voice of no one else. But if I am close enough to the other who speaks to hear his breath and feel his effervescence and his fatigue, I almost witness, in him as in myself, the awesome birth of vociferation. As there is a reflexivity of the touch, of sight, and of the touch-vision system, there is a reflexivity of the movements of phonation and of hearing; they have their sonorous inscription, the vociferations have in me their motor echo. *This new reversibility and the emergence of the flesh as expression are the point of insertion of speaking and thinking in the world of silence.*[12] (My italics).

This is to say that "what is lived is lived-spoken" in an order of "immediation" that is the articulation of Being.[13] Being becomes an openness in the form of a world or a field structured as a topography in which the figure appears only to obscure the horizon. The act of speaking presents a meaning of the lived-experience to the body-subject only at the price of denying this experience to any other body-subject. What is lived-spoken is finally known only to the subject as lived. Yet, it is the very reflexitivity of lived and lived-spoken in the individual body-subject that allows him to posit the intentional object which another can know by *his* presence-at-the-world.

---

10   M. M-P., *Praise*, p. 56.
11   M. M-P., *Praise*, p. 57.
12   M. M-P., *Visible*, p. 144. See Richard M. Zaner, "Merleau-Ponty's Theory of the Body-Proper as *Etre-au-monde*", *Journal of Existentialism* VI, no. 21 (Fall, 1965), pp. 31-39. [Note: the French *corps propre* is alternately translated as "body-proper" and "lived-body".]
13   M. M-P., *Visible*, p. 126.

Now it is at the heart of my present that I find the meaning of those presents which preceded it, and that I find the means of understanding others' presence at the same world; and it is the actual practice of speaking that I learn to understand. There is finality only in the sense in which Heidegger defined it when he said approximately that finality is the trembling of a unity exposed to contingency and tirelessly recreating itself. And it is to the same undeliberated and inexhaustable spontaneity that Sartre was alluding when he said that we are "condemned to freedom".[14]

Merleau-Ponty conceives of the act of speaking as an intentional history of the individual that comes to be the dialectic of being and other being. "He does not speak only of himself, of his own perspective, and for himself; he speaks for all".[15] The act of speaking becomes the ontological genesis that envelops the For-Itself and the For-the-Other in a dialectic system of four terms : "my being for me, my being for the other, the for itself of another, and his being for me".[16] The fundamental proposition that these four terms demonstrate is "That it is being that speaks within us and not we who speak of being".[17] The lived *gestalt* of speaking therefore requires that in the act of articulation the body-subject be no more that it perceives. This is to say, the lived-body experience is *one* in perception and expression as immanence and transcendence are one in presence. In the act of speaking one constitutes an evidence of being that is "real" and not "very possible" or "probable" which is sustained only so long as more speaking does not emerge to alter the *gestalt*. Speaking is the dialectic of perception in reverse.[18]

Metaphysics begins with the "opening out upon 'another', and is found everywhere...".[19] The specification of existence becomes the taking up of a *de facto* situation by the body-subject in a movement from singularity (as one's sexual existence) to generality (as one's social existence).[20]

The reason why I am able to understand the other person's body and existence "beginning with" the body proper [lived-body], the reason why the compresence of my "consciousness" and my "body" is prolonged into the compresence of my self and the other person, is that the "I am able to" and the "the other person exists" belong here and now to the same world, that the body proper is a

[14] M. M-P., *Signs*, p. 97.
[15] M. M-P., *Visible*, p. 79.
[16] M. M-P., *Visible*, p. 80.
[17] M. M-P., *Visible*, p. 194.
[18] M. M-P., *Visible*, p. 40.
[19] M. M-P., *Phenomenology*, p. 168.
[20] M. M-P., *Phenomenology*, p. 169.

premonition of the other person, the *Einfuhlung*, an echo of my incarnation, and that a flash of meaning makes them substitutable in the absolute presence of origins.[21]

Thus, "it is a question of a power — of an I can".[22] This ontology may be clearer in the following formulation. The existence of "one" or "we" is always lived through the modality of the "I". Yet, how does a lived-I properly become a plural "we" in the sense of a "one" which is existence ? Merleau-Ponty asserts that it is the act of speaking that has this existential power, this being "able to" "see" as the other "sees". "Then, through the concordant operations of his body and my own, what I see passes into him...".[23] "But, then, the truth of a being is not its essence, or what it has finally become. It is rather its existence, its active becoming".[24]

The ontological bond of subjectivity with intersubjectivity is manifest in communication as the "nuclei of signification about which the transcendental life pivots, specified voids".[25] Communication becomes the chiasm or intentional "encroachment" which finally "leads to the rejecting of the notion of subject, or to the defining of the subject as a field, as a hierarchized system of structures opened by an inaugural *there is*".[26] Just as each gesture points to its object with silent validity and as each perception grasps that presence of the visual dimension of "seeing", the act of speaking becomes that pointing and circumscribing which prescribes that *there is* a manifest intentionality. One's speech intends his Being and makes his Being an object for himself and Others. In speaking the body comes to know its subject and the subject is aware of its primordiality in the body. Indeed, what is lived is the ontological positing of what is lived-spoken.

In speaking of the creative power of Cézanne's painting Merleau-Ponty suggests the ontological semiotic that inhabits all expression as the dialectic of perception. "He gradually learned that expression is the language of the thing itself and springs from its configuration".[27] The very structure of existence that is perceptible is also an expression of meaning; existence speaks. "It is this Visibility, this generality of the

21   M. M-P., *Signs*, p. 175.
22   M. M-P., *Visible*, p. 225.
23   M. M-P., *Visible*, p. 142.
24   M. M-P., *Praise*, p. 65, n. I.
25   M. M-P., *Visible*, p. 239.
26   M. M-P., *Visible*, p. 239.
27   M. M-P., *Phenomenology*, p. 322.

Sensible in itself, this anonymity innate to Myself that we have previously called flesh, and one knows there is no name in traditional philosophy to designate it".[28] In this sense it is not "we" who speak as that existential "I" that transcends the "flesh, it is the truth that speaks itself at the depths of speech".[29] The dialectic of Being is precisely the Becoming-nature of man which is the Becoming-man of nature. Speaking is the lived-*gestalt* which is always open to Becoming-man of nature. Speaking is the lived-*gestalt* which is always open to Becoming and as such is Existence.

It is these existentials that make up the (substitutable) *meaning* of what we say and of what we understand. They are the armature of that "invisible world" which, with speech, begins to impregnate all the things we see — as the "other" space, for the schizophrenic, takes possession of the sensorial and visible space —— Not that it becomes a visible space in its turn: in the visible there is never anything but ruins of the spirit, the world will always resemble the Forum, at least before the gaze of the philosopher, who does not completely inhabit it ——
Our "interior life": a world in the world, a region within it, a "place from which we speak" (Heidegger) and into which we introduce the others by true speech.[30]

In the act of communication the speaking body-subject becomes the witness of its own existence inasmuch as its active becoming is a primordial ontogenesis.

"History is other people; it is the interrelationships we establish with them, outside of which the realm of the ideal appears as an alibi".[31] For Merleau-Ponty history is the record of the primordial transgression of the "I" into the "we" of communication. This is to say, the systematic approximation of the objective which is interpersonal is nonetheless the transcendental subjectivity of the late Husserl, whom Merleau-Ponty follows. In this sense the transcendental descends into history.

Or as we might put it, the historical is no longer an external relation between two or more absolutely autonomous subjects but has an interior and is an inherent aspect of their very definition. They no longer know themselves to be subjects simply in relation to their individual aspects, but in relation to one another.[32]

History is thus rendered as the maieutic of Being in the process of Becoming. What is spoken in the presence of the Other is spoken in my

[28] M. M-P., *Visible*, p. 139.
[29] M. M-P., *Visible*, p. 185.
[30] M. M-P., *Visible*, p. 180.
[31] M. M-P., *Primacy*, p. 25.
[32] M. M-P., *Signs*, p. 107. An excellent example occurs in *Phenomenology*, p. 130.

own presence and in the very act of speaking one is led "to rediscover as the reality of the interhuman world and of history a surface of separation between me and the other which is also the place of our union, the unique *Erfullung* of his life and my life".[33]

The separation and union of the speaker and the other publicize the existential modality of personal history as the "locus of the projections and introjections" which are the very "inner framework of intersubjectivity".[34] The act of speaking is the constant affirmation of the lived-existence that separates and unites body and subject *as* Body-subject and Other. Speaking as the expressing-perception which is the perceiving-expression constitutes that finality or truth which is the lesson of Hegelian dialectic and the Heideggerian metaphysics. This is to say, speaking is the trembling of a unity exposed to the activity of Becoming whose permanence maintains its progress by returning back into itself. There is only one phenomena which affirms this ontology of speaking by denying the silence that gives rise to expression. "Death is *the act of one person alone*. In the confused mass of being, death cuts out that particular zone which is ourselves".[35] Death is precisely that void of Being in which the *act speaks* with finality because the silence which is the possibility of speaking speech (parole parlante) does not exist. Therefore, "it is in the world that we communicate, through what, in our life, is articulate".[36]

Hence each one knows that he himself and the others are *inscribed* in the world; what he feels, what he lives, what the others feel and live, even his dreams or their dreams, his illusions and theirs, are not islets, isolated fragments of being: all this, by reason of the fundamental exigency of our constitutive nothingness, is *of being*, has consistence, order, meaning, and there is a way to comprehend it.[37]

Within the ontological act of speaking there is a moment in which "I" am "you" as the lived-body gathers itself up into the semiotic of perception-expression which is gesture — the act that aims beyond itself. The structure of signs displays at the moment of "presence" a meaning which "overflows into the other person when the act of speaking binds them into a single whole. Mind is no longer set apart but springs up

---

[33] M. M-P., *Visible*, p. 234.
[34] M. M-P., *Visible*, p. 234.
[35] M. M-P., *Signs*, p. 201.
[36] M. M-P., *Visible*, p. 11.
[37] M. M-P., *Visible*, p. 63.

beside gestures and words as if by spontaneous generation".[38] This is to suggest that speaking as a reciprocal, intentional reference marks out the intentional limit of analysis (perception). In semiotic terms the presence of signs is the immanent meaning of the transcendent act in which "speaking" is speech as ontology. In the act of speaking the latent intentionality of perception is a constant process of intentionality in Being.[39] In short, speaking is ontology manifest in a semiology of Becoming. Being does not precede Becoming; Being is the *a priori* existence of an active Becoming of phenomena that appear primordially in the intentional act of speaking in a world of other Body-subjects.

Within speaking and semiology Maurice Merleau-Ponty posits a phenomenological theory of existential communication that is, indeed, an introduction to the prose of the world. By extricating Merleau-Ponty's theory in the present study, an attempt is made to complete an intention that was never allowed to blossom into existence. "My works in preparation aim to show how communication with others, and thought, take up and go beyond the realm of perception which initiated us to the truth".[40]

---

[38] M. M-P., *Signs,* p. 235.
[39] M. M-P., *Visible,* pp. 243-244.
[40] M. M-P., "An Unpublished Text by Maurice Merleau-Ponty: *A Prospectus of His Work*" in *Primacy,* p. 3.

BIBLIOGRAPHY

I. PRIMARY SOURCES

A. Merleau-Ponty's Books, Articles, Lectures, and Essays in the Chronological Order of Publication; Annotated

1935
"Christianisme et ressentiment", *La Vie Intellectuelle* XXXVI, no. 2 (June 10), pp. 278-306.
[This is a review of Max Scheler's book: *Über Ressentiment und moralisches Werturteil*]

1936
"Etre et avoir", *La Vie Intellectuelle* XLV (October 10), pp. 98-109.
[This is a critical review of Gabriel Marcel's book: *Etre et avoir*]
"L'Imagination", *Journal de Psychologie Normale et Pathologique* XXXIII nos. 9-10 (November-December), pp. 756-761.
[This is a review of Jean-Paul Sartre's book: *L'Imagination*]

1939
M. M-P., *et al.* "L'Agrégation de philosophie", exposé G. Friedmann, *Bulletin de la Société Française de Philosophie* XXXVIII, pp. 117-158.
[Société Française de Philosophie, séance du 7 mai 1938]

1942
La Structure du comportement (Paris: Presses Universitaires de France).
[Original manuscript completed in 1938]

1943
"Les Mouches", *Confluences* III, no. 25 (September-October), pp. 514-516.
[This is a review of Jean-Paul Sartre's play: *Les Mouches*]

1944
Review of Hans Herter's *Altes und Neues zu Platons Kritias*, *Rheinisches Museum für Philologie* XCII, pp. 236-265.

1945
Phénoménologie de la perception (Paris: Editions Gallimard).
"Le Roman et la métaphysique", *Cahiers du Sud* XXII, no. 270 (March-April), pp. 194-207.

[Incorporated in *Sens et non-sens*]
"La Guerre a eu lieu", *Les Temps Modernes* I, no. 1 (October), pp. 48-66.
[Incorporated in *Sens et non-sens*]
"La Querelle de l'existentialisme", *Les Temps Modernes* I, no. 2 (November), pp. 344-355.
[Incorporated in *Sens et non-sens*]
"Le Doute de Cézanne", *Fontaine* VIII, no. 47 (December), pp. 80-100.
[Incorporated in *Sens et non-sens*]

1946
"Pour la vérité", *Les Tempts Modernes* I, no. 4 (January), pp. 577-600.
[Incorporated in *Sens et non-sens*]
"Le Culte du héros", *Action,* no. 74 (February 1), pp. 12-13.
[Incorporated in *Sens et non-sens* under the title "Le Héros, l'homme"]
"Foi et bonne foi", *Les Temps Modernes* I. no. 5 (February), pp. 769-782.
[Incorporated in *Sens et non-sens*]
"Autour du marxisme", *Fontaine* IX, nos. 48-49 (February), pp. 309-331.
[This is a critical review of Thierry Maulnier's book: *Violence et conscience.* Incorporated in *Sens et non-sens*]
"A propos d'une conférence de Maurice Merleau-Ponty sur les aspects politiques et sociaux de l'existentialisme", summarized by Jean Wahl, *Renaissances* V, no. 51, pp. 678-679; reprinted in *Fontaine* IX, no. 51 (April, 1946), pp. 678-679.
[This lecture was delivered on March 23, 1946 at the Institut d'Etudes Politiques de l'Université de Paris. The original lecture is not available]
"L'Existentialisme chez Hegel", *Les Temps Modernes* I, no. 7 (April), pp. 1311-1319.
[Incorporated in *Sens et non-sens*]
"Marxisme et philosophie", *Revue Internationale* I, no. 6 (June-July), pp. 518-526.
[Incorporated in *Sens et non-sens*]
"Le Yogi et le prolétaire", *Les Temps Modernes* II, no. 13 (October), pp. 1-29; no. 14 (November, 1946), pp. 253-287; no. 16 (January), pp. 676-711.
[Revised text incorporated in *Humanisme et terreur* that is the basis of material in Part I, Chapters 1 and 2, Part II, Chapters 1 and 2]
"Deux philosophies de l'Europe (marxisme-existentialisme)", *La Nef* III, no. 24 (November), pp. 87-98.
[This discussion with Karl Jaspers and others took place in September, 1946 at the *Rencontres Internationales de Genève*; reprinted in *Rencontres Internationales de Genève*; Neuchâtel: Editions de la Baconnière, 1946, pp. 252-256]
"Crise de conscience européenne", *La Nef* III, no. 24 (November), pp. 66-73.
[This discussion with Marcel Raymond and others took place in September, 1946 at the *Rencontres Internationales de Genève*; reprinted in *Rencontres Internationales de Genève,* Neuchâtel: Editions de la Baconnière, 1946, pp. 74-77]

1947
Humanisme et terreur. Essai sur le problème communiste (Paris: Editions Gallimard).
[Essays included:
   "Les Dilemmes de Koestler".
   "L'Ambiguïté de l'histoire selon Boukharine".
   "Le Rationalisme de Trotsky".
   "Du Prolétaire au commissaire".
   "Le Yogi et le prolétaire".]
"La Liberté chez Leibnitz", *Cours de l'Université Lyon* (Lyon: Année scolaire).
[The original lecture is not available]

"Indochine S.O.S." (unsigned editorial), *Les Temps Modernes* II, no. 18 (March), pp. 1039-1052.
[Incorporated in *Signes* under the title "Sur l'Indochine"]
"Pour les rencontres internationales", *Les Temps Modernes* II, no. 19 (April), pp. 1340-1344.
"Apprendre à lire", *Les Temps Modernes* II, no. 22 (July), pp. 1-27.
[This article contains material used in the *Preface* of *Humanisme et terreur*]
"Le Métaphysique dans l'homme", *Revue de Métaphysique et de Morale* LII, nos. 3-4 (July-October), pp. 290-307.
[Incorporated in *Sens et non-sens*]
"Le Cinéma et la nouvelle psychologie", *Les Temps Modernes* III no. 26 (November), pp. 930-943.
[Incorporated in *Sens et non-sens*]
"Le Primat de la perception et ses conséquences philosophiques", *Bulletin de la Société Française de Philosophie* XLI, no. 4 (December), pp. 119-153.
[This lecture was delivered on November 23, 1946 to the *Société Française de Philosophie*]
"En un combat douteux", (editorial signed T.M.), *Les Temps Modernes* III, no. 27 (December), pp. 961-964.
"Lecture de Montaigne", *Les Temps Modernes* III, no. 27 (December), pp. 1044-1060.
[Incorporated in *Signes*]
"Notes sur 'Les Cahiers de la Pléiade, avril 1947'", *Les Temps Modernes* III, no. 27 (December), pp. 1151-1152.
"Un Auteur scandaleux", *Le Figaro Littéraire* (December 6), n.p.
[Incorporated in *Sens et non-sens*]

1948
"Ame et corps chez Malebranche, Maine de Biran, Bergson", *Cours de l'Université de Lyon* (Lyon: Année scolaire).
[The original lecture is available under the title *L'Union de l'âme et du corps chez Malebranche, Biran et Bergson. Notes prises au cours de Merleau-Ponty à l'école normale supérieure (1947-1948)* (Bibliothèque d'histoire de la philosophie). Paris: Vrin, 1968]
"Language et communication", *Cours de l'Université de Lyon* (Lyon: Année scolaire).
[The original lecture is not available]
Sens et non-sens (Paris: Les Editions Nagel).
[Essays included:
    "Le Doute de Cézanne".
    "Le Roman et la métaphysique".
    "Un Auteur scandaleux".
    "Le Cinéma et la nouvelle psychologie".
    "L'Existentialisme chez Hegel".
    "La Querelle de l'existentialisme".
    "Le Métaphysique dans l'homme".
    "Auteur et maxisme".
    "Maxisme et philosophie".
    "La Guerre a eu lieu".
    "Pour la vérité".
    "Foi et bonne foi".
    "Le Héros, l'homme".]
"Jean-Paul Sartre ou autour d'un auteur scandaleux", *Le Figaro Littéraire* (January 3), n.p.
[Incorporated in *Sens et non-sens*]

"Le 'Manifesto communiste' à cent ans", *Le Figaro Littéraire* (April 3), n.p.
"Complicité objective" (editorial signed T.M.), *Les Temps Modernes* IV, no. 34 (July), pp. 1-11.
"Communisme-anticommunisme", *Les Temps Modernes* IV, no. 34 (July), pp. 175-188. [Incorporated in *Signes* under the title "La Politique paranoiaque"]
J.-L. Dumas. "Les Conférences", *La Nef* V, no. 45 (August), pp. 150-151. [This article is a summary of a lecture given by M. M-P., entitled "L'Homme et l'object". The original lecture is not available]

1949
La Structure de comportement; précédé d'une philosophie de l'ambiguité par Alphonse de Waehlens. New (2nd) Edition (Paris: Presses Universitairies de France).
"Humanisme surréaliste et humanisme existentialiste". Lecture delivered at the Collège Philosophique, 1949. [The original lecture is not available]
"Note sur Machiavel", *Les Temps Modernes* V, no. 48 (October), pp. 557-593. [Incorporated in *Signes*]
"Commentaire (à propos de Georg Lukacs)", *Les Temps Modernes* V, no. 50 (December), pp. 1119-1121. [Incorporated in *Signes* under the title: "Marxisme et superstition". This original commentary was proceded by an article on Lukacs written by F. Ernal]

1950
"Les Jours de notre vie" (editorial co-signed by Jean-Paul Sartre), *Les Temps Modernes* V, no. 51 (January), pp. 1153-1168. [Incorporated in *Signes* under the title: "L'URSS et les camps"]
"Mort d'Emmanuel Mounier", *Les Temps Modernes* V, no. 54 (April), p. 1906.
"Réponse à C. L. R. James" (editorial signed T.M.), *Les Temps Modernes* V, no. 56 (June), pp. 2292-2294.
"L'Adversaire est complice" (editorial signed T.M.) *Les Temps Modernes* V, no. 57 (July), pp. 1-11.

1951
"Machiavélisme et modernité" in *Umanesimo e scienze politica* (Ed. Enrico Castelli. Milan), pp. 297-308. [This paper was originally sent to the *Umanesimo e scienze politica Congress,* Rome-Florence, in September, 1949; incorporated in *Signes*]
"L'Homme et l'adversité" in *La Connaissance de l'Homme au XXe siècle*. Vol. 1951: Rencontres Internationales de Genève (Neuchâtel: Editions de la Baconnière), pp. 57-75; discussion, pp. 215-252. [Incorporated in *Signes* without the discussion. Lecture delivered on September 10, 1951]
"Le Philosophe et la sociologie", *Cahiers Internationaux de Sociologie* X, pp. 55-69. [Incorporated in *Signes*]

1952
"Sur le phénoménologie de langage" in *Problèmes actuels de la phénoménologie*. Ed. H. L. Van Breda (Bruxelles: Desclée de Brouwer), pp. 91-109. [This lecture was presented on April 13, 1951 to the *Premier Colloque de Phénoménologie*. Incorporated in *Signes*]
"Der Mensch und die Widerstandigkeit des Daseins", *Merkur* VI, pp. 801-821.
"Le Langage indirect et les voix du silence", *Les Temps Modernes* VII, no. 80 (June),

pp. 2113-2144; VIII, no. 81 (July, 1952), pp. 70-94.
[Incorporated in *Signes*]

1953
*Eloge de la philosophie: Leçon inaugurale faite au Collège de France, le jeudi 15 janvier,
1953.* (Paris: Editions Gallimard).
"Les Relations avec autrui chez l'enfant, première partie", *Les Cours de Sorbonne*
(Paris: Tournier et Constants).
"Les Science de l'homme et la phénoménologie. Introduction et première partie: le
problème des sciences de l'homme selon Husserl", *Les Cours de Sorbonne* (Paris:
Tournier et Constants).
"Le Monde sensible et Le Monde de l'expression", *Annuaire du Collège de France*
(Paris: Imprimerie Nationale), pp. 145-150.
[Incorporated in *Résumés*]
"Recherches sur l'usage littéraire de langage", *Annuaire du Collège de France* (Paris:
Imprimerie Nationale), pp. 150-155.
[Incorporated in *Résumés*]

1954
"Matériaux pour une théorie de l'histoire", *Annuaire du Collège de France* (Paris:
Imprimerie Nationale), pp. 180-187.
[Incorporated in *Résumés*]
"Le Problème de la parole", *Annuaire du Collège de France* (Paris: Imprimerie Natio-
nale), pp. 175-179.
[Incorporated in *Résumés*]
"Forum" in *L'Express*. October 2, p. 3.
"Forum" in *L'Express*. October, 9, p. 3.
"Sur l'érotisme" in *L'Express*. October 16, pp. 3-4.
[Incorporated in *Signes*]
"La France va-t-elle se renouveler" in *L'Express*. October 23, pp. 3-4.
"Les Femmes sont-elles des hommes?" in *L'Express*. November 6, p. 4.
"Les Peuples se fâchent-ils?" in *L'Express*. December 4, pp. 3-4.
"Sur les faits divers" in *L'Express*. December 18, pp. 3-4.
[Incorporated in *Signes*]

1955
Les Adventures de la dialectique (Paris: Editions Gallimard).
[Essays included:
    "La Crise de l'entendement".
    "Le Marxisme 'occidental'".
    "Pravda".
    "La Dialectique en action".
    "Sartre et l'ultra-bolchevisme".
    "Epilogue".]
"L'"Institution' dans l'histoire personnelle et publique", *Annuaire du Collège de
France* (Paris: Imprimerie Nationale), pp. 157-160.
[Incorporated in *Résumés*]
"Le Problème de la passivité: le sommeil, l'inconscient, la mémoire", *Annuaire du
Collège de France* (Paris: Imprimerie Nationale), pp. 161-164.
[Incorporated in *Résumés*]
"Sur l'abstention".
[The origin of this article has not been discovered. Incorporated in *Signes*]
"D'Abord comprendre les communistes" in *L'Express*. January 8, pp. 8-9.

"A quoi sert l'objectivité?" in *L'Express*. January 29, p. 4.

"Comment répondre à Oppenheimer?" in *L'Express*. February 19, p. 3.

"Sur Claudel" in *L'Express*. March 5, pp. 3-4.

[Incorporated in *Signes*]

"M. Poujade a-t-il une petite cervelle?" in *L'Express*. March 19, p. 3.

"Les Papiers de Yalta" in *L'Express*. April 9, pp. 3-4.

[Incorporated in *Signes*]

"Einstein et la crise de la raison" in *L'Express*. May 14, p. 13.

[Incorporated in *Signes*]

"Où va l'anticommunisme?" in *L'Express*. June 25, p. 12.

"L'Avenir de la révolution" in *L'Express*. August 27, pp. 7-10.

[Incorporated in *Signes*]

1956

Les Philosophes célèbres (editor) (Paris: L. Mazenod).

[Essays included:

    "Avant-propos".

    [Incorporated in *Signes* under the title: "Partout et nulle part"]

    "Christianisme et philosophie".

    [Incorporated in *Signes*]

    "Le grand rationalisme".

    [Incorporated in *Signes*]

    "Le Découverte de l'histoire".

    "Le Découverte de la subjectivité".

    [Incorporated in *Signes*]

    "L'Existence et la dialectique".

    [Incorporated in *Signes*]

    "L'Orient et la philosophie".

    [Incorporated in *Signes*]

    "Les Fondateurs".

"La Philosophie dialectique", *Annuaire du Collège de France* (Paris: Imprimerie Nationale), pp. 175-179.

[Incorporated in *Résumés*]

"Textes et commentaires sur la dialectique", *Annuaire du Collège de France* (Paris: Imprimerie Nationale), pp. 179-180.

[Incorporated in *Résumés*]

"Rencontre est-ouest à Venise", *Comprendre* XVI (September), pp. 202-301.

[This article reports the public discussions held in nine sessions, March 26-31, 1956. A condensation and selection of extracts appears in "Entre Merleau-Ponty, Sartre, Silone et les écrivains soviétiques: premier dialogue est-ouest à Venise", *L'Express*. October 19, 1956, pp. 21-24].

"Sur la destalinisation" in *L'Express*. November 23, pp. 13-17.

[Incorporated in *Signes*]

1957

"Le Concept de Nature: I. Eléments de notre concept de Nature. II. La Science contemporaine et les indices d'une nouvelle conception de la Nature", *Annuaire du Collège de France* (Paris: Imprimerie Nationale), pp. 201-217.

[Incorporated in *Signes*]

"La Psychoanalyse et son enseignement", *Bulletin de la Société de Philosophie* LI, no. 2 (April-June), pp. 65-104.

[This article reports a group discussion. The only comment by M. M-P. occurs at pp. 98-99]

1958

"Le Concept de Nature (suite): L'Animalité, le corps humain, passage à la culture", *Annuaire du Collège de France* (Paris: Imprimerie Nationale), pp. 213-219.
[Incorporated in *Résumés*]
"Du moindre mal à l'union sacrée" in *Le Monde*. June 5, n.p.
[Incorporated in *Signes* under the title: "Sur le 13 mai 1958".]
"La Démocratie peut-elle renaitre en France?" (Interview) in *L'Express*. July 3, pp. 15-17.
[Incorporated in *Signes* under the title: "Demain..."]
"Sur Madagascar" (Interview) in *L'Express*. August 21, n.p.
[Incorporated in *Signes*]
Les Relations avec autrui chez l'enfant : Introduction (Paris: Centre de documentation universitaire).
Les Sciences de l'homme et la phénoménologie (Paris: Centre de documentation universitaire).

1959

"Le Philosophe et son ombre" in *Edmund Husserl: 1859-1959*. Ed. H. L. Van Breda and J. Taminiqux (The Hague: Martinus Nijhoff), pp. 195-220.
[Incorporated in *Signes*]
"Réflexions générales sur le sens de cette tentative (l'ontologie de la Nature) et sur la possibilité de la philosophie aujourd'hui", *Annuaire du Collège de France* (Paris: Imprimerie Nationale), pp. 229-237.
[Incorporated in *Résumés* under the title: "Possibilité de la philosophie". Both titles reported in this reference are editorial constructions as M. M-P. never titled it himself].
"De Mauss à Claude Lévi-Strauss", *La Nouvelle Revue Française* VII, no. 82 (October) pp. 615-631.
[Incorporated in *Signes*]

1960

Signes (Paris: Librairie Gallimard).
[Essays included:
    "Le Langage indirect et les voix du silence".
    "Sur la phénoménologie du langage".
    "Le Philosophe et la sociologie".
    "De Mauss à Claude Lévi-Strauss".
    "Partout et nulle part".
    "Le Philosophe et son ombre".
    "Bergson se faisant".
    "Einstein et la crise de la raison".
    "Lecture de Montaigne".
    "Note sur Machiavel".
    "L'Homme et l'adversité" [Discussion omitted.]
    "Propos".]
"Préface" in *L'Œuvre de Freud et son importance pour le monde moderne* by A. Hesnard (Paris: Payot), pp. 5-10.
"Husserl aux limites de la phénoménologie", *Annuaire du Collège de France* (Paris: Imprimerie Nationale), pp. 169-173.
[Incorporated in *Résumés*]
Eloge de la philosophie et autres essais (Paris: Editions Gallimard).

"Nature et Logos: le corps humain", *Annuaire du Collège de France* (Paris: Imprimerie Nationale), pp. 173-176.
[Incorporated in *Résumés*]
"Bergson se faisant", *Bulletin de la Société Française de Philosophie* LIV, no. 1 (January-March), n.p.
[Incorporated in *Signes*. This lecture was given with the title "Hommage solennel à Henri Bergson" on 19 May 1959 before the *Bergson Congress (Xe Congrès de la Société de Philosophie de Langue Française)* in the Grand Amphitheatre de la Sorbonne]
"La Volonté dans la philosophie de Malebranche", *Bulletin de la Société Française de Philosophie* LIV, no. 3 (July-September), pp. 97-140.
[This article reports a discussion which included M. M-P. held on December 19, 1959]

1961
"L'Ontologie cartesienne et l'ontologie d'aujourd'hui: Philosophie et non-philosophie depuis Hegel", *Annuaire du Collège* (Paris: Imprimerie Nationale), p. 163.
[This is the announcement of the course that M. M-P. was to have presented at the Collège de France during 1961. The lecture is not available]
"L'Œil et l'esprit", *Art de France* I, no 1 (January), n.p.; reprinted in *Les Temps Modernes* XVII, nos. 184-185 (November), pp. 193-227. Published in book form: *L'Œil et l'esprit* (Paris: Editions Gallimard) 1964.
[The original article and the book reprint both contain illustrations chosen by M. M-P.].
"Cinq notes sur Claude Simon", *Méditations,* no. 4 (Winter), pp. 5-9.

1962
Gilbert Ryle. "La Phénoménologie contre *The Concept of Mind*" in *La Philosophie analytique.* (Philosophie No. IV: Cahiers de Royaumont.) Trans. André Gombay. (Paris: Editions de Minuit), pp. 65-84; discussion, pp. 85-104.
[The discussion includes remarks by Van Breda, Quine, Ayer, Merleau-Ponty, Wahl, and Alquié]
André A. Devaux. "Idéalisme, critique et positivisme phénoménologique (L'Esquisse d'un dialogue)", *Giornale di metafisica* XVII, pp. 72-91.
[This article reports a discussion between Joseph Moreau and M. M-P.].
"Un Inédit de Maurice Merleau-Ponty", Note d'introduction par Martial Gueroult, *Revue de Métaphysique et de Morale* LXVII, no. 4 (October-December), pp. 401-409.
[This article is a personal communication sent to Martial Gueroult written by M. M-P late in 1952 or early in 1953 after his appointment to the faculty of the Collège de France, and submitted for publication after M. M-P.'s death].

1964
L'Œil et l'esprit (Paris: Editions Gallimard).
[Reprint in book form of an article of the same title published in 1961].
Le Visible et l'invisible suivi de notes de travail. Texte établi par Claude Lefort, accompagné d'un avertissement et d'une postface (Paris: Editions Gallimard).

1965
"Husserl et la notion de Nature (Notes prises au cours de Maurice Merleau-Ponty)". Transcribed by Xavier Tilliette, *Revue de Métaphysique et de Morale* LXX, pp. 257-269.
[This article contains notes joined together from two lectures given by M. M-P. on March 14 and 25, 1957].
Eloge de la philosophie et autres essais. (Vol. 75: Collection Idées.) (Paris: Editions Gallimard).

1966
"La Philosophie de l'existence", *Dialogue* V, no. 3 (December), pp. 307-322.
[This article reports the transcript of a broadcast made by M. M-P. on November 17, 1959 on the program *Conférence* on Radio-Canada. The broadcast version is a text edited by M. M-P. from his remarks without notes to the *Maison canadienne de la cité universitaire de Paris* early in 1959].

1967
"Pages d'introduction à la Prose du Monde", Introductory Note by Claude Lefort, *Revue de Métaphysique et de Morale* LXXII, no. 2 (April-June), pp. 139-153.
[This article reports a fragment originally intended for inclusion in *Le Visible et l'invisible* which was apparently abandoned by M. M-P.].

1968
L'Union de l'âme et du corps chez Malebranche, Biran et Bergson (Bibliothèque d'histoire de la philosophie). Notes prises au cours de Maurice Merleau-Ponty, recueillis et rédigées par Jean Deprun (Paris: Vrin).
[Book reprint of the 1948 lecture: "Ame et corps chez Mallebranche, Maine de Biran, Bergson".]
Résumés de cours. Collège de France, 1952-1960 (Paris: Editions Gallimard).
[Résumés included:
"Le Monde sensible et le Monde de l'expression".
"Recherches sur l'usage littéraire du langage".
"Le Problème de la parole".
"Matériaux pour une théorie de l'histoire".
"L'"Institution' dans l'histoire personnelle et publique".
"Le Problème de la passivité: le sommeil, l'inconscient, la mémoire".
"La Philosophie dialectique".
"Textes et commentaires sur la dialectique".
"Le Concept de Nature: I. Eléments de notre concept de Nature. II. La science contemporaine et les indices d'une nouvelle conception de la Nature".
"Le Concept de Nature (suite). L'Animalité, le corps humain, passage à la culture".
"Possibilité de la philosophie".
"Husserl aux limites de la phénoménologie".
"Nature et Logos: le corps humain".]

1969
La Prose du Monde. Ed. Claude Lefort (Paris: Editions Gallimard).

B. Translations of Merleau-Ponty's Original French Treatises in the Chronological Order of Publication; Annotated

1946
"Cézanne's Doubt", abridged translation by Juliet Bigney, *Partisan Review* XIII, no. 4 (September-October), pp. 464-478.
[This translation omits approximately 100 lines of the text dealing with a discussion of Freud's analysis of Léonard de Vinci's psychological state as an artist, in particular his alleged homosexuality].

1956
"What is Phenomenology?" Trans. John F. Bannan, *Cross Currents.* VI (Winter), pp. 59-70.

[This article is a translation of the "Preface" to *Phénoménologie de la perception*].

1957
La Estructura del comportamiento. Precedido de *Una Filosofia de la ambiguedad* de Alphonse de Waelhens. Trans. Enrique Alonso (Buenos Aires).
Fenomenologia de la perception. Anon. trans. (Mexico: Fondo de Cultura Economica).

1958
Elogio della filosofia. Trans. Enzo Paci (Torino).

1962
"Bergson se faisant" in *The Bergsonian Heritage*. Ed. Thomas Hanna (New York: Columbia University Press), pp. 133-149.
Elogio de filosofia. Trans. António Braz (Lisboa: Guimaraes Editores).
Phenomenology of Perception (International Library of Philosophy and Scientific Method). Trans. Colin Smith (New York: Humanities Press; London: Routledge and Kegan Paul).
Senso e non senso. Introduction and trans. Enzo Paci (Milano: Il Saggiatore).
Sinais. Trans. Fernando Gil (Lisboa: Minotaura).

1963
In Praise of Philosophy. Trans. John Wild and James M. Edie (Evanston, Ill.: Northwestern University Press).
"The Philosopher and Sociology" in *Philosophy and the Social Sciences*. Ed. Maurice Natanson (New York: Random House), pp. 487-505.
The Structure of Behavior. Trans. Alden Fisher (Boston: Beacon Press).

1964
The Primacy of Perception and Other Essays. Ed. James M. Edie (Evanston, Ill.: Northwestern University Press).
[Essays and their translators include:
"An Unpublished Text by Maurice Merleau-Ponty: A Prospectus of his Work".
Arleen B. Dallery.
"The Primacy of Perception and Its Philosophical Consequences".
James M. Edie.
"Phenomenology and the Sciences of Man".
John Wild.
"The Child's Relation with Others".
William Cobb.
"Eye and Mind".
Carleton Dallery.
"The Crisis of the Understanding".
Nancy Metzel and John Flodstrom.
"The Yogi and the Proletarian".
Nancy Metzel and John Flodstrom.]
Sense and Non-sense. Trans. Hubert L. Dreyfus and Patricia A. Dreyfus (Evanston, Ill.: Northwestern University Press).
Signs. Trans. Richard C. McCleary (Evanston, Ill.: Northwestern University Press).

1965
La Fenomenologia y los ciencias del hombre. Anon trans. (Buenos Aires: Edit Nova).
Fenomenologia della percezione. (No. 95: La Cultura.) Trans. Andrea Bonomi (Milano: Il Saggiatore).

'Umanismo e terrore' e 'Le avventure della dialectica' (No. 20: Argomenti.) Introduction by Andrea Bonomi and F. Madonia. Trans. Andrea Bonomi (Milano: Sugar).

1966
Humanisme und Terror, I-II. (Nos. 147-148: Edition Suhrkamp.) Trans. Eva Moldenhauer (Frankfurt: A. M., Suhrkamp).

1967
"What is Phenomenology?" in *Phenomenology.* Ed. Joseph J. Kockelmans (Garden City, New York: Anchor Books; Doubleday and Co., Inc.), pp. 356-374.
[This is a complete reprint of the *Preface* in *Phenomenology of Perception,* trans. Colin Smith]
"Difficulties Involved in a Subordination of Psychology" in *Phenomenology.* Ed. Joseph J. Kockelmans (Garden City, New York: Anchor Books; Doubleday and Co., Inc.), pp. 485-502.
[This is a reprint of pp. 64-78 of *The Primacy of Perception and Other Essays,* ed. James M. Edie].

1968
The Visible and the Invisible; followed by Working Notes. Ed. Claude Lefor, trans. Alphonso Lingis (Evanston, Ill.: Northwestern University Press).

1969
The Essential Writings of Merleau-Ponty. Ed. Alden L. Fischer (New York: Harcourt, Brace and World, Inc.).
[This volume contains reprints of various translations, principally those of the Northwestern University Press. Fischer has included a new translation by him: "Phenomenology and Psychoanalysis, *Preface* to Hesnard's *L'Œuvre de Freud*"].
Humanism and Terror: An Essay on the Communist Problem. Trans. with notes by John O'Neill (Boston: Beacon Press).
"The 'Sensation' as a Unit of Experience" in *Perception: Selected Readings in Science and Phenomenology.* Ed. Paul Tibbetts (Chicago: Quadrangle Books), pp. 234-247.
[This is a reprint of Chapter I (pp. 3-12) of *Phenomenology of Perception,* trans. Colin Smith]
"The Metaphysical in Man" in *Perception: Selected Readings in Science and Phenomenology.* Ed. Paul Tibbetts (Chicago: Quadrangle Books), pp. 318-330.
[This is a reprint of pp. 83-86, 92-98 of *Sense and Non-sense,* trans. Hubert L. Dreyfus and Patricia A. Dreyfus. Omitted in the reprint are pp. 86-92 of the original translation text].

1970
Themes from the Lectures at the Collège de France, 1952-1960. Trans. John O'Neill (Evanston, Ill.: Northwestern University Press).
The Prose of the World. Trans. John O'Neill (Evanston, Ill.: Northwestern University Press).

II. SECONDARY SOURCES

A. Reviews of Merleau-Ponty's Treatises

Alquié, Ferdinand. "Etude sur le comportement", *Cahiers du Sud* XXXI, no. 267 (August-September, 1944), pp. 48-54.

Anon. Review of *Les Aventures de la dialectique, L'Express* (May 28, 1955), p. 13.

—. "Making Sense of Consciousness", *The Times Literary Supplement*, no. 3318 (September 30, 1965), p. 883.

—. "Phenomenology", *The Times Literary Supplement*, no. 2300 (March 3, 1946), p. 106.

—. Review of *Phenomenology of Perception, Heythrop Journal* V (April, 1964), p. 235.

—. Review of *La Structure du comportement, Revue de Métaphysique et de Morale* L, no. 4 (October, 1945), pp. 307-308.

—. Review of *La Phénoménologie de la perception, Revue de Métaphysique et de Morale* LI, no. 2 (April, 1946), pp. 183-184.

Borne, Etienne. Review of *Les Aventures de la dialectique, La Vie Intellectuelle* XXVI, no. 7 (July, 1955), pp. 6-19.

Campbell, Robert. Review of *Sens et non-sens, Paru* LI (February-March, 1949), pp. 66-67.

Collins, J. Review of *The Structure of Behavior, Cross Currents* XIV (Fall, 1964), p. 460.

Cruz, J. Review of *In Praise of Philosophy, Philippine Studies* XII (October, 1964), p. 764.

De Beauvoir, Simone. Review of *La Phénoménologie de la perception, Les Temps Modernes* I, no. 2 (November, 1945), pp. 363-367.

Fisher, Alden L. Review of *Phenomenology of Perception, Modern Schoolman* XLII (November, 1964), pp. 100-104.

—. Review of *Sense and Non-Sense, Signs,* and *The Primacy of Perception and Other Essays, Modern Schoolman* XLVI, no. 4 (May, 1969), pp. 357-360.

G., Y. Review of *La Phénoménologie de la perception, Paru* XIV (January, 1946), pp. 99-101.

Gendlin, Eugene. Review of *The Structure of Behavior, Modern Schoolman* XIII (November, 1964), pp. 87-96.

Ginnane, W. J. Review of *In Praise of Philosophy* and *Phenomenology of Perception, The Australasian Journal of Philosophy* XLII, no. 1 (May, 1964), pp. 135-142.

Gurwitsch, Aron. Review of *La Phénoménologie de la perception, Philosophy and Phenomenological Research* X, no. 3 (March, 1950), pp. 442-444.

—. Review of *The Phenomenology of Perception.* Trans. Colin Smith, *Philosophical Review,* LXXIII (July, 1964), pp. 417-422.

Grenier, Jean. Review of *La Phénoménologie de la perception, L'Arche* III, no. 10 (October, 1945), pp. 135-136.

Hodges, Clark. Review of *The Primacy of Perception* and *Signs, Philosophy and Phenomenological Research* XXVI, no. 2 (December, 1965), pp. 271-274.

Holloway, M. Review of *In Praise of Philosophy, Modern Schoolman* XLI (November, 1963), p. 105.

Jouhet, Serge. "Maurice Merleau-Ponty: *Signes*", *La Table Ronde, no.* 160 (April, 1961), pp. 148-151.

Kaufman, Fritz. Review of *La Phénoménologie de la perception, Erasmus* II, nos. 7-8 (January 15, 1949), columns 202-206.

Lauer, Quentin. Review of *In Praise of Philosophy* and *Phenomenology of Perception, Thought,* XXXIX (Spring, 1964), p. 144.
—. Review of *The Structure of Behavior, New Scholasticism* XL (January, 1966) p. 126.

Le Blond, J. Review of *Les Aventures de la dialectique, Études* CCVII (November, 1955), pp. 209-219.

Lingis, Alphonso. Review of *La Prose du Monde, Man and World* III, no. 4 (November, 1970), pp. 406-414.

Patri, Aime. Review of *Humanisme et terreur, Paru* XLII (May, 1948), pp. 61-62.

Robinson. Review of *In Praise of Philosophy, Philosophy and Phenomenological Research* XXV, no. 1 (September, 1964), p. 151.

Sokolowski, R. Review of *Signs, New Scholasticism* XL (April, 1966), pp. 246-250.

Spiegelberg, Herbert. Review of *The Structure of Behavior, Modern Schoolman* XLII (November, 1964), p. 96.

Taylor, Charles. Review of *The Primacy of Perception* and *Signs, The Philosophical Review* LXXVI, no. 1 (January, 1967), pp. 113-117.

Van Lier, Henri. "A propos des *Aventures de la dialectique, philosophie et politique*", *La Revue Nouvelle* (1955), pp. 222-232.

Van Marter, Leslie Edward. Review of *In Praise of Philosophy, Ethics* LXXVII, no. 2 (January, 1967), pp. 154-158.

Warnock, Mary. "Down (again) with Descartes", *New Society* V, no. 140 (June, 3 1965), pp. 30-31.

B. Analyses of Merleau-Ponty's Treatises

1. Books

Bakker, Reinout. *Merleau-Ponty* (Wijsgerige monografieën.) Onder red. van B. Delfgaauw, G. R. Nuchelmans en J. Sperna Weiland (Baarn, Netherlands: Het Wereldvenster, 1965).
—. *Noodzakelijke samenwerking* (Groningen, Wottens: Antwerpen, Noord-Nederlands Boekbedrijf, 1965).

Bannan, John F. *The Philosophy of Merleau-Ponty* (New York: Harcourt, Brace and World, Inc., 1967).

Barral, Mary Rose. *Merleau-Ponty: The Role of the Body-Subject in Interpersonal Relations* (Pittsburgh: Duquesne University Press, 1965).

Bonomi, Andrea. *Esistenza e struttura: Saggio su Merleau-Ponty* (Milan: Il Saggiatore, 1967).

Centineo, Ettore. *Una Fenomenologia della storia. L'Esistenzialismo di M. Merleau-Ponty* (Palermo: Palumbo, 1959).

De Beauvoir, Simone. *J.-P. Sartre versus Merleau-Ponty* [Merleau-Ponty ou l'anti-sartrisme.] Trans. Anibal Leal (Buenos Aires: Ed. Siglo Veints, 1963).

Derossi, Giorgio. *Maurice Merleau-Ponty (Filosofi d'oggi)* (Torino: Edizioni di Filosofia, 1965).

De Waehlens, Alphonse. *Une Philosophie de l'ambiguité; L'Existentialisme de Maurice Merleau-Ponty.* (Vol. 9: Bibliothèque de philosophie de Louvain.) 3rd ed. (Louvain: Nauwelaerts, 1968). (First published in 1951: Louvain, Publications Universitaires de Louvain).

Drevet, Claude, 'La Honte', *Revue de Métaphysique et de Morale* LXXIV (December, 1969), pp. 406-416.

Fressin, Augustin. *La Perception chez Bergson et chez Merleau-Ponty* (Paris: Société d'éditions d'enseignement Supérieur, 1967).

Garaudy, R., Cogniot, G., Cavening, M., Desant, J.-T., Kanapa, J., Leduc, V., et Lefebvre, H. *Mésaventures de l'anti-marxisme de Maurice Merleau-Ponty. Avec une lettre de G. Lukács* (Paris: Editions Sociales, 1956).

Halda, Bernard. *Merleau-Ponty ou la philosophie de l'ambiguité.* (Vol. 72: Archives des Lettres Modernes.) (Paris: Les Lettres Modernes, 1966).

Hyppolite, Jean. *Sens et existence dans la philosophie de Maurice Merleau-Ponty.* (The Zaharoff Lecture for 1963.) (Oxford: The Clarendon Press, 1963).

Kaelin, Eugene F. *An Existential Aesthetic: The Theories of Sartre and Merleau-Ponty* (Madison, Wisconsin: The University of Wisconsin Press, 1962).

Kwant, Remy C. *The Phenomenological Philosophy of Merleau-Ponty.* (Vol. XV: Duquesne Studies; Philosophical Series.) (Pittsburgh: Duquesne University Press, 1963).
—. *De fenomenologie van Merleau-Ponty* (Utrecht: Het Spectrum, 1962).
—. *De stemmen van de stilte. Merleau-Ponty's analyse van de schilderkunst* (Hilversum: Paul Brand, 1966).
—. *From Phenomenology to Metaphysics: An Inquiry into the Last Period of Merleau-Ponty's Philosophical Life.* (Vol. XX: Duquesne Studies; Philosophical Series.) (Pittsburgh: Duquesne University Press, 1966).
—. *De wijsbegeerte van Merleau-Ponty.* 2nd Ed. (Utrecht and Antwerp: Aula-Boeken, 1968).
—. *Mens en expressie in het licht van de wijsbegeerte van Merleau-Ponty* (Utrecht and Antwerp: Aula-Boeken, 1968).

Langan, Thomas. *Merleau-Ponty's Critique of Reason* (New Haven: Yale University Press, 1966).

Maier, Willi. *Das Problem der Leiblichkeit bei Jean-Paul Sartre und Maurice Merleau-Ponty.* (Vol. VII: Forschungen z. Paedagogik und Anthropologie.) (Tübingen: Max Niemeyer, 1964).

Moreau, Joseph. *L'Horizon des esprits. Essai critique sur "La Phénoménologie de la perception"* (Paris: Presses Universitaires de France, 1960).

O'Neill, John. *Perception, Expression, and History.* (Evanston, Ill.: Northwestern University Press, 1970).

Pie, Eliseo Touron del. *El Hombre, el mundo y Dios en la fenomenologia de Merleau-Ponty.* (Madrid: Revista estudio, 1961).

Ravagnán, Luis Maria. *Merleau-Ponty*. (Buenos Aires: Centro editor de America Latina, 1967).

Robinet, André. *Merleau-Ponty: Sa vie, son œuvre, avec un exposé de sa philosophie* (Paris: Presses Universitaires de France, 1963).

Schrader, George A. *Existential Philosophers: Kierkegaard to Merleau-Ponty* (New York: McGraw Hill Book Co., 1967).

Semerari, Giuseppe. *Da Schelling a Merleau-Ponty: Studi sulla filosophia contemporanea* (Bologna: Cappelli, 1962).

Thévénaz, Pierre. *De Husserl à Merleau-Ponty: Qu'est-ce que la phénoménologie?* Intro. Jean Brun (Neuchâtel: Editions de la Baconnière, 1966).

Tilliette, Xavier. *Philosophes contemporaines: Gabriel Marcel, Maurice Merleau-Ponty, Karl Jaspers; textes et études philosophiques* (Paris - Bruges: Desclée de Brouwer, 1962).

—. *Le Corps et le temps dans la 'Phénoménologie de la perception'* (Basel: Verlag für Recht und Gesenschaft, 1964).

2. *Articles and Essays.*

Alquié, Ferdinand. "Une Philosophie de l'ambiguité: L'Existentialisme de Maurice Merleau-Ponty", *Fontaine* II, no. 59 (April, 1947), pp. 47-70.

—. "Maurice Merleau-Ponty", *Cahiers du Sud* XLVIII, nos. 362-363 (September-November, 1961), pp. 153-155.

Andry, Colette. "La Vie d'un philosophe", in *L'Express* (May 11, 1961), pp. 34-35.

Anon. "Maurice Merleau-Ponty" in *Grand Larousse Encyclopédique* (Paris, 1963) VII, p. 273.

Anon. "Merleau-Ponty, fenomenologo existencialista", *Filosofia* (1958), pp. 291-293.

Antunes, M. "Significacao de M. Merleau-Ponty", *Brotéria* (Lisboa), LXXIV, no. 5 (1962), pp. 546-560.

Bakker, Reinout. "Der Andere Mensch in der Phänomenologie Merleau-Ponty", *Evangelische Ethik* I (1960), pp. 10-26.

—." De leer van 'de ander' in de fenomenologie van Merleau-Ponty" in *Handelingen v. h. 25e Nederlands Filologencongres, 1958* (Groningen, 1958), pp. 86-88.

—. "De geschiedenis in het denken van Merleau-Ponty", *Wijsgerig perspectief op maatschappij en wetenschap* VI (1965-1966), pp. 44-56.

Ballanti, Graziella. "L'Esistenzialismo di Merleau-Ponty", *Rivista di Filosofia Neoscolastica* XLIV, no. 5 (September-October, 1952), pp. 458-461.

Ballard, Edward G. "The Philosophy of Merleau-Ponty", *Tulane Studies in Philosophy* IX (1960), pp. 165-187.

—. "On Cognition of the Pre-Cognitive", *Philosophical Quarterly* XI, no. 44 (July, 1961), pp. 238-244.

Bannan, John F. "Philosophical Reflection and the Phenomenology of Merleau-Ponty", *Review of Metaphysics* VIII, no. 3 (March, 1955), pp. 418-422.

—. "Merleau-Ponty on God", *International Philosophical Quarterly* VI, no. 3 (September, 1966), pp. 341-365.

—. "The 'Later' Thought of Merleau-Ponty", *Dialogue* V. no. 3 (December, 1966), pp. 383-403.

Barral, Mary Rose. "Merleau-Ponty on the Body", *The Southern Journal of Philosophy* VII, no. 2 (Summer, 1969), pp. 171-179.

Bataillon, M. "Éloge prononcé devant l'Assemblée des Professeurs du Collège de France, 25 juin 1961", *Annuaire du Collège de France* (Paris: Imprimerie Nationale, 1961), pp. 37-40.

Bayer, Raymond. "Merleau-Ponty's Existentialism", *University of Buffalo Studies* (Monographs in Philosophy) XIX, no. 3 (1951), pp. 95-104.

—. "Merleau-Ponty et l'existentialisme", *Revue Philosophique de la France et de l'Étranger* LXXXVII (January-March, 1962), pp. 107-117.

Beerling, R. F. "Maurice Merleau-Ponty", *De Gids. Algemeen cultureel maandblad* CXXVI, no. 5 (Supplement, 1963), pp. 391-407.

Bergeron, André. "La Conscience engagée dans le régime des significations selon Merleau-Ponty", *Dialogue* V, no. 3 (December, 1966), pp. 373-382.

Biemel, Walter. "Sartres Widerpart: Maurice Merleau-Ponty in Deutschland", *Die Zeit* XXI, no. 42 (1966), s. 29.

Blanco, Domingo. "Vida y conocimiento en la filosofia de Merleau-Ponty", *Rivista de Filosofia* XX (1961), pp. 177-195.

Bonomi, Andrea. "Materialismo storico e questione esistentenziale", *Aut Aut*, no. 75 (1963), pp. 66-72.

Bouet, Michel-M. "Le Problème de l'intériorité objective dans la psychologie phéno-ménologique de M. Merleau-Ponty", *Les Etudes Philosophiques*, III, no. 3-4 (July-December, 1948), pp. 297-374.

Brus, B. Th. "De taal bij Merleau-Ponty", siehe auch Raymond Aron, *Nederlandsch Tijdschrift voor de Psychologie en haar Grensgebieden* XIII, no. 1 (1958), pp. 26-80.

—. "Een samenvatting van de Zienswijzen van M. Merleau-Ponty met betrekking tot de taal", *Algemeen Nederlands Tijdschrift voor Wijsbegeerte en Psychologie* LVI (1963-1964), pp. 75-87.

Brusch, Jean-Louis. "Maurice Merleau-Ponty", *Marginales* XVI, nos. 80-81 (November-December, 1961), pp. 60-62.

Burgers, Antoon. "De houding van Bergson en Merleau-Ponty ten opzichte van de wetenschappen", *Tijdschrift voor Filosofie* XXVII (1965), pp. 262-297.

Busch, Thomas. "Merleau-Ponty and the Problem of Origins", *Philosophy Today* XI, no. 2 (Summer, 1967), pp. 124-130.

Gaillois, Roland-P. "Note sur l'analyse réflexive et la réflexion phénoménologique" in *Deucalion* I (Paris: Editions de la Revue Fontaine, 1946).

—. "Destin de l'humanisme marxiste", *Critique* IV no. 22 (March, 1948), pp. 243-251.

—. "Le Monde vécu et l'histoire" in *L'Homme, le Monde, l'Histoire* (Paris: Arthaud, 1948), pp. 7-24.

Capizzi, Antonio. "Figure dell'ateismo francese dei Dopoguerra", *Giornale Critico della Filosofia Italiana* XLV (October-December, 1966), pp. 541-586.

Carr, David. "Maurice Merleau-Ponty: Incarnate Consciousness" in *Existential Philosophers: Kierkegaard to Merleau-Ponty*. Ed. George A. Schrader, Jr. (New York: McGraw Hill Book Co., 1967), pp. 369-429.

Cazabon, Gilles. "Deux approches antithetiques du probleme du comportement", *Revue Philosophique de Louvain*, LXVII (November, 1969), pp. 546-581.

Ceriotto, C. L. "Lenguaje y reflexión según Merleau-Ponty", *Philosophia*, no. 29 (1964), pp. 50-58.

Charlesworth, James H. "Reflections on Merleau-Ponty's Phenomenological Description of 'Word'", *Philosophy and Phenomenological Research* XXX (June, 1970), pp. 609-613.

Charron, Ghyslain. "Du Langage: La Linguistique de Martinet et la phénomenologie de Merleau-Ponty", *Revue de l'Universite d'Ottawa* XL (April-June, 1970), pp. 260-283.

Chatelet, François. "M. Merleau-Ponty et la dernière mode de l'anticommunisme", *La Nouvelle Critique* VII, no. 67 (July-August, 1955), pp. 30-48.

Christianus. "Sainte Antigone", *La Vie Intellectuelle* XV, no. 1 (January, 1947), pp. 1-4.

Cowley, Fraser. "L'Expression et la parole d'après Merleau-Ponty", *Dialogue* V, no. 3 (December, 1966), pp. 360-372.

Daly, James. "Merleau-Ponty's Concept of Phenomenology", *Philosophical Studies* XVI (1967), pp. 137-164.

De Beauvoir, Simone. "Merleau-Ponty et le pseudosartrisme", *Les Temps Modernes* X, nos. 114-115 (April-May, 1955), pp. 2072-2122. Reprinted in *Privileges* (Paris: Editions Gallimard, 1955).

Debray, Régis. "Avec *Signes* Merleau-Ponty veut faire parler l'histoire", *Arts* III, no. 802 (January, 1961), n.p.

Deguy, Michel. "Maurice Merleau-Ponty", *La Nouvelle Revue Française* IX, no. 102 (June, 1961), pp. 1118-1120.

—. "A propos de *Signes*", *La Nouvelle Revue Française* IX no. 99 (1961), pp. 481-485.

—. "*Le Visible et l'invisible*", *La Nouvelle Revue Française* XII, no. 138 (1964), pp. 1062-1072.

Delgaauw, B. "De inaugurale rede van Maurice Merleau-Ponty", *Studia Catholica* XXVIII (1953), pp. 137-139.

Delfino, R. "S. I. Cuerpo y alma en Merleau-Ponty", *Ciencia y Fe* XX (1964), pp.37-76

Derossi, Giorgio. "Maurice Merleau-Ponty dall' (ambiguità) al trascendentalismo corporeo", *Filosofia* XIV (1963), pp. 387-411.

—. "L'Emergenza del percepito e del significato dal progretto intenzionale corporeo in Merleau-Ponty", *Filosofia* XV (1964), pp. 127-153.

—. "Tempo, soggetto, cogito e conscenza intenzionale diretta (non-mediate) in Merleau-Ponty", *Filosofia* XV (1964), pp. 587-715.

—. "Dalla percezione alla vizione. L'Ontologie negatieve dell'ultimo Merleau-Ponty", *Filosofia* XVI (1965), pp. 333-357.

Derrida, Jacques. "La Forme et le Vouloir-dire; Note sur la phénoménologie du langage", *Revue Internationale de Philosophie* XXI (1967), pp. 277-299.

De Waelhens, Alphonse. "Over de betekenis van het œuvre van Maurice Merleau-Ponty", *Tijdschrift voor Filosofie* (1950), pp. 477ff.

—. "De taalphilosophie volgens M. Merleau-Ponty", *Tijdschrift voor Filosofie* XVI, no. 4 (Supplement, 1954), pp. 402-408.

—. "La Philosophie du langage selon M. Merleau-Ponty" in *Existence et signification* (Louvain: Editions E. Nauwelaerts, 1958), pp. 123-141.

—. "In Memoriam Maurice Merleau-Ponty", *Tijdschrift voor Filosofie* XXIII, no. 2 (June, 1961), pp. 340-347.

—. "Maurice Merleau-Ponty", *Ephemerides-theologicae Lovanienses,* XXXVII (1961), p. 935.

—. "Maurice Merleau-Ponty", *Revue Philosophique de Louvain* LIX, no. 62 (May, 1961), pp. 378-380.

—. "Situation de Merleau-Ponty", *Les Temps Modernes* XVII, nos. 184-185 (October,

1961), pp. 377-398. Trans. by Rosemary Lauer as "The Philosophical Position of Merleau-Ponty", *Philosophy Today* VII, no. 2 (Summer, 1963), pp. 134-149.

——. "Maurice Merleau-Ponty", *Revista Portuguesa de Filosofia* XVIII (1962), p. 176.

——. "Merleau-Ponty: philosophe de la peinture", *Revue de Metaphysique et de Morale* LXVII, no. 4 (October-December, 1962), pp. 431-449.

Douglas, Kenneth. "A Critical Bibliography of Existentialism (The Paris School)", *Yale French Studies*, Special Monograph no. 1 (1950), items nos. 201-229. [M. M-P. Bibliography to 1950; incomplete].

Drevet, Claude. "La Honte", *Revue de Metaphysique et de Morale* LXXIV (October-December, 1969), pp. 406-416.

Dreyfus, Hubert L., and Todes, S.J. "The Three Worlds of Merleau-Ponty", *Philosophy and Phenomenological Research* XXII, no. 4 (June, 1962), pp. 559-565.

Dufrenne, Mikel. "Maurice Merleau-Ponty", *Les Études Philosophiques* XVII, no. 1 (1962), pp. 81-92.

——. "Les Aventures de la dialectique ou les avatars d'une amitié philosophique (Merleau-Ponty)" in *Jalons*. (Vol. XX: Phaenomenologica.) (The Hague: Martinus Nijhoff, 1966), pp. 169-173. Reprint from *Combat*, September 29, 1953.

Ecker, David W. "How to Think in Other Categories: The Problem of Alternative Conceptions of Aesthetic Education", *Journal of Aesthetic Education* IV (April, 1970), pp. 21-36.

Ecole, Jean. "Rentrée au Collège de France avec M. Merleau-Ponty", *Revue Thomiste* LIII (1953), pp. 193-196.

Edie, James M. "Recent Developments in Phenomenology", *American Philosophical Quarterly* I, no. 2 (April, 1964), pp. 115-128.

Egebak, Niels. "Maurice Merleau-Ponty" in *Indskifter: Essays om Foenomenologi og Aestetik* (Fredensborg: Arena-Forfatterns Forlag, 1967), pp. 92-111.

Estrabou, Elma. "La Significatión del tiempo en la filosofia de Merleau-Ponty", *Revista de Humanidades (Córdoba)* II, no. 5 (1962), pp. 58-66.

Fausta, Falco. "La Fluidificazione dell'assoluto in M. Merleau-Ponty", *Atti della Accademia delle Scienze di Torino. Classe di Scienze Morali, Storiche e Filologiche* XCV (1960-1961), pp. 405-458.

Ferraris, Anna. "L'Apertura all'alterità nella Filosofia di Maurice Merleau-Ponty", s.a. Bergson, *Atti della Accademia delle Scienze di Torino. Classe di Scienze Morali, Storiche e Filologiche* XCVII, no. 1 (Supplement, 1962-1963), pp. 249-291.

Fisher, Alden L. "Maurice Merleau-Ponty" in *New Catholic Encyclopedia*. Ed. William J. McDonald (New York: McGraw Hill), 1967, IX, p. 687.

Fontan, Pierre. "Le Primat de l'acte sur l'énonce. A propos de *La Phénoménologie de la perception*", *Revue Philosophique de Louvain* LIII, no. 37 (February, 1955), pp. 40-53.

Fragata, Júlio. "A Filosofia de Merleau-Ponty", *Revista Portuguesa de Filosofia*, XIX (1963), pp. 113-141.

G., J. "Maurice Merleau-Ponty", *Humanitas (Tucuman)* IX, no. 14 (1961), pp. 288-289.

Gandillac, Maurice de. "Maurice Merleau-Ponty (1908-1961)", *Revue Philosophique de la France et de l'Étranger* LXXXVII (January-March, 1962), pp. 103-106.

Gerber, Rudolph J. "Merleau-Ponty: The Dialectic of Consciousness and World", *Man and World* II, no. 1 (February, 1969), pp. 83-107.

Gillan, Garth. "The Temporality of Language and the Symbolic", *Philosophy and Rhetoric* III, no. 1 (Winter, 1970), pp. 13-39.

Grene, Marjorie. "The Aesthetic Dialogue of Sartre and Merleau-Ponty", *Journal of the British Society for Phenomenology* I, no. 2 (May, 1970), pp. 59-72.

Greppi, Alessandra. "'Le Visible et l'invisible' di M. Merleau-Ponty", *Rivista di Filosofia Neo-scolastica* LIX (1967), pp. 238-244.

Hanly, C. M. T. "Phenomenology, Consciousness and Freedom", *Dialogue,* V no. 3 (December, 1966), pp. 323-345.

Hayen, André. "Le Phénoménologie de M. Merleau-Ponty et la métaphysique", *Revue Philosophique de Louvain* L, no. 25 (February, 1952), pp. 102-123.

Haymond, William S. "Merleau-Ponty on Sensory Perception", *Modern Schoolman* XLIV, no. 2 (January, 1967), pp. 93-111.

Holz, Hans Heinz. "Situierung eines Deukers. Bemerkungen zu Maurice Merleau-Ponty", *Festschrift zum achtzigsten Geburtstag von Georg Lukacs, hrsg. von Frank Benseler,* Neuwied, 1966 (Supplement, 1966), pp. 317-329.

Hyppolite, Jean. "A Chronology of French Existentialism", *Yale French Studies,* no. 16 (Winter, 1955-1956), pp. 100-102.
—. "Existence et dialectique dans la philosophie de Merleau-Ponty", *Les Temps Modernes* XVII, nos. 184-185 (October, 1961), pp. 228-244.

Jacques, J. H. "Exorcizing the Ghost in the Machine", *The Listener* LXXIV, no. 1893 (July, 1965), pp. 49-51.

Jelly, F. "A Thomist Dialogues with Merleau-Ponty", *Dominicana* LII (Fall, 1967), pp. 242-250.

Joliolt, Régis. "Le Problème de l'absolu dans la philosophie de M. Merleau-Ponty", *Tijdschrift voor Filosofie* XIX, no. 1 (March-June, 1957), pp. 53-100. Abridged trans. by M. Delphine and Alphonse Spilly, "The Problem of God in the Philosophy of Merleau-Ponty", *Philosophy Today* VII, no. 2 (Summer, 1963), pp. 150-164.

Jung, Hwa Yol. "The Radical Humanization of Politics: Maurice Merleau-Ponty's Philosophy of Politics", *Archiv für Rechts und Sozialphilosophie* LIII, no. 2 (1967).

Kaelin, E. F. "Merleau-Ponty, Fundamental Ontologist", *Man and World* III (February, 1970), pp. 102-115.

Kemp, Peter. "La Philosophie du langage de Merleau-Ponty", *Danish Yearbook of Philosophy* IV (1967), pp. 7-11.

Kockelmans, Joseph J. "Ruimtewaarneming en ruimte volgens Merleau-Ponty" *Tijdschrift voor Filosofie* XIX. no. 3 (1957), pp. 372-427.
—. "Merleau-Ponty's Phenomenology of Language", *Review of Existential Psychology and Psychiatry* III, no. 1 (Winter, 1963), pp. 39-82.
—. "Merleau-Ponty's View on Space-Perception and Space", *Review of Existential Psychology and Psychiatry* IV, no. 1 (Winter, 1964), pp. 69-105.
—. "Merleau-Ponty on Sexuality", *Journal of Existentialism* VI, no. 21 (Fall, 1965), pp. 9-29.
—. "Maurice Merleau-Ponty" in *Phenomenology* (Garden City, New York: Anchor Books; Doubleday and Co., Inc.) 1967, pp. 349-355.

Kuhn, Helmut. "Existentialismus und Marxismus. Zu Merleau-Ponty's Philosophie der Zweideutigkeit", *Philosophisches Jahrbuch* LXII (1953), pp. 327-346.

Kullman, Michael, and Taylor, Charles. "The Pre-Objective World", *Review of Metaphysics* XII, no. 1 (Issue 45, September, 1958), pp. 108-132.

Kwant, Remy C. "Menselijke existentie en geschiedenis volgens het wijsgerig denken van Maurice Merleau-Ponty", *Alg. Nederl. Tijdschrift voor Wijsbegeerte en Psychologie* (1954), pp. 230-247. Summary in French.

—. "Transcendeert Merleau-Ponty het realisme?" *Tijdschrift voor Filosofie* XVI (Supplement, 1954), pp. 236-264. Summary in English.

—. "De harmonische uitgroei van een wijsbegeerte, Naar aanleiding van de laatste publicatie van Maurice Merleau-Ponty", *Studia Catholica* XXX, no. 3 (1955), pp. 203-219.

—. "De historie en het absolute. Kritische analyse van de opvatting van Merleau-Ponty", s.a. H. Bergson, *Tijdschrift voor Filosofie* XVII (1955), pp. 255-305. Summary in French.

—. "De zingedachte van Maurice Merleau-Ponty", *Bijdragen der Phil. en Theol. Fac. N. en Z. Nederland Jez.* (1955), pp. 1-31.

—. "Maurice Merleau-Ponty : de hoop in de wereld", *Kultuurleven* (1956), pp. 137-145.

—. "De geslotenheid van Merleau-Ponty's wijsbegeerte", *Tijdschrift voor Filosofie* XIX (1957), pp. 217-272. Summary in French.

—. "De verhouding tussen wijsbegeerte en psychologie in het denken van Maurice Merleau-Ponty", *Annalen v. h. Thijmgenootschap* XLVI, no. 2 (1957), pp. 164-181.

—. "Merleau-Ponty's zienswijze omtrent de waarheid", *Handelingen v. h. XXIIe Vlaams Filologencongres* (1957), pp. 74-78.

—. "In memoriam M. Merleau-Ponty", *Streven* XIV (1960-1961), pp. 946-960.

—. "De wijsbegeerte van Merleau-Ponty", *Algemeen Nederlands Tijdschrift voor Wijsbegeerte en Psychologie* LIV (1961-1962), pp. 1-21.

—. "Levensechte wijsbegeerte. Naar aanleiding van de dood van Maurice Merleau-Ponty", *Tijdschrift voor Psychologie (Gawein)* X (1961), pp. 71-81.

—. "De ontwikkeling van Merleau-Ponty's denken", *Tijdschrift voor Filosophie* XXVI, no. 4 (Supplement, 1964), pp. 627-669.

—. "De autonomie van de wijsbegeerte volgens Merleau-Ponty", *Algemeen nederlands Tijdschrift voor Wijsbegeerte en Psychologie, Assen.* LVIII (1966), pp. 122-135.

—. "Merleau-Ponty and Phenomenology" in *Phenomenology.* Ed. Joseph J. Kockelmans (Garden City, New York: Anchor Books; Doubleday and Co., Inc., 1967), pp. 375-392. Reprint from Kwant's book *The Phenomenological Philosophy of Merleau-Ponty*, pp. 153-168.

—. "Merleau-Ponty's Criticism of Husserl's Eidetic Reduction" in *Phenomenology.* Ed. Joseph Kockelmans (Garden City, New York: Anchor Books; Doubleday and Co., Inc., 1967), pp. 393-408. Reprint from Kwant's book *From Phenomenology to Metaphysics,* pp. 156-169.

—. "The Human Body as the Self-Awareness of Being (An Inquiry into the Last Phase of Merleau-Ponty's Philosophical Life)", *Review of Existential Psychology and Psychiatry* VIII, no. 2 (Spring, 1968), pp. 117-134. Originally printed in *Humanitas* II (1966), pp. 43-62.

—. "De Mens als Oorsprong", *Tijdschrift voor Filosofie* XXXI (September, 1969), pp. 441-470.

Lacan, Jacques. "Maurice Merleau-Ponty", *Les Temps Modernes* XVII, nos. 184-185 (October, 1961), pp. 245-254.

Lacas, Pierre-Paul, "Représentation et expression de CORPS; la pensée contemporaine de Schilder à Merleau-Ponty le secret du corps est-il les profondeurs de l'ame?" *AS (L'Art Sacré),* no. 1 (premier trimestre, 1969), pp. 3-22.

Lacroix, Jean. "Un Philosophe de l'ambiguité: Maurice Merleau-Ponty" in *Panorama de la Philosophie Française Contemporaine.* Deuxième édition augmentée (Paris: Presses Universitaires de France, 1968), pp. 137-144. (First published in 1966).

Lagueux, Maurice. "Merleau-Ponty et la linguistique de Saussure", *Dialogue* IV, no. 3 (1965), pp. 351-364.

—. "Y a-t-il une philosophie de l'histoire chez Merleau-Ponty", *Dialogue,* V no. 3 (December, 1966), pp. 404-417.

Langan, Thomas. "Maurice Merleau-Ponty: In Memoriam", *Philosophy and Pheno menological Research* XXIII, no. 2 (December, 1962), pp. 205-216.

Lanigan, Richard L. "Rhetorical Criticism: An Interpretation of Maurice Merleau-Ponty", *Philosophy and Rhetoric* II, no. 2 (Spring, 1969), pp. 61-71.

—. "Merleau-Ponty's Phenomenology of Communication", *Philosophy Today* XIV, no. 2 (Summer, 1970), pp. 79-88.

Lauer, Quentin. "Four Phenomenologists [Scheler, Heidegger, Sartre, Merleau-Ponty]", *Thought* XXXIII (Summer, 1958), pp. 183-204.

Le Blond, Jean-Marie. "Le Sens de l'histoire et l'action politique", *Études* (November, 1955), pp. 209-219.

Lefebvre, Henri. "M. Merleau-Ponty et la philosophie de l'ambiguité", *Pensée,* no. 68 (July-August, 1956), pp. 44-58; no. 73 (May-June, 1957), pp. 37-52.

Levine, Stephen K. "Merleau-Ponty's Philosophy of Art", *Man and World* II, no. 3, (August, 1969), pp. 438-452.

Lewis, Philip E. "Merleau-Ponty and the Phenomenology of Language", *Yale French Studies,* nos. 36-37 (October, 1966), pp. 19-40.

Lysis. "Merleau-Ponty, critique de Charles Maurras", *La Nation Française,* no. 502 (July 7, 1965), pp. 14-15.

Mansion, Suzanne. "Aristotle's Theory of Knowledge and French Phenomenology", *International Philosophical Quarterly* VI, no. 2 (May, 1964), pp. 183-199.

Martius, Diamantino. "O Comunismo existencialista de M. Merleau-Ponty", *Revista Portuguesa di Filosofia* IX, (1953), pp. 225-250.

Mays, Wolfe. "Whitehead and the Philosophy of Time", *Studium Generale* XXIII (1970), pp. 509-524.

Merleau-Ponty, Maurice. [Special Issue.] *Aut Aut,* no. 66 (November, 1961), pp. 481-576.

Merleau-Ponty, Maurice. [Special Issue]. *Les Temps Modernes* XVII, nos. 184-185 (October, 1961), pp. 193-436.

Meyer, Rudolf W. "Maurice Merleau-Ponty und das Schicksal des franzosischen Existentialismus", *Philosophische Rundschau* V, no. 3 (1955), pp. 129-165.

Millet, Louis. "Sur la Leçon inaugurale de Maurice Merleau-Ponty dans la chaire de Bergson au Collège de France", in *Les Études Bergsoniennes* (Paris: Albin Michel, 1956) IV, pp. 230-233.

Monasterio, X. O. "Paradoxes et mythes de la phénoménologie", *Revue de Métaphy-sique et de Morale* LXXIV (July-September, 1969), pp. 268-280.

Monnerot, Jules. "Liquidation et justification", *La Nef* IV, no. 27 (February, 1947), pp. 8-19.

Montpellier, Gerard de. "La Psychologie est-elle la science du comportement?", *Revue Philosophique de Louvain* LXVIII (May, 1970), pp. 174-192.

Montull, Tomàs. "Maurice Merleau-Ponty y su filosofia", *Estudios Filosoficos* XI (1962), pp. 371-414; XII (1963), pp. 81-133.

—. "Merleau-Ponty: Ambiguedad existencial del cuerpo", *Estudios Filosoficos* XII (1964), pp. 271-317.

—. "Merleau-Ponty: Fenomenologia y campo fenoménico", *Estudios Filosoficos* XIII (1964), pp. 41-80.

Moreau, André. "Merleau-Ponty et Berkeley", *Dialogue* V, no. 3 (December, 1966), pp. 418-424.

Murphy, Richard T. "A Metaphysical Critique of Method, Husserl and Merleau-Ponty", *Boston College Studies in Philosophy* I (1966), pp. 175-207. Reprinted in *The Quest for the Absolute*. Ed. F. J. Adelmann (The Hague: Martinus Nijhoff, 1966), pp. 175-207.

Natanson, Maurice. "The Fabric of Expression", *Review of Metaphysics* XXI, no. 3 (Issue no. 83, March, 1968), pp. 491-505.

Ojea, G. Puente. "Fenomenologia y Marxismo en le pensamiento de M. Merleau-Ponty", *Cuadernos Hispanoamericanos* XXVI (1956), pp. 295-326; XXIX (1959), pp. 221-256.

—. "Existencialismo y Marxismo en la pensamiento de Merleau-Ponty", *Cuadernos Hispanoamericanos* XXX (1957), pp. 41-88.

Olafson, Frederick A. "A Central Theme of Merleau-Ponty's Philosophy" in *Phenomenology and Existentialism*. Ed. R. N. Lee and M. Mandelbaum (Baltimore: John Hopkins Press, 1967), pp. 179-205.

—. "Maurice Merleau-Ponty" in *The Encyclopedia of Philosophy*. Ed Paul Edwards (New York: Macmillan Co. and The Free Press, 1967), V, pp. 279-282.

O'Neill, John "Situation and Temporality", *Philosophy and Phenomenological Research* XXVIII (March, 1968), pp. 413-422.

O'Mahony, Brendan E. "The Rediscovery of Language", *Studies* LIII (Spring, 1964), pp. 72-84.

P., P. "Merleau-Ponty", *Giornale Critico della Filosofia Italiana* XLII (1963), pp. 426-427.

Papi, Fulvio. "Libertà e marximo in Merleau-Ponty", *Atti del XII Congresso internatzionale di filosofia, 1958* XII (Venice, September 12-18, 1958), pp. 361-368. *Storia della filosofia moderne e contemporanea* (Firenze, 1961).

Pariente, Jean-Claude. "Lecture de Merleau-Ponty, I-II" *Critique* XVIII, no. 186 (November, 1962), pp. 957-974; no. 187 (December, 1962), pp. 1066-1078.

Patri, Aimé. "Bibliographie", *Paru* XXXVII (December, 1947), pp. 51-52. [Lists materials cited in *Humanisme et terreur*; incomplete.]

Philippe, M.-D. "Exposé de la phénoménologie de M. Merleau-Ponty", *Nova et Vetera* (1951), pp. 132-146.

—. "Réflexions sur la phénoménologie de M. Merleau-Ponty", *Nova et Vetera* (1951), pp. 198-209.

Pietersma, Henry. "Husserl's Concept of Philosophy", *Dialogue* V, no. 3 (December, 1966), pp. 425-442.

Plinval, George de. "Quand la vérité passe à travers M. Merleau-Ponty", *Ecrits de Paris* (February, 1953), pp. 37-44.

Pontalis, J.B. "Note sur le problème de l'inconscient chez Merleau-Ponty", *Les Temps Modernes* XVII, nos. 184-185 (October, 1961), pp. 287-303.

Poole, R.C. "Indirect Communication. 2. Merleau-Ponty and Lévi-Strauss", *New Black Friars* XLVII, no. 555 (1966), pp. 594-604.

Racette, Jean. "Le Corps et l'âme, la chair et l'esprit, selon Merleau-Ponty", *Dialogue* V, no. 3 (December, 1966), pp. 346-359.

Rauch, Leo. "Sartre, Merleau-Ponty and the Hole in Being", *Philosophical Studies (Ireland)* XVIII (1969), pp. 119-132.

Revel, Jean-François. "Apprendice 3. Un roi sans couronne" in *Pourquoi des philosophes?* 2. *La Cabale des dévots.* (No. XVII: Libertés.) Edit. augmentée (Paris: Jean-Jacques Pairvert, 1965). First published as No. I: Libertés c. 1957.

Ricœur, Paul. "Hommage à Merleau-Ponty", *Esprit* XXVI, no. 6 (June, 1961), pp. 1115-1120. Reprinted from *Nouvelles Littéraires,* May 11, 1961.

Robert, J. D. "Le Sort de la philosophie à l'heure des sciences de l'homme", *Revue des Sciences Philosophiques et Théologiques* XLI (October, 1967), pp. 573-616.

Rouart, Julien. "'La Structure du comportement' de Maurice Merleau-Ponty" in *L'Evolution psychiatrique année 1947,* no. 1 (Paris: Desclée de Brouwer, 1947), pp. 333-350.

Rozitchner, Leon. "Merleau-Ponty: La Ambiguedad como revelación de la crises", *Imago Mundi* III, nos. 11-12 (March-June, 1956), pp. 199-207.

Said, Edward W. "Labyrinth of Incarnations: The Essays of Maurice Merleau-Ponty", *Kenyon Review* XXIX, no. 1 (January, 1967), pp. 54-68.

Sartre, Jean-Paul. "Merleau-Ponty vivant", *Les Temps Modernes,* XVII, nos. 184-185 (October, 1961), pp. 304-376; reprinted in *Situations IV* (Paris: Editions Gallimard, 1964). Trans. by Benita Eisler in *Situations* (Greenwich, Connecticut: Fawcett Publications, Inc., 1966), pp. 156-226.

—. "Merleau-Ponty" in *Pourquoi des philosophes?* Ed. Jean-François Revel (Paris: Jean-Jacques Pairvert, 1964). First published as No. 1: Libertés c. 1957.

Scharfstein, Ben-ami. "Bergson and Merleau-Ponty: A Preliminary Comparison", *Journal of Philosophy,* LII, no. 14 (July 7, 1955), pp. 380-386.

Schmitt, Richard. "Maurice Merleau-Ponty, I-II", *Review of Metaphysics* XIX, no. 3 (March, 1966), pp. 493-516; no. 4 (June, 1966); pp. 728-741.

—. "Phenomenology" in *The Encyclopedia of Philosophy.* Ed. Paul Edwards ((New York: Macmillan Co. and The Free Press, 1967) VI, pp. 135-151.

Schulte, Gunter. "Von Sinn der Wahrnehmung", *Tijdschrift voor Filosofie* XXXI (December, 1969), pp. 732-748.

Scotti, Guiseppina. "Originarietà e relazione in Merleau-Ponty", *Aut Aut* VII, no. 38 (March, 1957), pp. 172-184; no. 39 (May, 1957), pp. 295-309.

—. "Originalità e relazione nella *Phénoménologie de la perception*", *Aut Aut* VII, no. 41 (September, 1957), pp. 436-442.

—. "Sulla percezione in Merleau-Ponty", *Aut Aut* VII, no. 42 (November, 1957). pp. 512-523.

Semerari, Guiseppe. "Critica e projetto dell'uomo nella fenomenologia di Maurice Merleau-Ponty", *Il Pensiero* V, no. 3 (September-December, 1960), pp. 329-359.

—. "Existenzialismo e marxismo nella fenomenologia della percezione", *Rivista di filosofia* LII, no. 2 (April, 1961), pp. 167-191; no. 3 (July, 1961), pp. 330-353.

Sérant, P. "Maurice Merleau-Ponty et la pensée de gauche", *Revue des Deux Mondes* (July 1, 1955), pp. 117-127.

Sheridan, James F. "On Ontology and Politics: A Polemic", *Dialogue* VII, no. 3, (December, 1968), pp. 449-460.

Shiner, Larry. "A Phenomenological Approach to Historical Knowledge", *History and Theory* VIII, no. 2 (1969), pp. 260-274.

Simon, Gérard. "Le Visible et l'invisible", *Lettres Françaises,* VI no. 1032 (June 4-10, 1964), no. 1033 (June 11-17, 1964); no. 1034 (June 18-24, 1964), n.p.

Sinari, Ramakant. "The Phenomenology of Maurice Merleau-Ponty", *Philosophical Quarterly (India)* XXXIX, no. 2 (July, 1966), pp. 129-140.

Smith, Colin. "The Concept as Expression" in *Contemporary French Philosophy* (London: Methuen and Co., Ltd, 1964), pp. 114-136.

—. "The Notion of Object in the Phenomenology of Merleau-Ponty", *Philosophy* XXXIX, no. 148 (April, 1964), pp. 110-119.

—. "Sartre and Merleau-Ponty: The Case for a Modified Essentialism", *Journal of the British Society for Phenomenology* I, no. 2 (May, 1970), pp. 73-79.

Spiegelberg, Herbert. "French Existentialism: Its Social Philosophies", *Kenyon Review,* XVI, no. 3 (Summer, 1954), pp. 446-462.

—. "The Phenomenological Philosophy of Maurice Merleau-Ponty (1908-1961)" in *The Phenomenological Movement.* 2 vols. (Vols. V and VI: Phaenomenologica.) 2nd ed. (The Hague: Martinus Nijhoff, 1965) II, pp. 516-562. (First published in 1959-1960).

—. "Husserl's Phenomenology and Existentialism", *Journal of Philosophy* LII, no. 2 (January 21, 1960), pp. 62-74.

Strasser, Stephen. "Phenomenological Trends in European Psychology", *Philosophy and Phenomenological Research* XVIII, no. 1 (September, 1957), pp. 18-34.

—. "De betekenis van Merleau-Ponty voor de wijsgerige anthropologie", *Gawein* XII (1964), pp. 208-224. Reprinted in *Bouwstenen voor een Filosofische Anthropologie.* (Vol. XII: Paul Brand Paperbacks.) (Hilversum, Antwerpen: Paul Brand, 1965), pp. 313-332.

—. "Merleau-Ponty's bijdrage tot de sociaalfilosofie: Interpretatie en critiek", *Tijdschrift voor Filosofie* XXIX (1967), pp. 427-465.

Sturani, Enrico. "André Robinet: Merleau-Ponty, sa vie, son œuvre, avec un exposé de sa philosophie, Paris, 1963", *Rivista di Filosofia* LV, no. 3 (1964), pp. 350-352.

—. "Letture di Merleau-Ponty", *Revista di Filosofia* LVIII (April-June, 1967), pp. 164-182.

Thévenaz, Pierre. "Qu'est-ce que la phénoménologie?", *Revue de Théologie et de Philosophie* II, no. 3 (1952), pp. 294-316, Reprinted in *What is Phenomenology and Other Essays.* Ed. and introduced by James M. Edie. Trans. James M. Edie, Charles Courtney, and Paul Brockelman (Chicago: Quandrangle Press, 1962).

Tibbetts, Paul. "Some Recent Empirical Contributions to the Problem of Consciousness", *Philosophy Today* XIV (Spring, 1970), pp. 23-32.

Tilliette, Xavier. "Merleau-Ponty ou la mesure de l'homme", *Archives de Philosophie,* XXIV, nos. 3-4 (July-December, 1961), pp. 399-413.

—. "Une Philosophie sans absolu", *Études* CCCX (September, 1961), pp. 215-229.

—. "Maurice Merleau-Ponty, o la medida del hombre", *Razón y Fe* CLXV (February 1962), pp. 127-136.

—. "Le Corps et le temps dans la *Phénoménologie de la perception*", *Studia Philosophia. Jahrbuch der Schweizer Philosophischen Gesellschaft* XXIV (1964), pp. 193-209.

Toscano, Giuseppe. "'In der Welt sein di Maurice Merleau-Ponty", *Teoresi,* XIX (1964), pp. 149-223.

Ullmo, Jean. "Une étape de la pensée politique", *Critique* II, no. 98 (July, 1955), pp. 625-643.

Uranga, E. "Maurice Merleau-Ponty: Fenomenologia y existencialismo", *Filosofia y Letras* XV, no. 30 (1948), pp. 219-242.

Van Breda, H. L. "Maurice Merleau-Ponty et les Archives-Husserl à Louvain",

Revue de Métaphysique et de Morale LXVII, no. 4 (October-December, 1962), pp. 410-430.

Vandenbussche, Frans. "The Problem of God in the Philosophy of Merleau-Ponty", *International Philosophical Quarterly* VII, no. 1 (March, 1967), pp. 45-67.

—. "Het godsprobleem in de filosofie van Maurice Merleau-Ponty", *Bijdragen. Tijdschrift voor Philosophie en Theologie* XXVIII, no. 1 (Supplement, 1967), pp. 63-81.

Van Haecht, L. "In Memoriam Maurice Merleau-Ponty (1908 - 3 mei 1961)", *Dietsche Warande en Belfort* CVI (1961), pp. 350-353.

Verstraelen, Eugene. "Language Analysis and Merleau-Ponty's Phenomenology of Language", *Saint Louis Quarterly* IV (1966), pp. 325-342.

Viano, Carlo. "Esistenzialismo e umanesimo in Maurice Merleau-Ponty", *Rivista di Filosofia* XLIV, no. 1 (January, 1953), pp. 39-60.

Virasoro, Manuel ."Merleau-Ponty y el mundo al nivel de la percepcion", *Ciencia y Fe* (1957), pp. 147-155. Trans. by Michael Correa as "Merleau-Ponty and the World of Perception", *Philosophy Today* III, no. 1 (Spring, 1959), pp. 66-72.

Vita, Luis Washington. "Maurice Merleau-Ponty" in *Monologos y Dialogos.* (No. 34: Colecao Ensaio.) (Sao Paulo: Conselho Estodual de Cultura, Comissao de Literatura, 1964).

—. "M. Merleau-Ponty (1908-1961). In Memoriam", *Revista Brasileira de Filosofia,* XI (1961), pp. 272-274.

Vuillemin, Jules. "La Méthode indirecte de Maurice Merleau-Ponty", *Critique* ,no. 211 (December, 1964), pp. 1007-1016.

Wahl, Jean. "A propos d'une conférence du Maurice Merleau-Ponty sur les aspects politiques et sociaux de l'existentialisme", *Renaissances,* LI (1964), pp. 678-679.

—. "Cette pensée", *Les Temps Modernes* XVII, nos. 184-185 (October, 1961), pp. 399-436.

Waldenfels, Bernhard. "Gedenken an Maurice Merleau-Ponty", *Zeitschrift für Philosophische Forschung,* XVI (1962), pp. 406-413.

—. "Das Problem der Leiblichkeit bei Merleau-Ponty", *Philosophisches Jahrbuch* LXXV (1967-1968), pp. 347-365.

Warnock, Mary. "Maurice Merleau-Ponty" in *Existentialism,* Opus Series no. 52 (London and New York: Oxford University Press, 1970), pp. 71-91.

Zaner, Richard. "Existentialism as a Logos of Man. The Case for M. Merleau-Ponty", *Memorias del XXXIII Congresso Internacional de Filosofia* V (September 7-14, 1963), pp. 409-421. Reprinted in book form (Vol. V: Communicaciones libres.) (Mexico: Universidad Nacional Autónoma de Mexico, 1964).

—. "Merleau-Ponty's Theory of the Body-Proper" in *The Problem of Embodiment* (The Hague: Martinus Nijhoff, 1964), pp. 127-197.

—. "Merleau-Ponty's Theory of Body-Proper as *Être-au-Monde*", *Journal of Existentialism* VI, no. 21 (Fall, 1965), pp. 31-39.

—. "Piaget and Merleau-Ponty: A Study in Convergence", *Review of Existential Psychology and Psychiatry* VI, no. 1 (Winter, 1966), pp. 7-23.

Zani, L. "Fenomenologie dell'essere in Maurice Merleau-Ponty", *Rivista di Filosofia Neoscolastica* XLIX, nos. 5-6 (September-December, 1957), pp. 542-549.

Zuidema, S. U. "Een confrontatie tussen Barths theologische theologie en Merleau-Ponty's filosofische filosofie", *Philosophia Reformata* (1959), pp. 90-96.

3. *Unpublished Materials*

Anzieu, Didier. "Thèses et diplómes d'études supérieures de philosophie", *Essais et Études Universitaires* II (1946), pp. 115-121. A propos des thèses de Polin: Création et compréhension de valeurs; Bontonier: L'angoisse; Merleau-Ponty: Phénoménologie de la perception.

Barral, Mary Rose. "Merleau-Ponty: The Role of the Body in Interpersonal Relations". Unpublished Ph. D. dissertation, Department of Philosophy, Fordham University, 1963. [Revised and published under the title *Merleau-Ponty: The Role of the Body-Subject in Interpersonal Relations*. Pittsburgh: Duquesne University Press, 1965].

Bruzina, Ronald Charles. "Logos and Eidos: A Study in the Phenomenological Meaning (concept) according to Husserl and Merleau-Ponty". Unpublished Ph. D. dissertation, Department of Philosophy, University of Notre Dame, 1966.

Cantwell, Peter W. "Merleau-Ponty: Towards a Phenomenological Psychology of Real Knowledge". Unpublished Ph. D. dissertation, Department of Philosophy, Catholic University of America, 1966.

Delfino, Richardo. "Cuerpo y alma en Merleau-Ponty". Dissertatione ad laurean in Facultate Philosophia Santi Michaels (San Miguel, Argentina, 1964).

Lanigan, Richard L. "Speaking and Semiology: Maurice Merleau-Ponty's Phenomenological Theory of Existential Communication". Unpublished Ph. D. dissertation, School of Communications, Southern Illinois University, 1969.

McCleary, Richard Calverton. "Ambiguity and Freedom in the Philosophy of M. Merleau-Ponty". Unpublished M.A. thesis, Department of Philosophy, University of Chicago, 1954.

Murphy, Richard Timothy, "Phenomenology and the Dialectic: A Study of Pre-Reflexive Consciousness in the Phenomenological Theories of Husserl, Sartre, and Merleau-Ponty". Unpublished Ph. D. dissertation, Department of Philosophy, Fordham University, 1963.

Sandrini, F. "La Fenomenologia di Merleau-Ponty e il rapporto dialettico". Dissertation pour le doctorat en Philosophie, Université Catholique de Louvain, Institut Supérieur de Philosophie, 1957.

Szaszkiewicz, Georgius. "Relation entre le comportement et la connaissance selon Merleau-Ponty: Intelligence, liberté, et réflexion". Dissertatione ad laurem in Facultate philosophia Pontificiae Universitatis Gregorianae, Roma, 1962.

Taylor, Darrell Dewayne. "Husserl and Merleau-Ponty and the Problem of the Cultural Studies". Unpublished Ph. D. disseratation, Department of Philosophy, University of Southern California, 1966.

III. ADDITIONAL REFERENCES

A. Books

Aranguren, J. L. *Human Communication*. Trans. Frances Partridge (New York: McGraw-Hill Book Co., 1967).

Arendt, Hannah. *The Human Condition* (Garden City, New York: Doubleday & Co., Inc., 1959).

Arnheim, Rudolf. *Film as Art* (Berkeley: University of California Press, 1960).

Baird, A. Craig. *Rhetoric: A Philosophical Inquiry* (New York: The Ronald Press Co., 1965).

Barrett, William. *Irrational Man: A Study in Existential Philosophy* (Garden City, New York: Doubleday & Co., Inc., 1962). (First published in 1952).

Blackmur, R. P. *Language as Gesture: Essays in Poetry* (New York: Harcourt, Brace and Co., 1935-1952).

Brazin, André. *What is Cinema?* Trans. Hugh Gray (Berkeley: University of California Press, 1967).

Britton, Karl. *Communication: A Philosophical Study of Language* (New York: Harcourt, Brace, & Co., 1939).

Brown, Charles T., and Van Riper, Charles. *Speech and Man* (Englewood Cliffs, New Jersey: Prentice-Hall, Inc., 1966).

Chisholm, Roderick. *Realism and the Background of Phenomenology* (Glencoe: The Free Press, 1960).

Cioran, E. M. *The Temptation to Exist*. Trans. Richard Howard (Chicago: Quadrangle Books, 1968). (First published as *La Tentation d'exister* in 1956: Paris, Librairie Gallimard).

Cook, Olive. *Movement in Two Dimensions*; *A Study of the Animated and Projected Pictures which Preceded the Invention of Cinematography* (London: Hutchinson, 1963).

Dance, Frank E. X. (ed.). *Human Communication Theory: Original Essays* (New York: Holt, Rinehart, & Winston, Inc., 1967).

De Beauvoir, Simone. *Privileges* (Paris: Editions Gallimard, 1955).

—. *The Ethics of Ambiguity*. Trans. Bernard Frechtman (New York: The Citadel Press, 1964).

DeLaguna, Grace Andrus. *Speech: Its Function and Development* (Bloomington: Indiana University Press, 1963). (First published in 1927).

Dufrenne, Mikel. *Language and Philosophy*. Trans. Henry B. Veatch (Bloomington: Indiana University Press, 1963).

Edie, James M. (ed.). *An Invitation to Phenomenology* (Chicago: Quadrangle Books, 1965).

—. *Phenomenology in America* (Chicago: Quadrangle Books, 1967).

Farber, Marvin. *Phenomenology as a Method and as a Philosophical Discipline* (Buffalo: University of Buffalo, 1928).

—. (ed.). *Philosophic Thought in France and the United States* (Buffalo: University of Buffalo, 1950).

Feldman, Joseph, and Feldman, Harry. *Dynamics of the Film* (New York: Hermitage House, Inc., 1952).

Fogarty, Daniel. *Roots for a New Rhetoric* (New York: Russell & Russell, 1968). (First published in 1959, New York, Bureau of Publications, Teachers College, Columbia University).

Foucault, Michel. *Les Mots et les choses: une archéologie des sciences humaines* (Paris: Éditions Gallimard, 1966).

Gurwitsch, Aron. *Studies in Phenomenology and Psychology* (Evanston, Ill. Northwestern University Press, 1966).

Gusdorf, George. *Speaking (La Parole)*. Trans. Paul T. Brockelman (Evanston, Ill.: Northwestern University Press, 1965).

Heidegger, Martin. *Being and Time*. Trans. John Macquarrie and Edward Robinson (New York: Harper & Row, 1962). (First published as *Sein und Zeit* in 1927: Tübingen, Neomarius Verlag).

—. *Existence and Being*. Trans. D. Scott, R.F. C. Hull, and A. Crick (Chicago: Henry Regnery Co., 1949). (First published in 1927).

—. *What is Philosophy?* Trans. W. Kluback & J. T. Wilde (New York: Twayne Publishers, Inc., 1956).

—. *Introduction to Metaphysics*. Trans. Ralph Manheim (New Haven, Connecticut: Yale University Press, 1959).

Hegel, G. W. F. *The Phenomenology of Mind*. Trans. J. B. Baillie (New York: Harper & Row, Publishers, Inc., 1967). (First published in 1910).

Husserl, Edmund. *Ideas: General Introduction to Pure Phenomenology*. Trans. W. R. Boyce Gibson (New York: Collier Books, 1962). (First published as *Ideen zu einer reinen Phänomenologie und phänomenologischen Philosophie* in 1913).

—. *Cartesian Meditations*. Trans. Dorion Cairns (The Hague: Martinus Nijhoff, 1960).

—. *Phenomenology and the Crisis of Philosophy*. Trans. Quentin Lauer (New York: Harper & Row, Publishers, 1965).

—. *The Paris Lectures*. Trans. Peter Koestenbaum. 2nd. ed. (The Hague: Martinus Nijhoff, 1967).

—. *Logical Investigations* (London: Routledge and Kegan Paul, 1970). Vols I and II.

Jaspers, Karl. *Reason and Existenz*. Trans. William Earle (New York: The Noonday Press, 1955). (First published in 1935).

—. *Truth and Symbol (from Von Der Wahrheit)*. Trans. J. T. Wilde, W. Kluback, and W. Kimmel (New York: Twayne Publishers, 1959). (First published in 1947).

Johnstone, Jr., Henry W. *Philosophy and Argument* (University Park: The Pennsylvania State University Press, 1959).

Koffka, Kurt. *Principles of Gestalt Psychology* (London: Routledge & Kegan Paul, Ltd., 1962). (First published in 1935).

Kohler, Wolfgang. *Gestalt Psychology* (New York: The New American Library, Inc., 1947).

Kwant, Remy C. *Encounter* (Pittsburgh: Duquesne University Press, 1960). (First published in 1959).

—. *Phenomenology of Language* (Pittsburgh: Duquesne University Press, 1965).

Laing. R. D. *The Politics of Experience* (New York: Ballatine Books, 1967).

Lauer, Quentin. *Phenomenology: Its Genesis and Prospect* (New York: Harper & Row, Publishers, Inc., 1965). (First published as *The Triumph of Subjectivity* in 1958: New York, Fordam University Press).

Lawson, John Howard. *Film: The Creative Process*; *The Search for an Audio-Visual Language and Structure* (New York: Hill and Wang, 1964).

Lévi-Strauss, Claude. *Structural Anthropology*. Trans. Claire Jacobson & Brooke G. Schoepf (Garden City, New York: Doubleday & Co., Inc., 1967). (First published in 1958).

—. *The Scope of Anthropology*. Trans. Sherry O. and Robert A. Paul (London: Jonathan Cape, 1967). (First published in 1960 as *Leçon Inaugurale*).

—. (with Georges Charbonnier). *Conversations with Claude Lévi-Strauss*. Trans. John and Doreen Weightman (London: Jonathan Cape, 1969). (First published in 1961 as *Entretiens avec Claude Lévi-Strauss*).

—. *Totemism*. Trans. R. Needham (Boston, 1963).

—. *The Savage Mind*. Anon. trans. (Chicago: University of Chicago Press, 1966).

Luijpen, William A. *Existential Phenomenology* (Pittsburgh: Duquesne University Press, 1960).

Malraux, André. *The Voices of Silence: Man and His Art*. Trans. Stuart Gilbert (New York: Doubleday & Co., Inc., 1953).

Matson, Floyd W., and Montagu, Ashley. *The Human Dialogue: Perspectives on Communication* (New York: The Free Press, 1967).

Marle, Rene. *Introduction to Hermeneutics*. Trans. E. Froment and R. Albrecht (New York: Herder & Herder, 1967).

Morin, Edgar. *Le Cinema ou l'homme imaginaire: Essai d'anthropologie sociologique* (Paris: Les Editions de Minuit, 1956).

Morris, Charles W. *Signs, Language, and Behavior* (New York: Prentice-Hall, Inc., 1946). Reprinted in Charles Morris, *Writings on the General Theory of Signs* (The Hague: Mouton, 1972).

—. *Signification and Significance: A Study of the Relation of Signs and Values*. (Studies in Communication). (Cambridge, Massachusetts: M. I. T. Press, 1964). Chapter I is reprinted in Charles Morris, *Writings on the General Theory of Signs* (The Hague: Mouton, 1972).

McGuire, Jeremiah C. *Cinema and Value Philosophy* (New York: Philosophical Library, 1968).

McHugh, Peter. *Defining the Situation: The Organization of Meaning in Social Interaction* (Indianapolis: Bobbs-Merrill Co., Inc., 1968).

Naess, Arne. *Interpretation and Preciseness: A Contribution to the Theory of Communication* (Oslo: Skrifter Norske Vid. Akademi, 1953).

Natanson, Maurice. *Literature, Philosophy, and the Social Sciences: Essays in Existentialism and Phenomenology* (The Hague: Martinus Nijhoff, 1962).
—. *Philosophy of the Social Sciences* (New York: Random House, 1963).
—. *Philosophy, Rhetoric, and Argumentation* (University Park, Pennsylvania: The Pennsylvania State University Press, 1965).
—. *Essays in Phenomenology* (The Hague: Martinus Nijhoff, 1966).

Ogden, C. K., and Richards., I. A. *The Meaning of Meaning: A Study of the Influence of Language upon Thought and of the Science of Symbolism* (New York: Harcourt, Brace, & Co., Inc., 1923).

Peirce, Charles Sanders. *Collected Papers of Charles Sanders Peirce*. 6 vols. Ed. Charles Hartshorne and Paul Weiss, 1931-35. Vols. 7-8 ed. A. W. Burks, 1958. (Cambridge: Harvard University Press).

Peters, J. M. L. *Teaching About the Film* (New York: Columbia University Press, 1961).

Pudovkin, V. I. *Film Technique and Film Acting: The Cinema Writing of V. I.Pudovkin*. Trans. Ivor Montagu (New York: Lear Publishers, Inc., 1949).

Reichenback, Hans. *Elements of Logic* (New York: Macmillan Co., 1947).
—. *The Rise of Scientific Philosophy* (Berkeley: University of California Press, 1963).

Révész, Géza. *Thinking and Speaking—A Symposium* (Amsterdam: North-Holland Publishing Co., 1954).

Richards, Ivor Armstrong. *Principles of Literary Criticism* (New York: Harcourt, Brace, & World, 1925).

Richardson, W. J. *Martin Heidegger: Through Phenomenology to Thought* (The Hague: Martinus Nijhoff, 1964).

Ricœur, Paul. *Fallible Man: Philosophy of the Will.* Trans. Charles Kelbley (Chicago: Henry Regnery Co., 1965).

—. *Husserl: An Analysis of His Phenomenology.* Trans. Edward G. Ballard and Lester E. Embree (Evanston, Ill.: Northwestern University Press., 1967).

Rotenstreich, Nathan. *On the Human Subject: Studies in the Phenomenology of Ethics and Politics* (Springfield, Ill.: Charles C. Thomas, Publishers, 1966).

Russell, Bertrand. *The Analysis of Mind* (London, 1921).

—. *An Inquiry into Meaning and Truth* (New York, 1940).

—. *A History of Western Philosophy* (New York: Simon and Schuster, 1945).

—. *Logic and Language* (London: George Allen & Unwin, 1956).

—. *The Basic Writings of Bertrand Russell, 1903-1956.* Ed. R. E. Egner and L. E. Denonn (New York: Simon & Schuster, 1961).

—. and Whitehead, A. N. *Principia Mathematica* (London and New York, 1910-1913).

Sartre, Jean-Paul. *The Psychology of Imagination.* 4th ed. (New York: The Citadel Press, 1966). (First published in 1940).

—. *Existentialism* (New York: Philosophical Library, 1947).

—. *The Emotions: Outline of a Theory.* Trans. Bernard Frechtman (New York: Philosophical Library, 1948).

—. *Being and Nothingness: An Essay on Phenomenological Ontology.* Trans. Hazel E. Barnes (New York: Philosophical Library, 1956). (First published as *L'Etre et le Néant* in 1949: Paris, Libraire Gallimard).

Saussure, Ferdinand de. *Course in General Linguistics.* Ed. Charles Bally, Albert Sechehaye, and Albert Riedlinger. Trans. Wade Baskin (New York: McGraw-Hill Book Co., 1966).

Spottiswoode, Raymond. *A Grammar of the Film: An Analysis of Film Technique* (Berkeley: University of California Press, 1967).

Steiner, George. *Language and Silence: Essays on Language, Literature, and the Inhuman* (New York: Atheneum, 1967).

Stephenson, Ralph, and Debrix, J. R. *The Cinema as Art* (Baltimore: Penguin Books, 1965).

Strasser, Stephan. *Phenomenology and the Human Sciences.* Trans. Henry J. Koren (Pittsburgh: Duquesne University Press, 1963).

Strauss, Erwin W. (ed.). *Phenomenology: Pure and Applied* (Pittsburgh: Duquesne University Press, 1964).

—. and Griffith, Richard M. (eds.). *Phenomenology of Will and Action* (Pittsburgh: Duquesne University Press, 1967).

Thévenaz, Pierre. *What is Phenomenology and Other Essays.* Ed. James M. Edie (Chicago: Quadrangle Press, 1962).

Wahl, Jean. *A Short History of Existentialism.* Trans. Forrest Williams and Stanley Maron (New York: The Philosophical Library, 1949).

Wann, T. W. (ed.). *Behaviorism and Phenomenology: Contrasting Bases for Modern Psychology* (Chicago: University of Chicago Press, 1965).

Wiseman, Gordon, and Barker, Larry. *Speech--Interpersonal Communication* (San Francisco: Chandler Publishing Co., 1967).

Zaner, Richard M. *The Problem of Embodiment: Some Contributions to a Phenomenology of the Body* (The Hague: Martinus Nijhoff, 1964).

B. Articles and Essays

Aldrich, Virgil C. "Expression by Enactment", *Philosophy and Phenomenological Research* XVI, no. 2 (December, 1955), pp. 188-200.

Anderson, Raymond E. "Kierkegaard's Theory of Communication", *Speech Monographs* XXX, no. 1 (March, 1963), pp. 1-14.

Bemis, James L., and Phillips. Gerald M. "A Phenomenological Approach to Communication Theory", *Speech Teacher* XIII (November, 1964), pp. 262-269.

Blyth, John. "What is a Sign?", *Philosophy and Phenomenological Research* XIII, no. 1 (September, 1952), pp. 28-41.

Carr, David. "Incarnate Consciousness" in *Existential Philosophers: Kierkegaard to Merleau-Ponty*. Ed. George Schrader (New York: McGraw-Hill, 1967).

Caton, Hiram. "Speech and Writing as Artifacts", *Philosophy and Rhetoric* II, no. 1 (Winter, 1969), pp. 19-36.

Chisholm, Roderick M. "Intentionality and the Theory of Signs", *Philosophical Studies* III, no. 4 (June, 1952), pp. 56-63.

Cumming, Robert. "Existence and Communication", *Ethics* LXV, no. 2 (January, 1955), pp. 79-101.

Douglas, Kenneth. "A Critical Bibliography of Existentialism (The Paris School)", (Vol. I: Yale French Studies) in *A Critical Bibliography of Existentialism* (New York: Krous Reprint, 1966). (First published in 1950).

Ducasse, C. J. "Symbols, Signs, and Signals", *Journal of Symbolic Logic* IV, no. 2 (1939), pp. 43ff.
—. "Some Comments on C. W. Morris' 'Foundations of the Theory of Signs'", *Philosophy and Phenomenological Research* III, no. 1 (1942-1943), pp. 43-54.

Earle, William. "Phenomenology and Existentialism" *Journal of Philosophy* LVII, no. 2 (January 21, 1966), pp. 75-84.

Edie, James M. "Expression and Metaphor", *Philosophy and Phenomenological Research* XXIII, no. 4 (June, 1963), pp. 538-561.
—. "Phenomenology as a Rigorous Science", *International Philosophical Quarterly* VII, no. 1 (March, 1967), pp. 21-30.

Fales, Walter. "Phenomenology of Questions", *Philosophy and Phenomenological Research* IV, no. 1 (September, 1943), pp. 60-75.

Farrell, B. A. "Intentionality and the Theory of Signs", *Philosophy and Phenomenological Research* XV, no. 4 (June, 1955), pp. 500-511.

Fen, Sing-nan. "Situation as an Existential Unit of Experience", *Philosophy and Phenomenological Research* XI, no. 4 (June, 1951), pp. 555-560.

Funt, David. "Roland Barthes and the *Nouvelle critique*", *Journal of Aesthetics and Art Criticism* XXVI, no. 3 (Spring, 1968), pp. 329-340.

Gérard, J., and De Waelhens, Alphonse. "Bibliographie de l'existentialisme", *Revue Internationale de Philosophie* III (July, 1949), pp. 343-359.

Gerber, Rudolph J. "Structuralism in France", *Modern Schoolman* XLVI, no. 4 (May, 1969), pp. 301-314.

Godard, Jean-Luc. "Struggle on Two Fronts: A Conversation with Jean-Luc Godard", trans. D.C.D., *Film Quarterly* XXI, no. 2 (Winter, 1968-1969), pp. 20-35.

Gregg, Richard B. "A Phenomenologically Oriented Approach to Rhetorical Criticism", *Central States Speech Journal* XVII (May, 1966), pp. 83-90.

Hestenberg, Hans-Eduard. "The Phenomenology of Meaning as an Approach to Metaphysics", *International Philosophical Quarterly* I, no. 1 (February, 1961), pp. 85-124.

—. "Phenomenology and Metaphysics of the Human Body", *International Philosophical Quarterly,* III, no. 2 (May, 1963), pp. 165-200.

Husserl, Edmund. "Philosophy as a Strict Science", *Cross Currents* VI, no. 3 (Summer, 1956), pp. 227-246; no. 4 (Fall), pp. 325-344.

Ihde, Don. "Existentialism Today", *Journal of Thought* II, no. 4 (November, 1967), pp. 19-27.

—. "From Phenomenology to Hermeneutic", *Journal of Existentialism* VIII (Winter, 1967-1968), pp. 111-132.

—. "Rationality and Myth", *Journal of Thought* II, no. 1 (January, 1967), pp. 10-18.

—. "Some Parallels Between Analysis and Phenomenology", *Philosophy and Phenomenological Research,* XXVII, no. 4 (June, 1967), pp. 577-586.

Isenburg, Arnold. "Critical Communication", *Philosophical Review* LVIII (1949), pp. 330-344.

Kaufman, Fritz. "Jasper's Theory of Communication" in *The Philosophy of Karl Jaspers.* Ed. Paul Schilpp (Wilmette, Illinois: Open Court Publishing Co., 1957).

Kuntz, Paul G. "Order in Language, Phenomena, and Reality: Notes on Linguistic Analysis, Phenomenology, and Metaphysics", *Monist* XLIX, no. 1 (January, 1965), pp. 107-136.

Levin, David Michael. "On Lévi-Strauss and Existentialism", *American Scholar* XXXVIII, no. 1 (Winter, 1968-1969), pp. 69-82.

Martinet, Andre. "Structure and Language", trans. Thomas G. Penchoen, *Yale French Studies,* nos. 36-37 (October, 1966), pp. 10-18.

Morris, Charles Williams. "Foundations of the Theory of Signs" in *International Encyclopedia of Unified Science* (Chicago: University of Chicago Press, 1938). Vol. I, no. 2, pp. 2ff. Reprinted in Charles Morris, *Writings on the General Theory of Signs* (The Hague: Mouton, 1972).

Munson, Thomas N. "Heidegger's Recent Thought on Language", *Philosophy and Phenomenological Research* XXI, no. 3 (March, 1961), pp. 361-372.

—. "Wittgenstein's Phenomenology", *Philosophy and Phenomenological Research* XXIII (1962), pp. 37-50.

MacLeod, R. B. "Phenomenology: A Challenge to Experimental Psychology" in *Behaviorism and Phenomenology.* Ed. T. W. Wann (Chicago: University of Chicago Press, 1965).

McInerny, Ralph. "Ethics and Persuasion: Kierkegaard's Existential Dialectic", *Modern Schoolman* XXXIII (1956).

McGill, V. J. "Behaviorism and Phenomenology", *Philosophy and Phenomenological Research* XXVI (June, 1966), pp. 578-588.

Natanson, Maurice. "The Claims of Immediacy" in *Philosophy, Rhetoric and Argumentation.* Ed. Maurice Natanson and Henry W. Johnstone, Jr. (University Park, Pennsylvania: Pennsylvania State University Press, 1965), pp. 10-19.

—. "Phenomenology as a Rigorous Science", *International Philosophical Quarterly* VII, no. 1 (March, 1967), pp. 5-20.

Nemetz, Anthony. "The Problem of Philosophic Communication", *International Philosophic Quarterly* I, no. 2 (May, 1961), pp. 193-213.

Plessner, Helmuth. "On Human Expression" in *Phenomenology: Pure and Applied.* Ed. Erwin W. Straus (Pittsburgh: Duquesne University Press, 1964), pp. 63-74.

Pos, H.-J. "Phénoménologie et linguistique", *Revue Internationale de Philosophie* I, no. 2 (January 15, 1939), pp. 354-365.

Ricoeur, Paul. "Existence et herménéutique", *Dialogue* IV, no. 1 (1965), pp. 1-25.

—. "La Structure, le mot, l'événement", *Man and World* I (1967), pp. 10-30. Trans. as "Structure, Word, Event" in *Philosophy Today* XII, no. 2 (Summer, 1968), pp. 114-129.

Rotenstreich, Nathan. "Semantics, Typology and Phenomenology of Philosophy", *Philosophy and Phenomenological Research* XVII, no. 3 (March, 1957), pp. 353-361.

Russell, Bertrand. "The Philosophy of Logical Atomism", *Monist,* XXVIII (1918), pp. 495-527; XXIX (1919), pp. 32-63, 190-222, 345-380. Reprinted in *Logic and Language.* Ed. R. C. March (London: George Allen and Unwin, 1918).

—. "On Propositions: What They Are and How They Mean", *Proceedings of the Aristotelian Society* (Supplement II, 1919), pp. 1-43.

—. "Logical Atomism", *Contemporary British Philosophy* (1924).

Sacksteder, William. "Kinds of Theoretical Communication", *International Philosophical Quarterly* IV, no. 1 (February, 1964), pp. 110-121.

Sallis, John C. "Phenomenology and Language", *Personalist* XLVIII, no. 4 (Autumn, 1967), pp. 490-508.

Sayre, Woodrow W. "Communication as a First Principle in Philosophy", *Quarterly Journal of Speech* XXXIV, (April, 1948), pp. 128ff.

Scheffler, Harold W. "Structuralism in Anthropology", *Yale French Studies,* nos. 36-37 (October, 1966), pp. 66-68.

Schmitt, Richard. "Phenomenology and Analysis", *Philosophy and Phenomenological Research,* XXIII (1962), pp. 101-110.

—. "Phenomenology and Metaphysics", *Journal of Philosophy* LIX (1962), pp. 421-428.

Schrader, George A. "Inter-Personal Communication", *Review of Existential Psychology and Psychiatry* II, no. 1 (February, 1962), pp. 65-74.

Schrag, Calvin O. "The Phenomenon of Embodied Speech", *The Philosophy Forum* VII (1968), pp. 189-213.

Schutz, Alfred. "Language, Language Disturbances, and the Texture of Consciousness", *Social Research* XVII, no. 3 (September, 1950), pp. 365-394.

Stanage, Sherman M. "Linguistic Phenomenology and 'Person-Talk'", *Philosophy and Rhetoric* II, no. 2 (Spring, 1969), pp. 81-90.

Structuralism. [Special Issue.] *Yale French Studies,* nos. 36-37 (October, 1966).

Structuralismes: Idéologie et méthode. [Special Issue.] *Esprit* XXXV, no. 360 (1967), pp. 769-976.

Swenson, David F. "The Existential Dialectic of Soren Kierkegaard", *Ethics* XLIX, no. 3 (April, 1939), pp. 309-328.

Szathmary, Arthur. "Physiognomic Expression Again", *Journal of Aesthetics and Art Criticism,* XXV (Spring, 1967), pp. 307-312.

Taylor, Charles, and Ayer, A. J. "Symposium: Phenomenology and Linguistic Analysis", *Proceedings of the Aristotelian Society* XXXIII Supplement (July 10-12, 1959), pp. 93-110.

Turnbull, Robert G. "Linguistic Analysis, Phenomenology, and the Problems of Philosophy: An Essay in Metaphilosophy", *Monist* XLIX (1965), pp. 44-69.

Urban, Wilbur M. "The Dialectic of Meaning and Truth: Truth as Immanent Discourse", *Philosophy and Phenomenological Research* IV, no. 3 (March, 1944), pp. 377-399.

Wheelwright, Philip. "A Preface to Phenosemantics", *Philosophy and Phenomenological Research* II, no. 4 (June, 1942), pp. 511-519.

Wild, John. "An Introduction to the Phenomenology of Signs", *Philosophy and Phenomenological Research* VIII, no. 2 (December, 1947), pp. 217-233.

—. "Is There a World of Ordinary Language?", *Philosophical Review* LXVII (October, 1958), pp. 460-476.

—. "Authentic Existence", *Ethics* LXXV, no. 4 (July, 1965), pp. 227-239.

Zaner, Richard M. "Philosophy and Rhetoric: A Critical Discussion", *Philosophy and Rhetoric* I (Spring, 1968), pp. 61-77.

C. Unpublished Materials

Anderson, Raymond Eugene. "Kierkegaard's Theory of Communication". Unpublished Ph. D. dissertation, Department of Speech and Theater, University of Minnesota, 1959.

Brooks, Deems M. "Toward a Synthesis of Creative Communication in the Philosophy of Henry Nelson Wieman". Unpublished Ph. D. dissertation, Department of Speech, Southern Illinois University, 1968.

Carruth, Bruce Chandler. "An Exploratory Study of Phenomenological Interpersonal Relations". Unpublished Ph. D. dissertation, Department of Social Psychology, Vanderbilt University, 1958.

Christopherson, Myrvin F. "A Kierkegaardian Scheme of Criticism: A Comparative Study of the Critical Categories Deriving from Aristotelian and Kierkegaardian Theories of Communication". Unpublished M.S. thesis, Department of Speech and Theater, Purdue University, 1963.

—. "Soren Kierkegaard's Dialectic of Communication: An Approach to the Communication of Existential Knowledge". Unpublished Ph.D. dissertation, Department of Speech and Theater, Purdue University, August, 1965.

INDEX

A

abbreviations, 13.
abnormal, 102.
absence, 85, 90, 92, 104, 112, 122, 155, 166, 170, 172.
accent, 49.
accessory, 176.
act(s), 74, 102, 104, 127, 145, 153, 158, 169, 174, 192;
    according to Others, 130;
    consciousness of, 101;
    creative, 144;
    first philosophical, 131;
    intentional, 95, 103;
    of choice, 129;
    of experiencing, 103;
    of perception, 120;
    of speaking, 187, 194;
    — speaking, 208.
action, 101, 106, 113, 121, 171.
activity, 200;
    and passivity, 94n, 136;
    daily, 181.
actor, 171, 197.
adult, 109.
advent, 148, 159.
affirmation, 65-66.
age (of doubt), 23.
agency, 71, 87, 95, 106, 119, 121-2, 125, 132, 160.
aggression, 112, 114.
akten, bedeutungsgebende, 169.
Aldrich, Virgil C., 47n.
alexia, 162.
alibi, 103, 207.
algorithm, 83.
alter ego, 42, 159, 200.
ambiguity, 92-3, 119, 200;
    bad, 201.

analogy, 60, 65, 103, 111, 113, 173, 177-8.
analysis, 75;
    ordinary language, 30;
    phenomenological, 30, 209;
    semiological, 87.
analytic, 110.
Anderson, Raymond E., 36n, 37n.
anger, 47.
anonymity, 113.
anthropology, 117.
anosognosia, 123.
antinomy, apparent, 21, 27.
aphasiac, amnesic, 161.
appearing, modes of, 32.
appearance, 33, 99, 128, 143, 181.
a priori, 76, 99, 147, 159.
Aranguren, J. L., 80n.
archetype, 115, 138.
Arendt, Hannah, 115n.
argument (to persuade), 114.
articulation, 95, 167, 186, 204-5, 208.
assignment, 71.
assimilation, 178.
asynchronism, 171.
attachment, absolute, 130.
attention, 199.
audio, 199;
    — recording, 189;
    — tape, 109.
ausdruck, 133.
Ayer, A. J., 30n.

B

background, 120, 135.
Ballard, Edward G., 147n.
Bannan, John F., 140n.
Barker, Larry, 187n.
Barral, Mary Rose, 25n.

Barrett, William, 25n.
Barthes, Roland, 78ff., 86, 86n, 92n, 159n, 170, 179, 179n.
Bayer, Raymond, 16n, 88n.
bearing, 111.
Becoming, 206-7.
Bedeutung, 133.
behavior, 89, 99, 111, 188;
  analysis of, 100;
  human, 57, 59;
  patterns, 133.
Behaviorism, 17.
Being, 66, 75, 103, 116, 119, 135, 156, 188, 203-4, 205-6;
  — as-object, 110n;
  — for-itself, 39, 115, 150, 200;
  — for-the-other, 115, 200;
  — in-itself, 39, 150.
belief, 110.
Bergson, Henri, 157.
bifurcation, 126, 181.
Bigney, Juliet, 156n.
Black, Max, 63n.
Blackmur, Richard P., 48n.
Blyth, John H., 56n.
body, 21, 51, 81, 91, 99, 103-4, 109-10, 125ff., 128, 133, 152, 153, 188, 192.
  cultural, 128-9;
  geographical, 47;
  lived-, 48, 81, 92, 97ff., 118, 130ff., 166;
  natural, 128-9;
  phenomenal, 131;
  physical, 47;
  visual, 107, 109ff., 119.
Body-subject, 27, 91-2, 95, 173, 184, 196, 204, 208;
  lived-, 124, 147, 205.
books, the great, 193.
'bracketing', 134; see "reflection".
Brazin, André, 143n.
Britton, Karl, 29n.
Brown, Charles T., 187n.
Bukharin, 197.
Busch, Thomas, 45n.

C

camera, 171.
caress, 190.
category, 31, 174.
Caton, Hiram, 179n.
Cavell, Stanley, 31n.

certitude, 122.
Cézanne, 103, 156-7, 206.
chain, 118.
chaos, 100.
characters, 198.
Charbonnier, Georges, 185n.
chiasm, 94, 131, 138-9, 158, 167ff., 175, 195, 203.
child, 109, 178, 199.
Chisholm, Roderick M., 83n.
choice, 129;
  human, 126;
  of commitment, 166-7.
Christopherson, Myrvin F., 35, 36n.
cinema, see "film".
cinematography, 140.
Cioran, E. M., 161, 161n, 177, 177n.
circularity, 139, 175.
circumspection, 73.
clarification, 176.
class, 31, 62.
Claudell, 178.
Cleaver, Eldridge, 101, 101n.
close-up, 198-199.
code, symbolic, 175.
codification, 177.
coding, 168.
cogito, 149ff.;
  Cartesian, 34, 44;
  pre-reflective, 149;
  radical, 34, 44, 46, 97, 108, 120, 147ff.;
  tacit, 149;
  verbal, 149.
Commissar, 97.
commitment, risked, 167, 190, 195.
communicability, 68.
communication, passim;
  act of, 207;
  authentic-inauthentic, 35, 72;
  direct, 35, 37ff., 118;
  existential, 17, 22, 24, 35ff., 70, 133, 178, 196;
  in consciousness as such, 64-5;
  indirect, 35;
  in empirical existence, 64;
  inner, 100;
  in spirit, 70;
  instrumental, 187;
  M. M-P.'s theory of, 18-9, 137;
  oral, 191;
  philosophy of, 19;
  pre-, 148;

primordial, 35, 41, 124, 188-9, 191;
  rational, 70;
  refusal to, 167;
  risk of, 180;
  secondary, 191;
  semiotic, 191, 209;
  technique, 22;
  theory of, 80;
  true, 188, 209.
communion, 124;
  of Black Saints, 114.
comprehension, 159.
concept, 77.
conception, 23.
configuration, 136, 206.
conjecture, 141.
connotation, 55, 87.
consciousness, 40, 66, 75, 98-9, 101,
  181, 203;
  as such, 68;
  collective, 194;
  incarnate, 124;
  sign is, 74;
  state of, 91.
'consciousness of -', see "intentionality".
constants, 88.
constitution, 33, 177, 194.
constructa, 42, 131.
constructions, 83.
content, 67, 91.
contradiction, 137.
convention, 176, 178.
convergence, 73, 108.
conversation, 189, 194, 198.
co-possessive, 114.
co-present, 174.
Correa, M., 82n.
correlation, 22, 63, 80.
correspondence, 31, 89, 115.
counter-shock, 114.
creation, 19.
criticism, 23.
cryptographers, 183.
'crypto-nonsense', 64.
culture, 94, 180, 192, 201.
cypher, 37ff., 66ff., 70.

D

Daesin, 73.
Daly, James, 16n.
danger, 112.

Darstellung, 133.
data, 21.
death, 107, 180, 208.
De Beauvoir, Simone, 24, 24n.
Debrix, J. R., 141n, 171n.
decoding, 168.
decomposition, 197.
deduction, 99.
definition, in use, 27-8.
demiurgy, verbal, 177.
denotation, 55, 87.
depth, 103, 115, 138.
De Saussure, Ferdinand, 52, 77-8, 85-6,
  160, 168, 172, 174-5, 193.
Descartes, René, 27, 33, 98, 138, 150.
description(s), 88, 105, 120;
  definite, 64;
  phenomenological, 30ff., 98ff;
  theory of, 28, 62ff.
De Vinci, Leonard, 156.
De Waehlens, Alphonse, 18n, 25n,
  155n.
dialectic, 93, 95, 106, 108, 121, 125,
  129, 132, 158, 171-2, 174, 177, 186,
  194, 196, 205.
dialogue, 171;
  dramatic, 198-9;
  expository, 197;
  film, 197ff.;
  maieutic, 194ff., 199ff.;
  tonal, 197-8.
discourse, 26, 38-9, 59, 95, 118, 202n.
discussion, 195.
distance, 103.
distinction of degree, 113.
divergence, 73, 108, 116, 157, 168,
  195.
dream, 167, 181, 208.
Dreyfus, H. L., 18n, 145n.
Dreyfus, P. A., 18n.
dualism, 27, 65, 98, 152, 200, 203;
  Cartesian, 28, 45, 51ff., 148;
  denial of, 81;
  intersubjective, 107.
'dubbed', 172.
Ducasse, C. J., 57, 57n.
Dufrenne, Mikel, 29, 29n, 123, 123n.

E

Earle, William, 30n, 174n.
écart, 137, 157, 167.
ecstasy, 194.

Edie, James M., 18n, 26, 29n, 31n, 88n.
Edwards, Paul, 35n.
effect, 21.
ego, 135.
'eidetic intuiting', 31, 133.
Einfühlung, 46, 206.
Einklammerung, 33.
elements, 129, 171, 181, 189, 199, 201.
embody, 27, 76.
embrace, 128.
emotion, 111.
Empiricism, 162.
Encompassing, 68.
encounter, 42, 99, 175;
    originating, 138.
encroachment, 127, 206.
engage, 126.
'en soi et pour soi', 177.
entretien, 194.
epoché, 133ff.
erfullung, 208.
essence, 29, 32, 96, 176, 181;
    investigating general, 31;
    objective, 54;
    subjective, 54.
ethics, 200-201.
'être-au-monde', 40, 150-51, 154, 194, 204.
event, 79;
    interhuman, 195.
example, 31.
exchange, 203.
exegesis, theological, 183.
existence, 181;
    as consciousness, 137;
    as lived, 46;
    as thing, 137;
    corporeal, 110;
    empirical, 68;
    historical, 97;
    personal, 23, 146;
    sexual, 205;
    social, 23, 205;
    speaks, 206.
Existentialism, 42, 75, 200;
    ontological, 16;
    semiotic, 65ff.
existents, 68.
Existenz, 70.
experience, 90, 97, 102;
    being-an-, 100;
    brute, 100;
    felt, 125;

internal, 99;
    lived-, 94, 121, 173, 183, 190;
    lived-body, 17;
    non-positing, 120;
    personal, 23;
    pre-conscious, 120;
    pre-objective, 120;
    translation of, 95.
explain, 44.
explosion, 122.
expression, 90, 155ff., 168, 180, 195;
    acts of, 46, 95, 157;
    apparatus of, 94;
    existential, 189;
    facial, 46, 185;
    interpersonal, 42;
    personal, 42;
    primordial, 138.
exterior, 167, 201.
eye(s), 108, 177.

F

face, 111, 159.
fact, 23.
Fales, Walter, 16n.
falsity, 125.
family, 62.
Farrell, B. A., 169.
fashions, 139.
feeling, 189.
Feldman, Joseph and Harry, 198n.
Fen, Sing-nan, 21n.
field, 104, 121, 126, 130, 204, 206;
    intersubjective, 118;
    of freedom, 129.
figure, 141-2, 152, 172, 204;
    and background, 137.
film, 19, 140ff., 169ff., 173, 196ff.
finality, 119, 205.
finitude, 201.
Fisher, Alden L., 98n, 102n.
fixation, verbal, 178.
flesh, 99, 108, 127, 131, 137, 157, 168, 192, 204, 206-7.
flowers, 190.
flux, 182.
foreground, 135, 173.
form, 67, 76, 110, 122, 137, 159.
Forum, 207.
France, Collège de, 21, 80, 193.
freedom, 129ff.;
    condemned to, 125, 205;

conditioned, 129;
   field of, 129.
French, 192.
Funt, David, 170n.
fusion, 127.
future, 117, 178, 182.

G

generation, 209.
genesis, 97.
geography, 148.
gestalt, 32, 46, 135, 170, 174, 186,
   198-9;
   — function, 181;
   linguistic, 139;
   radical, 33, 46, 133ff., 135ff.;
   temporal, 140ff.
gesticulation, verbal, 185.
gesture, 41, 46ff., 85, 89, 94-5, 111,
   113, 115, 151, 157, 171, 178, 187,
   189, 196, 209.
God, 98.
Godard, Jean-Luc, 197, 197n.
grammar, 183, 188;
   pure, 53.
grillwork, 157.
ground, 53, 133, 141, 152;
   common-, 199;
   transcendent, 142.
grouping, 136.
Gueroult, Martial, 202.
Gurwitsch, Aron, 18n.

H

habituation, 178.
Hall, Edward T., 80n.
Hanna, Thomas, 118n.
hating, 101.
Haymond, William S., 143n.
head, 128.
hearer, audible-, 131.
hearing, 82, 177, 199, 204.
Hegel, G. W. F., 29, 42, 65, 106, 138,
   195.
Heidegger, Martin, 24, 25n, 26, 38,
   38n, 71ff., 71n, 95, 95n, 96n, 118,
   133, 135-6, 153, 175, 193, 200, 202,
   205, 207.
Henstenberg, Hans-Eduard, 133n.
here, 103, 108, 127, 205.
hermeneutics, 34, 183, 202.

hierarchies, 63, 140.
himself, 114.
history, 102, 147, 170, 205, 207.
homo loquens, 19.
homo sapiens, 22.
horizon, 116, 120, 137, 141, 152, 204.
Husserl, Edmund, 25-6, 26n, 29, 31-4,
   65, 76, 107, 118n, 124, 129, 133,
   135, 151-2, 161, 168, 193, 200.
hyper-reflection, 166.
hypostatization, 146.
hypothetical, 111, 112.

I

I, *passim*;
   as lived, 185, 199, 206-8;
   can, 34, 150, 153, 205-6;
   the philosophical, 146.
icon, 53, 174;
   film as maieutic, 196ff.
idea(s), 77, 144, 172.
Idealism, 17.
identity, 203.
ideology, 86.
'idle talk', 38, 72-3.
Ihde, Don, 27n, 181, 183.
ill, mentally, 102.
illness, 102, 123, 161.
illumination, 65ff.
illusions, 33, 208.
image, 74-6, 103, 107, 110, 113, 170,
   173, 197, 199;
   body (schema), 125;
   immanent, 142;
   introceptive, 109ff., 151;
   — portrait, 74.
imitation, 89.
immanence, 88, 90ff., 105, 113, 122,
   132, 138, 141, 167, 174, 205;
   paradox of, 91.
immediacy, claim to, 115.
immediation, 204.
incarnation, 111, 179, 206.
index, 53, 174.
indicating, 71-2.
individuals, 63, 205.
inference, 64.
information, 21, 157, 168.
inhabit, 111, 113, 127.
inhabitant, 113.
inner and outer, 129.
inscribed, 208.

institution, 177.
instrument, 64, 126, 180.
intellection, 99ff., 103, 119.
intellectualism, 99, 162, 123.
intentionality, 30, 46, 74, 109, 117,
  151-2, 185, 195, 199, 206;
  latent, 209;
  thetic, 152-3;
  operative, 152-3.
intentions, 95, 101, 111.
interaction, 52, 99.
intercorporeal, 113, 196, 208.
interior, 161, 178, 201.
interpretant, 53.
interpreter, 172, 176.
intersubjectivity, 42, 177, 184-5, 188,
  196, 205.
intonation, 47.
intrapersonal, 113, 199.
intrasubjective, 102.
intuition, phenomenological, 30.
intuitus mentis, 165.
invisible, 103, 105.
involvement, 73.
ipse, 113.

J

Jaspers, Karl, 24, 36n, 37, 37n, 38,
  65, 65n, 83.
jealousy, 111.
judge, 198.
jury, 198.

K

Kaelin, Eugene F., 82n.
Kant, Immanuel, 94n, 139.
Kierkegaard, Soren, 24, 35-8.
knowing,
  pre-, 127;
  silent, 127.
knowledge, 19, 133.
Kockelmans, Joseph J., 112n, 143n.
Koffka, Kurt, 102n.
Kullman, Michael, 145n.
kundgibt, 99.
Kuntz, Paul G., 30n.
Kwant, Remy, 110n, 170.

L

Laing, R. D., 21, 21n, 102, 102n, 121,
  121n.

Langan, Thomas, 26n, 46n.
language, 38, 50, 55, 90, 139, 160ff.,
  175ff.;
  and semiology, 78;
  as becoming, 165-6;
  as *gestalt,* 159;
  code (instrument), 162;
  consciousness of, 164;
  eidetic, 187;
  foreign, 183;
  ideal, 28, 62, 64;
  index, 163;
  ordinary, 63, 64, 170, 180, 187;
  phenomenology of, 161, 183;
  philosophy of, 26;
  private and public, 163;
  sign-, 148;
  thinking, 176.
langue, see "tongue".
Lanigan, Richard L., 179n.
Lauer, R., 155n.
lawyer, 198.
Lebenswelt, 16, 134-5, 148, 167, 175,
  190.
Leepa, Allen, 199n.
Lefort, Claude, 18n, 19n, 203n.
Levin, David M., 81n.
Lévi-Strauss, Claude, 80, 81n, 182,
  184n, 185n.
life, 107, 179, 199;
  daily, 181;
  interior, 207;
  intersubjective, 194;
  personel, 23;
  social, 80.
lighting, 142.
limb, phantom, 123.
linguistics, 159, 168, 176;
  diachronic, 83;
  structural, 26;
  synchronic, 83;
  transformational, 26.
listening, 94;
  and speaking, 94n, 139, 185, 191,
    194.
literature, 23, 179ff.
lived-spoken, 206.
living, 95, 132, 180.
locality, 105.
logic, 22, 28, 53, 55, 61, 190;
  in action, 50;
  incarnate, 50;
  of history, 124;

perceptual, 81;
pure, 63.
logos, 18, 157, 203ff.;
nascent, 120;
ontological, 202.
love, 190.
loving, 101.

M

MacLeod, R. B., 21-2, 22n, 23.
McCleary, Richard C., 18n.
Malraux, 204.
man, 22, 98;
behavioristic, 21;
of action, 23;
speaking, 83.
mankind, 111n.
Marsh, R. C., 63n.
Martinet, André, 84n.
mathematics, 22, 61.
matter, 79.
matrix, 167.
meaning, 21, 30, 62, 90, 94-5, 138,
168, 178, 207;
carnal, 168;
cognitive, 61n;
'condemned to —', 119, 126;
constitution of, 23;
existential, 49;
form, 47;
historical, 195;
immanent, 131, 190;
in difference, 87;
instrumental, 61n;
intentional, 147;
physiognomic, 22;
potential, 179;
pre-, 126, 167;
pre-condition to, 23;
pre-conscious, 147;
'pregnant', 90;
primordial, 89, 176;
private, 95;
public, 95;
real, 86;
sedimented, 49;
verifiability theory of, 61.
memory, 141.
mention and use, 176.
Merleau-Ponty, Maurice, *passim;*
analyses of, 221-235;

and Gilbert Ryle, 30n;
as author, 18, 81n, 147, 202ff.;
bibliography of, 210-18;
Collège de France, 18;
editor-in-chief, 17;
existential phenomenology, 77, 81ff.,
95-6, 118;
inaugural address, 18;
method, 98ff., 107, 134, 200;
on cinema, 197;
political director, 17;
primacy of speech, 80;
semiology, 78, 156, 174;
teacher, 17.
message, 168.
metalanguage, 86.
metamorphosis, 133.
metaphor, 60, 104.
metaphysical, 151, 193;
in man, 98;
problems, 28.
metaphysics, 200-202, 205.
metric, 198.
milieu, 118, 159, 199.
mind, 21, 51, 60ff., 81, 89, 100, 105,
116, 208;
savage, 184.
mirror, 109.
mobile, 143n.
modalities, 126.
mode, existential, 22.
model;
film as, 196;
ideal of language, 84;
of linguistic semiotic, 81.
modulations, 110.
moment, 167.
monads, 201.
monitoring, 194.
monologue, inner, 180.
montage, 141, 173.
Morin, Edgar, 174n, 199n.
Morris, Charles W., 54n, 54ff.
movement, 142, 143n, 195, 204-5;
actual, 61;
potential, 61;
sets of, 62.
movie, see "film".
Munson, Thomas N., 73.
myself, 107, 108ff.
Mysteries, Dionysian, 182.
myth, 181ff.;
per se, 181;

rational, 181.
mythos, 181.

N

name(s), 158;
    proper, 62ff.
naming, 52, 162-3.
Natanson, Maurice, 26, 115n.
Naturalism, 17.
nature, 18, 201, 203.
negatives, 112.
nervure, 82.
network, 117.
news items, 180.
Nietzsche, Friedrich, 36.
non-coincidence, 103.
non-verbal, 112.
nothingness, 24, 39, 100.
normal, 102.
novel, 179, 180.
now, 108, 127, 205.
nymphomania, 112.

O

object, 52-3, 63, 74, 93, 100, 101,
    108, 110, 120-21, 142, 190, 196;
    and subject, 27-8;
    intentional, 137, 145, 153, 204;
    intersubjective, 129;
    lived-, 103;
    of acquaintence, 64;
    of experience, 59;
    physical, 21, 77;
    'pure', 64;
    signs, 80.
objectivity, 37, 52, 59, 65, 120, 200.
Objectivism, 131.
observer, 93.
obsession, 132.
odor, 103.
Ogden, C. K., 58ff., 60n.
one, 127, 131, 206.
O'Neill, John, 19n, 20n, 119n, 203n.
ontogenesis, 122, 207.
ontologist, 102.
ontology, 202, 206, 209.
opacity, 182.
Operationalism, 28.
operations, 127.
opinion, 125.
organism, 197.

Organon, Aristotle's, 56.
Other, 68, 94, 102, 107, 158, 207-8.
outside, 110.

P

painter, 106.
painting, 113, 156, 178.
Palmer, Richard E., 183n.
'Pandora's Box', 179.
paradigm, 137, 140, 172;
    audio-visual, 173-4.
paradox, 104.
parallelism, 171.
parole, see "speaking".
parole parlante, 187, 191, 194.
parole parlée, 187, 191, 194.
participation, 128.
particulars, 62.
Pascal, Blaise, 98.
passivity and activity, 94n, 136, 140.
past, 117, 121, 182, 201.
Peirce, Charles Sanders, 52ff., 52n,
    168, 174.
people;
    and things, 48, 171;
    primitive, 181.
perceived-perceiving, 85, 139.
percept, 122.
perception, 76, 94, 97ff., 104, 115ff.,
    119, 122-4, 180;
    as synopsis, 119ff.;
    bodily, 112;
    counter-, 139;
    existential, 87;
    immediate, 32;
    intentional, 30, 209;
    object of, 77, 194;
    primacy of, 120, 172;
    psychic, 30;
    synaesthetic, 99;
    verbal, 122.
person, 21, 111, 121, 190;
    accused, 198;
    embodied, 27.
personal, 195.
perspective, 106, 138, 173, 184, 199;
    concatenation of, 118;
    deformation of, 32.
phantasms, 181.
phenomena;
    immediate, 33;
    in consciousness, 33;

mental, 29;
non-posited, 123;
physical, 29;
return to, 26.
Phenomenalism, 27ff., 75;
    linguistic, 27ff.;
    semiotic, 50ff.
Phenomenology, 27, 82, *et passim*;
    bi-polar, 45;
    definition of, 43-4;
    descriptive, 46;
    existential, 27, 81, 98;
    existential communication as, 20ff.;
    hermeneutic, 83;
    method, 16, 19, 30ff., 97ff., 124,
        134ff., 154;
    of origins, 45;
    radical, 43;
    semiotic, 125;
    static, 124;
    the term, 29.
phenosemantics, 166n.
Philosophical School of Paris, 24.
philosophy, 19, 102, *et passim*;
    and consciousness, 41;
    dialectical, 184;
    highest point of, 119;
    militant, 23, 41;
    triumphant, 23.
phonation, 204.
photograph, still, 144.
photography, 142.
physics, 28.
physiognomies, 48, 189.
Plessner, Helmuth, 189n.
Poetics, Aristotle's, 56.
poetry, 192.
'pointing', 62, 72, 115.
political, 23.
politics, 19.
polymorphism, 124, 137.
Ponge, Francis, 178.
Poole, R. C., 81.
Positivism, Logical, 28, 30.
possibility, 113.
potential, 113, 174.
'pour autrui', 195.
'pour soi', 195.
power, 123.
pragmatics, 56.
pre-conscious, 148ff.
pre-objective, 143ff.
presence, 40, 92, 95n, 104, 106, 111-

12, 130, 158, 170, 181, 204-5, 208;
    -at-the-world, see "être-au-monde";
    dialectic of, 123;
    essential, 131;
    synergic, 90, 127;
    synoptic, 82, 95, 121, 186;
    unitary, 97.
present, 117, 182, 201, 205.
presupposition, 135.
privacy, 114.
private and public, 126, 200.
probable, 205.
probability, 182.
process, 79;
    circular, 139.
projection-injection, 200, 208.
property, 203.
proposition(s), 54, 108, 200, 202, 205.
prose, 171, 180, 202.
prosecutor, 198.
Proust, 197.
proximal, 106.
'psyche', 107, 111ff., 117.
psychism, 184.
psychoanalysis, 102.
psychology, 19, 102;
    film and the new, 140ff.;
    Gestalt, 17, 136, 139;
    modern, 47;
    positive, 81.
public, 192.
Pudovkin, V. I., 198n, 199n.
pulsation, temporal, 117.

Q

quasilocality, 105.
questions, 15.

R

radio, 82.
rationality, 83, 183.
reacting, 95.
reading, 74, 103, 179, 193.
'ready-to-hand', 72.
real, 144, 205.
Realism, 18.
reality;
    lived-, 95, 111;
    objective, 29, 108;
    perceived, 172;
    psychic-, 102;

retrospective, 124;
  -through-communication, 64.
reason, genesis of, 196.
receiver, 121.
record, public, 114.
Rede, 202; see "speaking".
reduction;
  eidetic, 31, 135;
  phenomenological, 33, 120;
  philosophical, 135;
  reflective, 145ff.;
  scientific, 135;
  transcendental, 135.
reference, 59, 71, 209.
referent, 59.
reflection, 65ff., 182;
  First, 44, 120, 133;
  Second, 44, 133, 144ff.;
  Third, 44, 147ff.
reflective, 110.
Reichenbach, Hans, 60, 61n.
relata, 79.
relations, interpersonal, 200.
relationship, 112.
reliefs, 110.
remember, 140.
representamen, 53.
representations, 101.
research, 65ff.
resemblance, 103.
residue, 117.
response, 79, 121, 195.
result, 106.
reversibility, see "chaism".
revolution, 23.
rhetoric, 51, 53-4, 86;
  Aristotle's *Rhetoric*, 56;
  of risk, 114, 180.
rhythm, 170-71.
Richards, I. A., 59n; see "Ogden,
  C. K.".
Ricœur, Paul, 93, 93n, 152n.
risk, 114, 180.
roles, 106.
'round square', 64.
Russell, Bertrand, 28, 28n, 60ff.
Ryle, Gilbert, 30n.

S

sachverhalt, 184.
Said, Edward W., 168n.
Sartre, Jean-Paul, 24, 24n, 39-40,

74ff., 97, 97n, 125, 150, 178, 202,
  205.
Satz, 184.
Scheffler, Harold W., 80n.
Scheler, Max, 148.
schema, 86, 121, 125, 203.
Schilpp, Paul A., 62n.
schizophrenic, 207.
Schmitt, Richard, 34, 34n, 176n.
Schutz, Alfred, 81n.
science, 15-16, 55, 81;
  'strict', 26.
screen, film, 142, 172-3.
sedimented, 40, 67, 89, 130, 138,
  175ff., 180, 183, 190.
see, 44, 104, 119, 176, 179, 206.
seeing, 82, 102ff., 108, 119;
  -being seen, 94n, 139.
seer, visible, 131.
self, 76, 106;
  -awareness, 44.
semantics, 56, 59;
  thickness, 162, 178;
  triangle, 59.
Semantics, General, 53, 57.
semiology, 19, 51, 96, 158, 172, 209,
  et passim;
  as problematic, 76;
  linguistic, 56;
  of Bertrand Russell, 60ff.;
  of Charles S. Peirce, 52ff.;
  of Charles W. Morris, 54ff.;
  of C. K. Ogden and I. A. Richards,
    58ff.;
  of Hans Reichenbach, 60ff.;
  of Jean-Paul Sartre, 74ff.;
  of Karl Jaspers, 65ff.;
  of Martin Heidegger, 71ff.;
  of Maurice Merleau-Ponty, 80ff.,
    93;
  of music, 88n;
  of Roland Barthes, 78ff.;
  phenomenalistic, 59;
  phenomenological, 80ff.;
  realistic, 57-8;
  semiotic, 183.
semiotic, 53, 55;
  as existential phenomenology, 75;
  ontological, 200, 206;
  sight-sound, 173.
sensa, 27.
sensation, 23, 98ff., 103, 108, 116, 119,
  121, 171;

bodily, 133;
  felt, 99;
  psychological, 30.
sense(s), 34, 96, 103, 138, 172, 207.
sense-data, 26, 99.
sense-organs, 177.
sensitive-sensible, 131.
sentence, 113.
separation, 123, 137, 208.
sexuality, 111-12, 152.
shared, 200.
showing, 71.
shot(s), 141;
  long, 198;
  medium, 198.
side,
  same, 129;
  other, 144.
sign(s), 51ff., 57, 59, 71, 73-6, 85, 161,
  172, *et passim*;
  and signification, 85ff., 190;
  arbitrary, 58;
  as given, 75;
  as perceived, 92;
  cinematic, 174;
  classification, 58;
  conventional, 89;
  definition, 77, 86;
  determinate set of, 101;
  -existent, 91;
  formal, 58;
  -gestalt, 139;
  instrumental, 58;
  kinds of, 71;
  linguistic, 56;
  mental, 82;
  natural, 58, 89;
  ontical, 72;
  physical, 82;
  post-linguistic, 56;
  pre-established, 186;
  pre-linguistic, 56;
  proper, 58;
  qualified, 192;
  relation, 58;
  semiological, 79;
  subjective, 61.
signaling, 139.
'sign-function', 79.
signification, 80, 85ff., 170, 176, 186,
  190, 192, *et passim*;
  -becoming, 91;
  existential, 190;

fixed, 163;
  gestural, 114;
  immanent, 47;
  inter-individual, 196;
  is the sign, 103;
  lexical, 193;
  sign meaning, 22, 139;
  transcendence of, 93, 206.
signified, 77, 80, 87, 92, 101-2.
signifier, 77, 87, 101-2.
'signifying humus', 178.
sign-vehicle, 55.
silence, 87, 164ff., 172, 186, 190, 198,
  204;
  absence of sound, 165;
  as private awareness, 165;
  in dialectic, 165;
  non-language signification, 166;
  of perception, 166;
  transcendent, 191.
simultaneity, 104, 156.
Sinari, Ramakant, 147n.
singing, 82.
singularity, 205.
Sinn, Ausdrucks-, 169.
Sinngebung, 129.
Sinn, Zeichen-, 169.
site, 64.
situation, 129, 192;
  de facto, 146, 205;
  hermeneutical, 135;
  linguistic, 94;
  primordial, 135ff.
slow-motion, 142.
smile, 157, 178.
Smith, Colin, 17, 18, 43, 105n.
smoothness, 103.
socio-anthropology, 19.
sociopath, 114.
softness, 103.
solitude, 167.
soul, 99, 104, 112.
sound-image, 77, 198.
space;
  actual, 115;
  and time, 27, 127, 130, 173;
  centrifugal, 116;
  cultural, 115-16;
  disorientation, 143;
  intentional, 117;
  lived-, 97, 181, 207;
  topological, 116;
  virtual, 115-17, 142, 181.

spatiality, 115ff., 132, 140;
  in genesis, 131.
speaking, 49, 78, 82, 89, 94, 119,
  123-4, 139, 148, 159, 182, 184-5,
  188, 194, 202, 204, 207-8, *et passim*;
  act of, 15, 48, 112, 177, 187, 204,
  206, 209;
  as maieutic, 199ff.;
  existential, 187;
  'forgotten', 183;
  genetic act of, 50;
  man, 15;
  phenomenology of, 160, 183;
  philosophy of, 26;
  primacy of, 80;
  -speech, 78;
  -tone, 157.
spectator, 143n, 196, 199.
speech, 49, 90, 93, 113, 156, 159, 175,
  190ff., *et passim*;
  abortive, 176;
  act of, 113;
  agency of, 106;
  and semiology, 78;
  and thought, 122, 163, 192;
  as institution, 177;
  definition of, 191;
  empirical, 185;
  existential, 185;
  less speaking, 160, 175;
  originating, 186;
  philosophy of, 155;
  secondary, 186;
  sensible, 176;
  -speaking, 85;
  spoken-, 78.
Spiegelberg, Herbert, 16n, 30, 30n, 34,
  43, 45n, 134.
spirit, 68, 207.
spontaneity, 138, 186, 201, 205.
spontaneous, 128, 130, 136, 209.
Spottiswoode, Raymond, 141n.
sprachbegiff, 91.
Stalin, 197.
statement, 178;
  about sensa, 30;
  emotive, 59;
  rhetorical, 60;
  scientific, 59.
Stephenson, Ralph, 141n, 171n.
stimulus, 79, 121.
'strokes', 74.
Structuralism, 19, 168, 168n, 193.

structure, 79, 99, 111, 121, 131-2, 137,
  153, 169, 178, 183, 192, 203;
  expression of, 31;
  of experience, 99;
  philosophy of, 19n;
  semiological, 98;
  unique, 192;
  vital, 126.
style, 169, 178-9.
subject, 176;
  and object, 27-8, 138;
  speaking, 139, 161, 168, 184, 187ff.,
    190-91;
  transcendent, 65, 195.
subjectivism, 54, 75.
subjectivity, 65, 72, 110, 200, 207;
  as intersubjectivity, 42, 177, 194-5;
  primacy of, 65.
'subject-object', 126.
substance, 79, 108.
Swenson, David F., 36n.
sychronism, 171.
symbol, 53, 59, 63, 66, 77, 83, 162,
  174, 188, 204;
  being-as-a-, 67.
symbolic, 22, 119, 183.
synergism, 119, 122, 170, 202.
synopsis, 27, 45, 89, 119ff., 122ff.,
  125, 143, 170, 176, 199.
syntactics, 56.
syntagm, 92.
syntax, 92, 180, 188.
synthesis, 27, 29, 75, 98, 110, 120, 127,
  141;
  dialectic, 65ff.;
  imaginary, 74;
  perceptual, 74, 123;
  transitional, 45.
system, 79, 111-12, 115, 158, 168, 170,
  172, 184, 188;
  car-, 79;
  diacritical, 184;
  existential, 200;
  furniture-, 79;
  garment-, 79, 139;
  incarnate, 168;
  intersubjective, 184;
  language, 169, 178;
  music, 88n;
  self-world-others, 195;
  semiotic, 84;
  signifying, 95, 157;
  symbols, 133.

T

'talk', 38, 72-3, 169, 202n.
Taylor, Charles, 30n, 145n.
teleology, 139, 203.
telepathy, 112.
temporality, 46, 117ff., 131-32.
Temps Modernes, Les, 17.
tension, 143, 194.
theater, 105, 110.
themes, 19.
there, 108, 128, 138, 145, 185.
'there is', 206.
thing(s), 46, 71, 81, 99, 104;
  -itself, 83, 106, 179;
  perceiving, 126;
  physical, 61;
  themselves, 26, 84, 94n, 102, 119,
    125, 140, 196, 199, 206.
thinking, 119, 204.
thought, 59, 103, 105, 122, 172, 176;
  objective, 182;
  object of, 91;
  -speaking, 176, 191;
  -thinking, 85.
threat, 114.
time, 77, 117ff., 121, 130, 132, 182;
  actual, 173;
  and space, 27, 105, 143;
  crystallization of, 95;
  film, 143, 173;
  -less, 182;
  lived-, 97;
  natural, 117;
  pyramid of, 192.
Todes, S. J., 145n.
tokens, 55.
tongue, 175ff., 187, 189, 192.
topography, 204.
touch, 81, 119, 127, 158, 204;
  tangible-, 131.
transcendence, 70, 88, 90ff., 108, 113,
  132, 138, 153, 167, 174, 203, 205;
  cipher of, 95;
  paradox of, 91.
transformations, 88, 91, 103, 192.
translations of Merleau-Ponty, 217-19.
transmitter, 121.
trompe-l'œil, 106.
truth, 54, 64, 125, 143n, 145, 207, 208.
types;
  branching theory of, 63;
  theory of, 28, 61ff.

U

understanding, 39, 62, 82, 94, 133,
  205.
unity, 123, 135, 168, 198, 205, 208.
universality, 23, 96, 112, 180, 195, 201.
usage, 79, 88, 176, 181, 191;
  actual, 179;
  virtual, 179.
utterance(s), 21, 177.

V

Valéry, 178.
validity, material, 52.
value(s), 23, 84, 167, 175, 177, 180,
  194;
  sedimented, 183.
Van Riper, Charles, 187n.
variants, reflective, 115.
variation, 113;
  free imaginative, 32, 194.
'verbal chain', 50, 90.
verbalism, 160.
verification, 16, 112.
vertical, 184.
Vichynski, 197.
victim, 114.
video-tape, 110.
viewer, 141, 171, 173, 197.
Virasoro, Manuel, 82n.
visible, 18, 105, 112, 128, 203, 206.
vision, 103-4, 127, 198, 204.
vocabulary, 183.
voice, 111, 204.
volition, acts of, 61.

W

Wann, T. W., 22n.
Wahl, Jean, 24n, 74n.
wave, temporal, 117.
Welch, Cyril, 96n.
'we-ness', 196, 206-7.
Weltanschang, 175, 190.
what, 125, 139, 146.
Wheelwright, Philip, 166n.
Whitehead, A. N., 63n.
whole, 32, 88, 119, 135, 139, 181, 201,
  208.
Wild, John, 18n, 30n, 57, 57n.
will to communicate, 96.
Wiseman, Gordon, 187n.

witness, 185, 207.
Wollen, Peter, 174ff., 174n.
word(s), 49, 62, 74, 77, 93, 106, 157,
  161, 170, 175, 185, 191, 198-9;
  movement of, 61;
  or noises, 140;
  physiognomy of, 162;
  there, 176.
world, 23, 38, 81, 102, 104, 111, 125,
  127, 133, 144, 155, 177, 181, 185,
  189, 195, 199, 202, 204, 208-9;
  experience of, 97;
  I and the, 139;
  objective, 28, 123;

'outside-', 30, 99.
worldhood, 72.
wortbegriff, 91.
writing, 62, 155, 179-80, 187;
  '— degree zero', 179.

Y

Yogi, 97.
you, 199, 208.

Z

Zaner, Richard M., 168n.

APPROACHES TO SEMIOTICS

edited by

THOMAS A. SEBEOK

1. THOMAS A. SEBEOK and ALEXANDRA RAMSAY, Eds.: Approaches to Animal Communication. 1969. Gld. 52,—
2. HARLEY C. SHANDS: Semiotic Approaches to Psychiatry. 1970. Gld. 58,—
3. TZVETAN TODOROV: Grammaire du Décaméron. 1969. Gld. 28,—
4. JULIA KRISTEVA, Ed.: Essays in Semiotics / Essais de Sémiotique. 1971. Gld. 110,—
5. PETER BOGATYREV: The Functions of Folk Costume in Moravian Slovakia. 1971. Gdl. 32,—
6. JULIA KRISTEVA: Le texte du roman. 1971. Gld. 38,—
7. THOMAS A. SEBEOK: Semiotics: A Survey of the State of the Art. 1971.
8. O. MICHAEL WATSON: Proxemic Behavior. 1970. Gld. 24,—
9. DAVID EFRON: Gesture and Environment. 1972.
10. PIERRE and ELLI KÖNGÄS MARANDA: Structural Models in Folklore and Transformational Essays. 1971. Gld. 34,—
11. G. L. BURSILL-HALL: Speculative Grammars of the Middle Ages. 1971. Gld. 70,—
12. HARLEY C. SHANDS: The War with Words. 1971. Gld. 23,—
13. JOSETTE REY-DEBOVE: Etude linguistique et sémiotique des dictionnaires français contemporains. 1971. Gld. 64,—
14. GARRICK MALLERY: Sign Language among North American Indians [1881]. 1972.
15. CLAUDE CHABROL: Le Récit féminin. 1971. Gld. 28,—
16. CHARLES MORRIS: Writings on the General Theory of Signs. 1971. Gld. 54,—
17. FRANÇOIS RASTIER: Idéologies et théories des signes. 1972.
18. JOSETTE REY-DEBOVE, Ed.: Recherches sur les systèmes signifiants. Symposium de Varsovie 1968. 1972.
19. RUDOLF KLEINPAUL: Sprache ohne Worte: Idee einer allgemeinen Wissenschaft der Sprache. 1972.
20. DOEDE NAUTA: The Meaning of Information. 1972.

Prices are subject to change
Titles without prices are in preparation

MOUTON · PUBLISHERS · THE HAGUE